Ebola
Stigma and Western
Conspiracy

Adrian Davieson, PhD

D1417380

ISBN: 1508775923
ISBN-13: 978-1508775928

DEDICATION

To the 30,000 Ebola infected patients, and over 11,000 victims claimed by Ebola in West Africa. This book is also dedicated to the healthcare workers from around the world who are in Liberia, Sierra Leone and Guinea, fighting the disease. An esteemed tribute to the World Health Organization, CDC, Doctors Without Borders (MSF), for their efforts to contain the disease and save mankind from another plague. A heartfelt dedication to the selfless African doctors and nurses who sacrificed their lives to save the lives of infected Ebola patients in Sub-Saharan Africa. Their sacrifice is akin to a martyrdom for a worthy cause! A special tribute to the memory of Thomas Eric Duncan whose promising life was cut short by Ebola. I would be remiss if I didn't mention the victims of police brutality in the U.S. and everywhere in the world – they are the unlikely victims of unjust societies worldwide!

CONTENTS

Prologue 1

Chapter 1: Ebola 16

Chapter 2: Controversies 23

Chapter 3: Is Ebola a Curse or a Blessing? 29

Chapter 4: The Influence of Belgian Nuns and Dr. Peter Piot 34

Chapter 5: African Flue or Western Ebola? 36

Chapter 6: Can the flu vaccine be used as an Ebola vaccine? 38

Chapter: 7 Thomas Eric Duncan 41

Chapter 8: Was Duncan a Villain or a Hero? 51

Chapter 9: Why Africa Continues to Suffer Degradation 55

Chapter 10: Africa's Economic Mobility and Setbacks 59

Chapter 11: Western Ebola Patients versus African Ebola Patients 67

Chapter 12: West African Countries Infected with Ebola Virus 72

Chapter 13: The unimportance of Africans/Blacks in the U.S 123

Chapter 14: Police Brutality/Killings of Black Men 158

Chapter 15: How Ebola Marginalized the African 173

Chapter 16: The Impact of Ebola and Police Brutality 193

Chapter 17: The 21st Century Ebola vs. 14th Century Black Death 202

Chapter 18: Conclusions 214

Epilogue: 230

References: 232

ISBN: 1508775923
ISBN-13: 978-1508775928

Printed in the United States of America

Designed by Adrian Davieson

THE HARBINGER OF DEATH

It sauntered through the dense mist, searching, and frolicking, with a mocking façade; and sometimes threatening with its fangs. But first it puts its victims at ease with easy demeanor, before pouncing with talons, and swooping everything in its paths! – Adrian Davieson.

Prologue

In a remote shanty village, 20 miles outside Monrovia, in the Margibi County, in tiny hooch, a frail looking dark skinned woman, of Grebo descent of the Kru tribe, lay on the earthen floor, groaning. For the past six hours since her husband rushed her from the farm where she had been cultivating maize, where she had suddenly collapsed, she has been groaning and crying that her stomach was cramping and hurting. She had vomited everywhere on the earthen floor. Within three hours since she started experiencing the pain that had kept her lying on the floor, her condition had worsened. Her husband had rallied around the village trying to arrange transportation to take her to the nearest hospital, five miles south of the village, in a nearby town; but transportation had been hard to get. Commercial vehicles usually avoided the village because of the potholes and impassable roads. The villagers depended on their motorcycles and bicycles to get around. In some cases, wheelbarrows are used to transport sick people, and heavy loads.

A month ago, a ten year old boy, from the Bong County, had been bitten by a rattle snake while he was helping his father in the farm. It had taken a couple of hours to get a wheelbarrow to transport the boy from the farm to the village clinic. There had been no motorcycles to borrow, and to use. The boy had died from the snake venom three hours later because it took too long to get the boy to the clinic, in a wheelbarrow. The poisonous zootoxins had spread too far in the boy's body before help came.

The only medical facility in the village was a small dispensary/clinic, managed by a former pharmacy apprentice who had learned his trade from another medicine dispenser, before being freed as an apprentice to open his own dispensary/clinic. The staff at the dispensary/clinic never learned their trade in any school. They had been apprentices who had been assistants and had been freed (graduated). Most village dispensaries/clinics are usually used for illegal abortions; and since the law in the land is hardly enforced, the dispensaries/clinics flout the law with impunity. Most of the drugs in the dispensaries/clinics have long expired, often shipped from abroad (overseas) by unscrupulous businessmen who usually bribe their way through customs to get the drugs through the corrupt system.

The woman lay dying as her five children surrounded her, weeping and wailing. They knew death was near and afoot. Their

1

mother was sweating profusely. One of the children, the oldest one among them, had put a wet dirty towel on her forehead to reduce the burning fever. As if the wet towel emitted a renewed life in the dying woman, she jerked. Soon, she was shaking as if suffering from epileptic seizures. The children were weeping uncontrollably as they watched helplessly as their mother lay dying.

Their father had gone everywhere to seek help to no avail. His eyes were red and bloodshot as if drunk. But he wasn't. Sorrow had paid an unwelcome visit. He had cried himself out. He knew his wife was dying. He also knew that the situation was out of his hand. There was nothing to do now but to wait for the local herbalist. The Herbalist would save her, he silently reassured himself while hoping and praying. He has already sent three people to get the herbalist. The herbalist was busy with other patients. He knew he has to wait his turn. Patience was something he has learned long ago. The tears kept streaming his cheeks as he watched his children wail and weep for their dying mother.

The herbalist eventually came two hours later. By the time he arrived, the woman was on the throes of death. There was very little he could do, even if he could do anything. As the herbalist started his incantations, and began to administer the mixed herbs he had prepared for her, the woman gave up the ghost, dead. There were specks of dried blood on her lips, part residue of the blood she had vomited when she had started to hemorrhage and her intestines had started to burn, and part remnant of bleeding from her mouth.

The herbalist helped prepare the funeral rites as was required by the custom and tradition of the land. The children cleaned up the vomits and blood as they wail and gnash their teeth. Death has struck, and their loved one was gone. Never to be seen! There was nothing they could do. They seemed to realize the reality of the moment as they kept cleaning the area their mother had lay and died.

As the funeral rites were concluded, the herbalist gathered his things, demanded for payment, changed his mind and headed out the door. He knew it was a bad time to ask for payment. Before leaving he chastised the man for not coming to him sooner. The widower understood the reproof, even though he had tried to get the herbalist sooner. It was a cultural thing to shift blames. He was the grieving one. He would take the blame as his forefathers before him had learned to do. It was just a lip service, the herbalist's way of offering condolences.

The herbalist has not been gone twenty minutes when the oldest of the five children, a girl of 19, started to sweat heavily on her forehead. She collapsed as her siblings watched helplessly, thinking she was still moaning the death of their mother. The father had gone to make preparation for the burial of their mother. Burial was a simple process in the village. It would be a conclusion of the rites the herbalist had started. A bottle of palm oil, along with a white piece of cloth, with a grass mat and grounded white native chalk that would be sprinkled on the body before it is wrapped and buried. The palm oil would be used to rub the forehead of the deceased as part of the native ceremony.

At the time the widower had returned to the village, on his way home from making burial arrangements, and buying materials required for the burial of his now deceased wife, an hour later, his oldest daughter was in the throes of death, vomiting and hyperventilating. Her body temperature was 103f. She was feverish and shaking on the sand, in front of their thatched hut. Her younger brother, whom she was older than by a couple of years, saw what was happening and recoiled with fear. He knew his sister was no longer moaning. She was dying. He could tell by the symptoms that were enveloping her weakening body that she was dying; just like their mother had died not too long ago. He ran, looking for his father. He found him at the edge of the village, with the elders, discussing the burial of his wife.

As the widower saw his son running towards him, he immediately knew something was amiss. The curse that has bedeviled his family was not done with him yet, he realized as he listened to his son's narration of the latest looming tragedy in his family. Before the son could finish his story, he ran toward his house, only to find his daughter grasping for her last breath of life. She was near death, minutes later, as he started to give her the medicine the herbalist had prepared for his deceased wife who had also experienced the same symptoms before her death.

He looked up but the oldest son was gone. He knew where he was headed. He could tell, and felt, that his daughter had few minutes left or was already dead. Denial was taking its effect in him. He refuses to accept the obvious that his daughter was already dead or half dead. The herbalist would arrive late he thought gloomily and by then his oldest daughter would be dead. He looked at his three remaining children who were now gathered fearfully, looking at their senior sister, as she lay dying in their father's arm.

In less than an hour, the oldest son sprinted back to the thatched hut he shares with his family. He came alone. The sadness on the boy's face told the grieving father all he needed to know. The father collapsed but quickly realized he had to be strong. He forced himself to, and cried in a loud piercing voice and quickly stopped. He can't do this in the presence of his children, he told himself. In a mechanical voice that seemed far away, he asked needlessly: "where is the herbalist?" as he looked at his son, who was too dazed to answer. The unfolding tragedies were too surreal. It was like a bad dream for the boy.

And just then, the boy started to scream as if suddenly realizing the tragedy that was befalling his family. The father asked the now wailing son again, about the herbalist he had gone to fetch. But the son was too caught up in his own grief, and wailing, to answer. The father shook him on his shoulder. "Where is the herbalist you went to get?" He asked his son again, amid his own grief and tears. "What use is the herbalist when the patient is dead?" the son shot back, with anger and grief. "Anyway, he is dead too. I met his family wailing and crying, the same way we are crying here. He was dead when I got to his compound," the son said with tears in his eyes and with increased wailing.

By the time dusk had arrived in the village of five thousand inhabitants, the widower and his oldest son were the only ones standing and alive, in their family. His wife and four other children had died of the same mysterious curse, after they had experienced the same symptoms that his wife had experienced. At first he had thought the gods had placed a curse on his family; until he heard about the deaths of the herbalist and the other villagers. He was more convinced than ever that the gods were angry with them in the village. What have they done to deserve the wrath of the gods? He asked himself.

After he had buried four of his children and his wife, he made up his mind. He would burn down the hut. It saddened him to think so. The thatched hut had been home for many years; but now the overwhelming sadness makes it a sorrowful abode. It bears so much sadness and pain, he thought. He took the kerosene that his now deceased wife often used to cook their food, sprinkle it on the thatched roof and set it ablaze. He hoped the curse would die and burn with the hut.

That night, he slept in his farm where he had taken refuge with his son. Sleep had been difficult as he tossed and turned throughout the short night. He had dreamt of his wife and children. They had all been smiling in the dream, beckoning him to join them. For reasons he could not understand, he had refused. He returned the next day to the village to find that the worst was not yet over. There were sorrows everywhere he went. Children were wailing and the women were weeping. He found that the curse that had bedeviled his family had visited all the households in his village. He ran to the house of the local village head, only to learn that he has also died from the curse that had taken his family.

One by one, he learned that he was not alone. His village was under attack by a mysterious curse. Walking with his son, and with no belongings, having burnt everything he possessed, he walked to the outskirt of the village and sat down on the grass, thinking of the next cause of action. He had no plan. He had never ventured going to the city. The only life he had known was in the village and its environs. It would be hard to make any plan when he has never had to do so. His son stood, waiting, not knowing what to say or do.

"Papa, we can go to the city of Monrovia and get a job. We will be safe in Monrovia. They have big hospitals and plenty of jobs there," the son said, but the father wasn't listening. He was still drowned in his sorrows.

And elsewhere in a small village, southeast of Koidu, in Sierra Leone, Nouhou Kossi, the bicycle repairer, was whistling to himself as he walked home from the shop where he repairs bicycles. Anyone looking at him would have thought he won the lottery. The day had been good in the shop for Kossi. A shop he had owned for thirty years, passed down from his grandfather who was a popular bicycle repairer in the village. The day had been profitable for him. It had been better than the day before when very few customers had come to the shop and didn't have any money. His wife will be happy today, he thought blissfully.

Lately he has not been a good provider because of the scarcity of money in his household. Spare parts had become hard to get. Sometimes when a bicycle is too old it can be very hard to fix without replacing the parts. He knew it was worthless to fix a bicycle that has spanned over 60 years and has served three generations. But he couldn't tell his customers that. If he did, he will be out of business. They would rather fix the old bicycle than buy a new one. He was glad that they did not have money to buy a new one. If they did, business will be really bad for him. Most of his fellow villagers were farmers and traders. Money was scarce.

He was half way home on his old motorcycle; and decided he would stop to buy baked bread from Foday's bakery. His wife and kids love fresh bread. He bought three loaves of bread and had just put them in a compartment at the bottom of the motorcycle when he heard someone screaming *papa! Papa!* As the voice drew nearer he recognized his oldest boy's voice and flinched, as if a bad omen was afoot. Has something happened? He wondered. He waited by the motorcycle as his son ran towards him.

"What is the matter, Amadu?" he asked his son. "Papa, mama is dying! You need to hurry up and come home now," the boy managed to say. Without waiting to say anything more, he quickly started the motorcycle as his son climbed in the backseat. He rode as fast as he could, in the potholed and narrow road. Erosion had created gullies and gulch, making the roads steep and impassable. But Nouhou was used to the roads. He grew up with the roads looking like that; and he couldn't remember if the roads have ever been paved or tarred. As he rode closer to home, with his son sitting at the back of the motorcycle, he thought he heard the disquiet weird sound of death, coming from his thatched roof hut. He became very worried now. Something has gone terribly wrong, he told himself, as he quickly jumped off the motorcycle, leaving his son to park it.

Amadi, his son, was strong enough to quickly park and position the motorcycle as it was about to fall to the ground. He parked the motorcycle where his father usually parks it, and ran after his father, into the small hut. What Nouhou and his son saw when they entered the hut almost paralyzed them with fear. The sight that greeted them was horrifying and too gory for them to even comprehend. His wife, Aminata, lay on the floor; tossing and twitching with pain. There was blood and vomits everywhere. Next to his wife lay his youngest son, listless and dead. Around him were blood and vomits. His youngest son's eyes were rolled back in his head, dead. He could tell his son had been dead for a while. The blood and vomits were dried and the remnants of the vomits and blood were still around the corners of his youngest son's mouth. Three feet away lay his granddaughter. He ran to her and by the cold stiffness of her body, he knew she had been dead for a while.

He turned to his oldest son, who had his hands folded on his head, crying. "Why didn't you come and get me from the store sooner?" Amid tears the boy said, "Papa, I was in the bush hunting and had just gotten home when I saw them like this. I quickly threw

6

down my bag when I saw them lying on the floor with blood and vomits everywhere; and ran to get you," he said, still crying. "Papa, are they dead, oh my God, what happened?" he said, still crying. "Yes, son, they are all dead, except for your mother, who is almost dead herself." He turned towards his wife again who now lay prostrate, and tried to revive her but found that it was no use. He looked at her pleading eyes, and kissed her. He gave her a goodbye kiss that seemed to bid her farewell. Something told him he shouldn't have done that. But it was too late or he didn't care. He closed her eyes with his hand, as fear gripped him.

She died immediately as if she had been waiting for him to arrive before dying. He looked up as if conjuring a divine succor. He looked down like a defeated man. He knew things will no longer be the same. He thought a terrible curse has been placed on his family by the gods! He felt the need to go to the village elder to inform him of the calamity that has befallen his family. He got up again, looked confused and started walking aimlessly. The look on his face was beginning to worry his son, Amadu, as he strides besides his distraught father. The father stopped again, and fell down as if struck by an unseen hand.

His father got unsteadily to his feet, and staggered toward the door as if in a trance. He had barely taken two steps, when he lurched forward, and fell again. He started vomiting and sweating. Soon he was bleeding from every pore in his body, and vomiting blood. The son knew the fate that had befallen his mother and siblings was also befalling his father. He was transfixed with fear, and confused. He was sweating. That was when he was caught in the cycle of death that had taken his family. If he had just left, he probably would have been saved. He did the unthinkable; he bent down to try to revive his father by cleaning his face with cold water and a piece of cloth. If he had followed his first mind to get help or run away from the evil harbinger of death, he would have been spared the agony of death that was about to befall him.

As he bent down to help his father, he started to convulse in a violent spasm. He started to have abdominal pains and muscular contraction. All at once! Before he knew what was happening to him, he started to vomit blood, lots of it. The convulsion was soon taken over by heavy hemorrhaging. He knew he was at the throes of death. He was too confused and too weak to think. He tried to fight the agony of death that was taking over his body and mind; but the abdominal pain was too heavy and painful for him. He tried to move his hand from his father's face, where he had placed it earlier, but couldn't. The hand lay where he had placed it earlier when he had tried to clean up his father's face. The small earthen bowl that he had filled with water lay upturned with the water now flowing with the vomit and blood around the family of Nouhou Kossi. Death had arrived, unsuspected, and within hours had claimed the entire family of Kossi.

A neighbor who was friends with the Kossi's family had not seen the family for a few days and decided to check on them. The neighbor could not remember a day he had not exchanged greetings with Nouhou. It was strange that he has not seen any member of the family the last couple of days, he thought. He had gone to the family's thatched hut to check on them. As he pushed open the bamboo door, he blinked twice to make sure he was not dreaming and having a nightmare. He shook his head as if trying to clear his head. He looked again to be sure. He could not believe what he was seeing. It was surreal, he thought. He saw the entire family lying dead in the same way, on the floor. He immediately thought a murder had taken place but he knew there was no foul play in what he was looking at. But he couldn't believe that an entire family could be so grotesquely dead in one spot.

All the members of the family were dead in the same grotesque manner. He had wept; and quickly ran to the village elder to report what he had seen. He had fetched the village voodoo priestess and village elders. As if listening to unseen commands, the villagers did not get close to the corpses. To them, the gods have spoken and the oracle must be consulted. The next morning the villagers gathered around the only tree in the center of the village to discuss the misfortune that had visited the village. It would take a week before the villagers discovered that Ebola had visited their little village. At that time, half of the villagers had died in the same way the Kossis had died.

And elsewhere in neighboring Guinea, Abdoulaye Mohamed woke up with a start as he realized he was getting late for school; when he finally cleared his eyes at 5:30am in the morning of Tuesday, in late February 2014. The nine year old knew he had a long walk before him to school and should have gotten up at 4:00am. Rubbing his eyes to clear the remaining sleep, he wondered why his parents hadn't come to wake him up. They usually wake him up. In the five years plus he has been going to school, he could not remember a day his parents didn't wake him up for school. He was very surprised, and pleasantly so, this morning. At least he got a few more minutes of sleep. He hadn't gone to bed early the night before. He had secretly been looking at the magazine his friend, Sidiki, had allowed him to borrow. In his nine years of age he has never seen naked beautiful white girls in such seductive poses, having wild sex in the pictures he saw in the magazine. He had gotten an instant erection as he had quickly looked through the pages, furtively watching the door to make sure his parents did not catch him.

He did not know how Sidiki got the magazine but he was glad that his friend had allowed him to borrow it. He had been so mesmerized by the sexual poses, the big penises and huge clitoris and tits in the magazine that he didn't know how it got so late. At the time he had realized it was late, it was already past 11pm and he knew he should have been asleep by 9pm. His parents had tucked him in bed around 8:25pm, after he had eaten his dinner of rice, stew, and chicken. It had been a festive day. His parents had prepared rice and stew with chicken, his favorite. He still could not understand why his parents had prepared such a meal on an ordinary day. He was usually treated to rice and stew with chicken only on Christmas and Easter. The day must have been special. He didn't know what was special about it but he was glad that he was served with rice and stew, along with chicken.

He had finally finished his food around 7:30pm, and had finished his homework of mathematics and science immediately afterward. At 8pm, he had quickly run to the back of the house where he had hidden the old penthouse magazine and retrieved it. He had told his parents he was going to the pit-latrine at the back of the house. His parents had showed concern that he was rushing to the latrine, minutes after he had finished his dinner. But he had assured them that he was alright, that nothing was wrong with him. After he had retrieved the old penthouse magazine, he had looked to make sure his parents and his nosy younger brother were not around to see him. He had quickly run to his room and had hidden the magazine under the grass mattress he sleeps in. He enjoyed sleeping in his grass mattress. His best friend sleeps in a mat at his house. He was the only one among his friends who sleeps in a mattress. His friends still sleep on the bare floor, and sometimes in a mat.

He stretched himself, feeling tired. He had not slept well. He had dreamt that he was with one of the beautiful girls in the magazine, holding and kissing her. In the dream, his friend, Sidiki had been watching him with envy as he fondled the girl's breasts and kisses her. He had learned the act of kissing from another boy, Fode, in school who often boasts of sleeping with lots of girls. Fode had said all he needed to do was to stick out his tongue and cover the girl's mouth with his, in a kiss. He had tried it once and liked it.

Though some of the other boys doubted Fode's stories of sexual exploits with girls, they had never stopped to envy him. Fode was the envy of many boys in school. He was handsome with mixed complexion. There was a rumor his father was a white French man. There was also a rumor that Fode's mother had traveled to France for prostitution and had been deported a few years later. She had arrived in Conakry, pregnant.

Rumor had it she had not known she was pregnant with a child until she had arrived home in her village, 15 miles outside Conakry. It had not mattered to her that she got pregnant without a husband. It was a taboo to come home to the village pregnant with a child and no husband. But Fode's mother had been different. She was beautiful and easily flaunts her beauty. She was also a proud beauty who never cared about gossips about her. She had traveled to a white man's land and was pregnant with a white baby. She was an exception to the tradition and taboo. She was the envy of the villagers, rather than an embarrassment. She was treated like a celebrity. They had hoped that one day the white man would come and visit his son; but he never came. It was fine with the villagers. After all, they have their own white man in Fode.

Fode often gets lots of presents from girls and he always shares the presents with his friends, including Abdoulaye, who usually gets most of the presents from him. Since Fode was not good in math, it was Abdoulaye who always helps him with complicated math. His friendship with Fode allows him to mingle with some of the cutest and prettiest girls in the school. The girls were always trying to be with Fode, because of his looks and also because he was half white!

Abdoulaye walked unsteadily towards his parents' bedroom, after making sure that he had carefully hidden the magazine in-between his books. He had promised to return the book. Since he only borrowed it for one day, he knew his time to see the magazine was up. He knew how his friend, Sidiki, gets when crossed. He did not want to get the boy angry. Sidiki was much bigger and taller than him and was also a few years older. There was a rumor that his parents almost didn't want to send him to school, that the pastor in the village had convinced the parents to send the boy to school. Sidiki was 13 years old and the biggest in class. He was always the one the other kids in their small gang lean on to fight off other boys who try to bully them in school. And it was Sidiki who had given him the old penthouse magazine. He knew the last person he would want to get angry was Sidiki. Even the teachers were afraid of Sidiki because of his size. At 13 years old, Sidiki was bigger and taller than most 18 year olds.

As Abdoulaye got closer to his parents' bedroom he started to feel uneasy. The feeling was surreal. As he approached the mud bed that was adjacent to the mud chairs, in the bedroom, the uneasy feeling grew stronger. He knew something was amiss as he got closer to the mud bed that his parents sleep in. He saw that the hurricane lamp was burning faintly, as if his parents were still asleep. He could not tell whether his parents were up or still asleep because the light from the kerosene lamp was so faint. He went back to his room to get his lamp. Since he never sleeps with his lamp on, he still had enough kerosene in it. He brought it, and entered the bedroom again. He saw his mother and father on the floor. The grass mattress on the mud bed had fallen to the ground. As he looked closer, he noticed that there were vomits and blood everywhere. Their eyes were rolled back in their heads. Though he was nine years old, he didn't have to be told that his parents were dead.

Abdoulaye screamed, ran out of the mud house to his uncle's house, three mud houses down. He got there just in time to see his uncle getting ready for the farm. The uncle was picking up his cutlass, hoe and bag, when he saw his nephew run into his house. He knew by the look on the boy's face that something bad had happened. Without waiting to ask the boy what had happened, he ran with him back to the boy's house, not bothering to tell his wife who had also been getting ready to go to the market when Abdoulaye ran into the house. His wife ran behind them as they ran back to the house of Mohamed, in that early morning of Tuesday in late February.

Five hours later, Abdoulaye, his uncle and his wife, were also dead. It would be days later before the villagers in the village found out that a curse had visited their village. By the time the name of the curse was unraveled, half of the inhabitants of the village had died. The same plague had also befallen the neighboring village where Abdoulaye's father, Ismael Mohamed, had gone to buy goods for his shop, where he had contracted the disease called Ebola, the day before.

Since March 2014, Ebola has ravaged the cities, towns and remote villages of Liberia, Guinea and Sierra Leone. In six months, since February 2014, over 9,000 West Africans have died from Ebola in the three countries; and over 30,000 people have been infected with the disease. The World Health Organization predicted that the situation will get worse before it gets better. According to the United Nations, the death rate since the Ebola outbreak has surpassed 70% as of October 14, 2014. And it was predicted by the United Nations that up to 10,000 new cases a week would occur in the three countries of Liberia, Sierra Leone and Guinea, in West Africa. The grim prediction seemed overblown, experts observed; but the speed the virus was spreading in the summer of 2014, had been alarming enough to debunk or accept any prediction. In December 2014, reported cases of new infections had lessened, compared with the summer of 2014 when the United Nations had first made its grim predictions.

In a faraway land, about 4,447 miles away, across the Atlantic Ocean, in the United States, in a small Texas town, two black teens are playing basketball in an abandoned old elementary school yard. The younger of the two teens appears gifted with quickness; and was adept in his ability to move the ball with minimum effort. The younger teen dribbles the basketball back and forth, and before the older teen knew it the ball was inside the basket! They kept playing for the next two hours. Just as they were about to stop to take a break, four white teens walked into the basketball court. They stood watching the two black teens play for several minutes.

After a while, their leader, a heavyset white teen who looked like he could be in his late 30s but was actually 18 years old, whispered something in the ears of his buddies who were standing next to him. The other white boys quickly drew closer, straining their ears to hear what the heavyset white teen was saying.

They didn't have to strain their ears too hard because they knew why they were at the basketball court. They hadn't come to play basketball. They knew the two young black teens would be at the basketball court at that time and had hatched a devious plan a week ago, to harm the boys. The two young black teens had not known that the four white teens had been watching them with binoculars for months as they would often come to the same basketball court to play. The white teens even knew the time that the two black teens would show up and the time they would leave. And on top of that, they knew that the old elementary schoolyard was a deserted and an isolated area where people hardly go to. And they also knew that the small dirt road that was once used by students to get to school had fallen into disuse. Shrubs and tall grasses had long taken over the once popular dirt road. Lately, the dirt road had witnessed five rapes, ten muggings and one murder. It was an area mostly frequented by drug peddlers and miscreants.

The town's officials had promised to demolish the school and possibly sell the land to a developer. But no developer had shown interests. With a population of just 6,500, the town was hardly a hub for commercial activities. Since the prospect of the town turning profits in any business venture was slim, potential businessmen and major retail stores had shunned the town. It wouldn't be worth the investment of hundreds of millions of dollars to major retailers and corporations. A Chinese conglomerate had shown interest in the land with intent to build a factory to manufacture cement in the place but the indigenes had resisted; and had turned down the proposal. An adult entertainment mogul had shown interest in buying the land to use it for adult entertainment and again, the residents had turned down the proposal. And since no immediate decision had been made to demolish and develop the land, the place had become a fertile ground for all sorts of criminal mischief.

In the ten years since the old elementary school had been closed and abandoned, it has made the news over five times for drug peddling, prostitution and gang activities. There had been unconfirmed rumors that white supremacists and skinheads with racist beliefs often use the old elementary schoolyard for meetings and clan activities. To a lot of the residents of the small town, skinheads no longer exist in the area. The only place where skinheads and white nationalists still exist was Vidor, where blacks are still not allowed after dark, and where blacks are still openly discriminated against.

As the four white teens watch the two black teens take a break, the heavily tattooed leader of the gang decided it was time to make a move. The heavyset white teen leader casually made his way towards the basketball center. As he approaches, the older of the two black teens saw him and suddenly stopped. He could tell by the racist and swastika tattoos in the body of the badly scared heavyset white teen that trouble was imminent. Though for his age he has not seen too many KKK (Ku Klux Klan) activists and activities, he has often heard stories. He could tell by the hatred burning in the eyes of the heavyset white teen that trouble loomed. He quickly nudged his smaller friend that they should scram. The younger black teen was still too caught up in the basketball game to see or comprehend the nudge or the trouble that was afoot. Just as he turned to see why his friend was nudging him, he caught sight of the heavyset white teen approaching them menacingly. The now fully alerted two young black teens also saw the remaining white skinheads. They knew for sure that all was not well, that trouble was afoot.

The black teens quickly scrammed and ran as fast as they could. But as fast as they ran, they could not outrun the four white teens who had spread themselves around the court and were now chasing them. As the black teens ran, it became obvious to them that they were losing the race. There would be no one nearby to rescue them, they thought. The nearest home was a mile away, and was an old dilapidated home that belonged to an old white farmer who lives alone. They knew not to expect any help from the old white farmer as he was known to disdain the sights of blacks in the town. So they ran as fast as they could. It was no use. The four white teens were closing in. Even though they felt they were losing the race and would probably be seriously beaten or killed if caught, they still ran as fast as they could.

They had almost given up hope of outrunning their chasers, when suddenly they ran upon a highway, and then suddenly they saw a police cruiser driving towards them. They felt a sigh of relief that somehow God had answered their prayers. They ran as fast as they could so that the police officer could see them. Since it was on the verge of sunset and it was still daylight, the officer saw them. The black teens looked over their shoulders and saw that the white skinheads had stopped chasing them, obviously because of the police car, they thought.

"Stop there and don't move!" the officer shouted as he stopped his police cruiser. The black teens stopped to obey the officer. "Put your hands above your head and fold them! And don't move them!" the officer said to the black teens who were already obeying him. The officer drew his .38 police special and walked cautiously towards the two black teens. He raised his gun as he was talking on his radio while he approaches the two black teens. "What have you stolen and which house did you burglarize?" the officer asked the teens. "We were just out in the old schoolyard playing basketball when four white boys chased us. We did not steal anything or burglarize any house," the older black teen said. "You are thieves, don't turn and don't move!" he screamed again. The younger black teen saw that they were facing worse danger than when they were being chased by the four white teens. They saw that their chances of survival were with the skinheads than with the cop. But it was too late!

The white police officer looked furtively at both sides of the highway. Seeing no one approaching, he released the safety on his gun, and just then the younger teen who had been watching the officer from the corner of his eyes darted off and ran. He had overheard the officer on the handheld radio saying two black teens had burglarized a home and were armed with weapons and resisting arrest. He knew what would follow. He had seen many of his friends killed by police officers with the same excuse of resisting arrest. His instinct told him to bolt and run for it and he did. Just as he was running toward the direction of his home, he heard the sounds of multiple gunshots and his friend's voice, "you have shot me officer! I did not commit any crime!" He knew he had to run faster. And he ran. The dying voice of his friend remained in his head until he luckily made it home.

He quickly called his friend's mother, a single mother, who works two jobs; and told her what had happened. He could hear the wailing and weeping of his friend's mother. He knew he should have done something but he also knew there was nothing he could have done. He would probably have been shot dead like his friend; if he had tried to help, he thought.

The local news had carried the news of the shooting. The police had said the boy had been fleeing from a home he had burglarized and when the police had tried to stop him he had pulled a gun on the officer who had shot him in self defense. A police spokesperson said a gun was recovered at the scene of the shooting. He knew his friend did not have a gun on him and did not even own a gun and had never touched a gun in his life. He wasn't surprised a month later when the grand jury refused to indict the officer, saying it was a justifiable homicide of self defense!

Chapter 1

Ebola

The name Ebola came from the Legbala headstream of the Mongala River, in Congo. The Legbala headstream was also known by the indigenes of Zaire as the Ebola River. The Legbala headstream is a tributary of the Congo River, in the northern part of the Democratic Republic of Congo. The river is said to have a length of 250 km.

In the native language of Ngbandi, Ebola, which is a derivative of Legbala, is known as the white water, with French and Belgian connections. During the Belgian and French colonial influence in sub-Saharan Africa, natives were often named after their colonial masters; and names were given to children, places and things that had colonial references. The French names, *Eau Blanche and L'Ebola,* were associated with the white water. Dr. Peter Piot, the renowned Belgian Ebola researcher, was said to have named Ebola after the Legbala headstream that the indigenes refer to as the Ebola River or white water, to prevent the village, Yambuku, from being stigmatized with the Ebola disease. Dr. Piot had wanted it known that it was the river rather than the people that had Ebola.

According to the CDC, "Ebola is a rare and deadly disease. The disease is caused by infection with one of the Ebola virus species (Zaire, Sudan, Bundibugyo, or Tai Forest virus). Ebola is spread by direct contact (through broken skin or mucous membranes in, for example, the eyes, nose, or mouth) with: blood or body fluids (such as urine, saliva, sweat, feces, vomit, breast milk, and semen) of a person who is sick with Ebola, objects (like needles and syringes) that have been contaminated with the virus, and infected fruit bats or primates (apes and monkeys)."

What has come to be known as Ebola is a virus known in the scientific community as a hemorrhagic fever that kills as soon as it is contracted, usually within days. The known symptoms of Ebola include fever, sore throat, muscle pain, headache, vomiting, diarrhea and sudden rise in body temperature to 103. If not immediately treated, Ebola can result in kidney and liver dysfunctions, which can result in internal and external hemorrhage. According to the World Health Organization, and the Center for Disease Control, low blood pressure due to loss of fluid and hemorrhage can result in death within days of contracting the virus.

The virus is usually contracted through body fluids. As at the end of November, 2014, the death toll resulting from Ebola, according to the BBC News, had exceeded 7,000 deaths. In the countries affected such as Liberia, Sierra Leone and Guinea, Ebola has devastated and ravaged lives, with Liberia and Sierra Leone recording the most deaths. BBC reported that 7,244 cases were reported in Liberia with 4,181 deaths, from March 2014 to August, 2014. In neighboring Sierra Leone, 6,802 cases of Ebola were reported with 1,453 deaths. In the neighboring country of Guinea, 2,123 cases of Ebola were reported with 1,284 deaths. The low figure in Guinea, according to World Health Organization was as a result of the drastic measures taken by the country's government to contain Ebola in that country.

The virus, according to the CDC, has some of the symptoms identified in the flu virus such as fever, weakness, body aches and breathing difficulties. Unlike the flu virus, Ebola has an experimental drug called ZMapp, along with "53 promising drug compounds," according to Time.com. In a report published by the Icahn School of Medicine at Mount Sinai and the National Institute s of Health (NIH), reported by Time.com, additional 10,000 drug compounds are being explored by scientists to see if "Ebola could be treated similarly to the treatments they've developed for viruses like HIV and Hepatitis." The compounds will, reportedly, be experimented and tested on animals "to see what effects they have on Ebola, as well as their side effects." The idea is to scan the 2,816 compounds already approved by the U.S. Food and Drug administration that are currently used for other ailments. The method will include using a virus-like particle that contains Ebola proteins and then calibrating it to identify drugs that could prevent Ebola "from infecting the human cells by 50%."

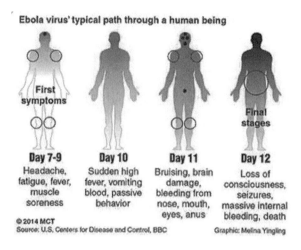

Ebola virus' typical path through a human being

First symptoms

Final stages

Day 7-9	Day 10	Day 11	Day 12
Headache, fatigue, fever, muscle soreness	Sudden high fever, vomiting blood, passive behavior	Bruising, brain damage, bleeding from nose, mouth, eyes, anus	Loss of consciousness, seizures, massive internal bleeding, death

© 2014 MCT
Source: U.S. Centers for Disease and Control, BBC

Graphic: Melina Yingling

Though not airborne, people in direct contact with infected patients are usually quarantined for a period of 21 days, for observation. "Ebola is not easily transmitted," President Obama said while urging Americans to avoid hysteria about Ebola. The president said "We can't just cut ourselves off from West Africa," saying that sealing off West Africa would only make things worse. President Obama was responding to nervous Americans and congressional members who were asking him to impose a travel ban on West Africans from Liberia, Sierra Leone and Liberia coming to America, according to Reuters.

Infected patients in Guinea, Liberia and Sierra Leone have been known to spread the disease through semen, breast feeding and improper burial of victims. Sub-Saharan Africans in the affected countries have contracted the virus through fruit bats that live in tropical and subtropical countries such as sub-Saharan Africa. Fruit bats feed on ripe fruits, pollen and nectar.

People living in tropical and subtropical countries can contract Ebola by coming in contact with fruit bats or through an animal that has been infected by a living or dead fruit bats, according to the World Health Organization.

When compared to major infectious diseases in the last decade, Ebola appears to be the most deadly. According to Time Magazine, agencies for disease control monitoring infectious diseases like the CDC, WHO, UNOCHA, Red Cross and FTS, indicated that Ebola maintains a giant share of 47% compared to tuberculosis (15%); polio (10%); SARS (9.6%); whooping cough (1%); measles (0.2%); and Swine flu (0.02%).

Health officials with both CDC and WHO opined that eating fruits infected by fruit bats can also lead to the Ebola infection. Bush meat, which is a common delicacy among sub-Saharan Africans have been known to be infected with Ebola. According BBC News Africa, bat-eating has been banned in some parts of West Africa, to curb Ebola in several sub-Saharan African countries. Guinea has banned the sale, distribution and consumption of bats to contain and prevent the spread of Ebola. Fruit-bats, a common delicacy in West Africa is reportedly responsible for the Ebola outbreak in several parts of southern Guinea. African hunters who hunt for animals in the forest often pick up dead animals which they sell in the open markets to traders and consumers. In most cases, the virus spreads through the hunter and those unlucky enough to buy such contaminated animals like fruit-bats.

Ebola first surfaced in June 1976, in south Sudan (now the sovereign state of South Sudan) and later that year in August, in Zaire (now the Democratic Republic of the Congo). At the time of the first known outbreak in Nzara, South Sudan, the virus infected 284 people; and killed 151 people. The first known patient of the disease was a store clerk in a cotton factory in Nzara. The infected store clerk had only lasted six days in the hospital before dying of the disease. The World Health Organization would later put a name on the virus as Ebola when a positive identification of the disease was obtained.

The disease occurred again in August 1976, in Yambuku, in a remote village in northern Zaire, in the Mongala District. At the time of the second outbreak in this small village, the victim was a headmaster, Mabalo Lokela. The World Health Organization had identified the same symptoms in the village headmaster that had been observed in the store clerk in Nzara back in June, and immediately knew another outbreak had occurred.

When the village headmaster had first contracted the disease it was assumed he had malaria, and was given quinine, a drug made from the bark of a tree and used for treating malaria. Malaria is very common in sub-Saharan Africa and is caused by mosquitoes. That assumption would change when Lokela started showing the symptoms of Ebola, immediately after a trip to Legbala, the mainstream of the Mongala River, which is a tributary of the Congo River. The village headmaster had been admitted to the Yambuku Mission Hospital when his condition had worsened. Three days after Lokela, the village headmaster, was admitted to Yambuku Mission

Hospital, he died. He had lasted 14 days after showing symptoms of Ebola.

The death of Lokela from the Ebola disease had created an epidemic. Those who had been in contact with Lokela had displayed the symptoms and had died of the disease. The ripple effect created by Lokela's death soon created a panic in the small village of Yambuku, to where it reached the central government in Kinshasa. President Mobutu Sese Seko, the then president of Zaire, had immediately ordered his Minister of Health to quarantine the villagers in Yambuku, including residents of Kinshasa, the capital, as part of the quarantine zone.

Under President Mobutu Sese Seko's directive, a martial law was imposed. With the martial law, schools and businesses were closed. The epidemic that led to the martial law and the shutdown of businesses and schools were, according to Dr. Peter Piot, a Belgian microbiologist known for his research in Ebola, not unrelated to the unnecessary injections of vitamins to pregnant women by Belgian nuns without first sterilizing the syringes. The bold steps taken by President Mobutu Sese Seko had helped contained the disease, which had stopped when Yambuku and Kinshasa were quarantined.

According to CDC, the second outbreak lasted 26 days. The quarantine of the Yambuku and Kinshasa zone lasted 14 days. Researchers led by Dr. Peter Piot opined that the disease had been contained because of the actions taken by President Mobutu Sese Seko to quarantine the areas affected. The researchers also concluded that the early discontinuation of the vitamin injections had also helped to make the disease to disappear. Incineration of Ebola medical wastes from Ebola patients in Zaire was also part of the process of containment, ordered by health officials, in 1976.

When the virus was first identified as Ebola in 1976 in sub-Saharan Africa, it was merely an outbreak that had occurred in Sudan and Zaire. Though it had killed 151 people, it had not created a global panic. The virus had disappeared as mysteriously as it had appeared when it was contained. According to the World Health Organization, a few lives were lost but none alarming since it had only occurred in the remote villages of the then southern Sudan and Zaire. In 2013, an outbreak occurred again, in Gueckedou, a town in southern Guinea, in the Nzerekore region of Guinea, near the Sierra Leonean and Liberian borders. During the 2013 outbreak, there was a brief but mild outbreak in sub-Saharan Africa, and the impact was not serious enough to attract global attention. Though the World

Health Organization had reported that several outbreaks occurred in 2013 in Guinea; they were small outbreaks and there was nothing major or catastrophic. It did not attain a momentous tragic proportion and catastrophe. It did not result in extreme misfortunes to create utter ruin and pandemic as has happened in Guinea, Sierra Leone and Liberia in 2014.

According to CNN, the latest outbreak first started in Guinea towards the end of 2013, when a 2 year old boy had been infected after eating an infected bush meat such as the meat of infected monkeys, antelope and squirrels. The virus had spread from the 2 year old to his immediate family, and from there a network of infections had culminated into several different chains of infections.

PATIENT ZERO

The World Health Organization traced the outbreak back to a single child in Guinea

EMILE, AGED 2
DIED DEC. 28, 2013

HIS SISTER

FAMILY FRIEND
IN SIERRA LEONE

HIS MOTHER

GUECKEDOU
HOSPITAL CHAIN

HIS GRANDMOTHER

DAWA CHAIN

HER DAUGHTER

CHAIN BURNS
OUT AFTER
12 MORE
CASES

A MIDWIFE

DAMDOU
POMBO CHAIN

A MIDWIFE

HER NEPHEW

SOURCE: World Health Organization

From Guinea, the virus had headed to neighboring Sierra Leone where, according to CNN "hundreds of deaths can be traced to the funeral of a widely respected traditional healer who died of Ebola after people came from Guinea seeking treatment from her."

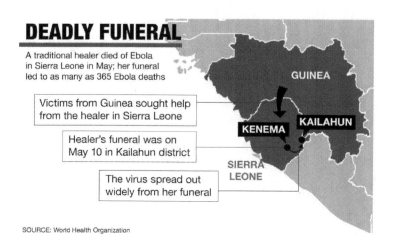

DEADLY FUNERAL

A traditional healer died of Ebola in Sierra Leone in May; her funeral led to as many as 365 Ebola deaths

Victims from Guinea sought help from the healer in Sierra Leone

Healer's funeral was on May 10 in Kailahun district

The virus spread out widely from her funeral

GUINEA

KAILAHUN

KENEMA

SIERRA LEONE

SOURCE: World Health Organization

Chapter 2

Controversies

The outbreak of Ebola in sub-Saharan Africa has become a scourge in West Africa. Officials with the World Health Organization reported that "new cases could reach 10,000 a week by December 2014," according to BBC News Africa. The New York Times reported that "Ebola virus ravaging West Africa has renewed the risk of political instability in a region barely recovering from civil war." Donald Trump, a billionaire developer, known for his bluntness, stated that "Africans should be banned from visiting and traveling to the United States," according to the media. In his tweet, Trump wrote "What the hell is Obama doing in allowing all of these potentially very sick people to continue entering the U.S.! Is he stupid or arrogant?"

With contempt for the presidency and President Obama, according to media reports, Trump would continue his tirade about the president, with unprecedented tweets. Utmost contempt for, and disregard to, the presidency and President Obama was not entirely unexpected of Trump who had unsuccessfully tried on numerous occasions to run for president. In his last attempt, in 2011-2012, he "couldn't make it to the GOP primaries," one political observer said. He had to withdraw his political aspiration for the presidency, out of embarrassment.

In another tweet, Trump wrote "President Obama - close down the flights from Ebola infected areas right now, before it is too late! What the hell is wrong with you?" For someone who "had filed more bankruptcies running businesses than any corporate executive, he would be qualified to give advice about running a country!" another political observer noted. As if not embarrassed, he would tweet again: "President Obama, I have an idea! Pretend that West Africa is Israel and then you will be able to stop the Ebola area flights." He was unabashedly referring to the conservative media reports and insinuations that President Obama does not like Israel and its Prime Minister, Benjamin Netanyahu.

According to Pew research and other notable, mostly conservative media polls, majority of Americans (58%) had agreed with Trump that there should be a travel ban, banning West Africans from travelling to the United States. In another conservative media (known for its biased reports) poll conducted whether a travel ban should be imposed, a majority of Americans reportedly opined that a travel ban be placed on visitors from West Africa. A school teacher who had visited her native country of Tanzania for vacation was placed on a 21 day observation for Ebola, by her school, in Texas.

The CDC warned that "Traveling to Sierra Leone could affect your ability to return home." Travelers leaving Sierra Leone are being screened at airports before departure. "If travelers are being screened before leaving Sierra Leone, why shouldn't travelers to that country be able to return home to the U.S.?" A Nigerian doctor living in Houston wondered.

The Ebola stigma also affected visitors to Dallas after Thomas Eric Duncan had tested positive for Ebola in that city. The Ebola hype and stigma would also transcend the West African sub-region as Americans from other parts of the U.S. were warned to avoid Dallas and to stay away from recent immigrants from West Africa. A visitor that traveled to Dallas from another part of the U.S. was put on 21 day incubation for attending a conference in Dallas, Texas.

A cruise ship with a suspected Ebola patient was refused docking in Mexico and Belize in October 2014 because of an Ebola scare. According to the U.K. based Independent Newspaper, passengers that were aboard the Carnival Magic cruise ship were refused dock in Mexico and Belize because the cruise ship they were in was reportedly carrying a Texas healthcare worker who had been exposed to Ebola virus at the Texas Presbyterian Hospital. One of the countries was quoted saying that the cruise ship was "like a floating petri dish." CNN reported one of its readers saying: ""I feel bad for sick people, but I don't understand the desire to be on the petri dish in the first place."

The Ebola scare on the Carnival Magic cruise ship had occurred when a Texas healthcare worker who had handled a blood sample of Thomas Eric Duncan was quarantined in her room, aboard the cruise ship, as a precaution. Though the healthcare worker later tested negative for the disease, the stigma had quickly broadened to include those who had been around Duncan, including those who had tested his blood sample. It didn't matter that the female healthcare worker was a supervisor and didn't personally test a sample of Duncan's blood. The fact that she was a healthcare worker working at the lab at the Texas Presbyterian Hospital when the test was done was enough to cause an Ebola scare. After all, Duncan had died in that hospital!

The already stigmatized sub-Saharan Africans continue to face several challenges like the one below, given by the CDC:

If you have symptoms of Ebola or a have high risk of exposure to Ebola, you will not be allowed to travel on commercial flights to the United States and potentially to other countries.

If you have symptoms of Ebola, you will not be able to travel until your symptoms go away, unless you are being medically evacuated to receive needed care.

If you have had a high risk of exposure to Ebola but are not sick, you will either have to arrange a charter flight home or stay in Sierra Leone until 21 days after your last exposure and authorities ensure it is safe for you to travel.

For Africans, especially Africans in the United States, it was as if Ebola was another excuse to degrade and marginalize them. The fear was confirmed when Thomas Eric Duncan, a Liberian who became infected with Ebola had died of the disease "untreated," according to his nephew, Josephus Weeks. The vexing opinions of several Africans were whether Duncan was allowed to die in order to contain the spread of the disease or whether Duncan was deliberately allowed to waste away in a ventilator while under sedation. The news report that Duncan woke up hungry and was asking for food, while supposedly on sedation and on a ventilator, attested to the poor treatment Duncan had received during his quarantine at the Texas Presbyterian Hospital, in Dallas.

A doctor, according to media reports, with the CDC, said the seasonal flu was more dangerous than the Ebola virus. A health official with the World Health Organization said the West had neglected to develop a cure and a vaccine for Ebola because the outbreak had not first occurred in the West. Another CDC health expert opined that a vaccine was not developed for Ebola because it was not profitable to do so since the countries affected were poor and would be unable to afford the vaccines.

The spread of the virus to Spain by a Spanish nurse who had treated a priest returning from West Africa, and the infection of a returning healthcare worker in London, and the United States, coupled with the arrival of Duncan with Ebola, had pushed the West to quickly develop the Zmapp and other experimental drugs.

During the research for this book, several Africans, in Africa and in the United States and the United Kingdom were interviewed. Most of the Africans interviewed in Africa were from West Africa, South Africa and North Africa, with several of them from sub-Saharan Africa, to see how they felt about the stigma that they had been brushed with. A Guinean Chemical Engineer, who lives in Austin, said he was not surprised that the West would see Africans as unwelcomed guests in the U.S. considering the weakened economic significance of Africa compared with Asians from China and India. When asked to elaborate, the Guinean chemical engineer, who asked for anonymity for fear of retaliation, said black Africans were only good for exploitation, never as equal partners in economic development.

A Nigerian attorney who lives in Houston was very blunt in his opinion. "Look at it this way, some Americans, like Donald Trump, look at West Africans as immigrants who came to the U.S. because of poverty in their homelands. To him and others, these West Africans are poor, miscreants, fraudsters, and crooks anyways, especially Nigerians. Why allow them here if they are bringing criminality to America, and worst of all, diseases that can kill Americans?"

The sentiments expressed by the Nigerian attorney appeared to be a near consensus among other Africans interviewed. The exceptions were North Africans from Egypt, Tunisia, Libya, Algeria, Morocco, and Mauritania. North Africans saw themselves as Arabs and unaffected by the stigma of Ebola. Their own issues were terrorism and instability in their homelands. An Egyptian salesman interviewed said he has never really seen himself as an African, let alone be touched by the Ebola stigma. The same response was received from a good majority of North Africans. A few North Africans, mostly Libyans and Tunisians, felt the stigma was unfair and racist.

The West Africans interviewed were unanimous in their opinion that being tarred with Ebola was unfair and racist. A Ghanaian who lives illegally in Houston and who was waiting for the immigration bill to pass that would allow illegal immigrants to file for legal papers, whose student visa had expired, said, while craving anonymity for obvious reasons, "if African leaders have not been too greedy and selfish, the African continent would be a wealthy continent. The continent has gold, diamond, uranium, oil, and all the mineral resources needed to enhance the lives of its citizenry like those in the advanced countries in the West. Why can't African leaders use these resources to enhance their countries? Why squander their riches and abandon their problems for the West to solve?"

It was easy to understand the frustration of the Ghanaian. Since finishing his education at a local university, he has been unable to secure an employment because of his illegal status. And to compound his situation, he was told he had to go back home to reapply for a visa to come back to the U.S. as an immigrant. To reapply for a visa to come back to the U.S., he would have to wait in his country for a period of five years, the same number of years he has been living in the U.S. illegally!

"If my country had been developed and there are gainful employment opportunities, why would I even want to remain here, or come here in the first place?" The Ghanaian added.
Most Africans, especially West Africans or sub-Saharan Africans felt their countries' wealth have been plundered, mismanaged and misused by their leaders.

"Shouldn't African leaders have been able to develop a vaccine if they were serious leaders?" a Liberian asked. He continued. "They could have. But they did not want to. They would rather wait for Western countries to do their jobs for them," he said, with sadness in his eyes and voice.

Though President Mobutu Sese Seko of Zaire, who led his country from November 1965 to May 16, 1997, had taken the initiative to quarantine the part of his country that were affected with Ebola in 1976, he could have also been able to fund a vaccine for Ebola if he wanted to. President Mobutu Sese Seko was reportedly one of the richest men in the world.

Instead of enriching his bank accounts with his country's revenues and aids from Western countries, he could have funded a scientific research into a vaccine for Ebola, says an insider with the World Health Organization. "Mobutu was installed, aided and supported by the U.S. and Belgium. Why didn't these countries support a vaccine development, knowing that Ebola outbreak had occurred twice in that region?" a Cuban healthcare expert asked, but the question was why Mobutu didn't try to harness the support of these rich countries toward developing a drug for a disease that had killed so many people in 1976 in the region.

Chapter 3

Is Ebola a Curse or a Blessing?

Like most tragedies, Ebola has had its disadvantages and advantages. With the West forced to pay attention to the once neglected but exploited sub-Saharan Africa, Ebola has compelled Western countries to pay attention. The most glaring disadvantages have been the stigmatization of Africa with Ebola. A Stigma that Dr. Peter Piot had wanted to avoid in 1976. Conversely, the obvious advantage is that the once snobbish Western countries are being forced to pay attention to Africa, especially sub-Saharan Africa. The Africa that was always allowed to perish with its endless tribal and civil wars, along with its 21st century ingrained terrorism and jihad, was now being rescued from the ravages of Ebola. The West has no choice but to come to the aid of Africa or the problems besetting Africa would come visiting the comforts of its cities and towns, as happened with the arrival of Thomas Eric Duncan in Dallas, with Ebola, on September 20, 2014, in the U.S.

Another compelling reason the West is focusing on eradicating Ebola is that Ebola is beginning to infect Westerners, especially those helping to fight the disease in West Africa. A Scottish nurse was recently transported to London after she had contracted the Ebola disease while helping to treat Ebola patients in Sierra Leone. In the U.S. over six healthcare workers, including nurses and doctors have been infected, and cured. An Italian doctor had also contracted the Ebola disease while treating patients with Ebola in Sierra Leone.

The doctor was later given the experimental drug to help combat and fight the deadly disease that has claimed the lives of thousands of West Africans. According to Yahoo News, the Italian doctor became the first Italian to be infected with Ebola.

The advantages have come to sub-Saharan Africa in the fom of scarce sophisticated medical equipment and well trained healthcare professionals such as nurses and doctors that are now arriving in West Africa. The West feared that there will be the likes of Thomas Eric Duncan arriving in their countries, if sub-Saharan Africa continues to be ignored with its diseases and miseries. There was also the fact that Ebola has transcended the African continent, with several Europeans and Americans infected with the disease.

For decades, Africa has been allowed to wallow in its self-inflicted poverty. The plight of suffering and fleeing West Africans are usually overlooked by Western media because it was thought that wars and strife were part of the African psyche. "If African children were dying of hunger, Western countries would look the other way," one African diplomat said. Why worry about Africa? After all, their leaders are corrupt and greedy enough to forsake their own people. Why shouldn't Idi Amin of Uganda, Mobutu Sese Seko of Zaire, and other African dictators and tyrants be allowed to kill their own people? It is just Africa, why waste human and material resources to rescue a people that were used to suffering and death?

If the same problems had been occurring in other parts of the world, save Africa, the West would have intervened with both humanitarian and military aids. Iraq was liberated of Saddam Hussein because he was a despot who was killing his own people. Idi Amin was allowed to kill, and to even eat his own people, with the West watching with amusement. It had taken a bold East African country, Tanzania, to take out Amin. "Where were the democracy-selling Western countries while Amin slaughtered his own people?" One African scientist asked. If Idi Amin had been an Arab dictator, in the Middle East or South America, attempts would have been made to topple and kill him.

With the West now refocusing its attention on Africa, especially on West Africa, Ebola patients would receive medications such as experimental drugs, and drugs for malaria and typhoid fever, including intravenous liquids and oral rehydration with water, sugar and salt. The plague being caused by Ebola would come to a minimal, if not abrupt stop, and there would be a sigh of relief that another catastrophe had been prevented. But will such a time come when Western countries would devote enough resources to eliminate Ebola in West Africa? If the dangerous precedent set by the Black Death is reenacted and is anything to go by, the West would understand that the Ebola disease is not confined to West Africa. Like the Black Death that started in Asia, "Ebola could transcend Africa and reach western countries also," an African healthcare expert said.

With the third outbreak of Ebola, in three West African countries, it was hard not to take action to find a vaccine, and to provide needed healthcare in Ebola ravaged countries of Liberia, Guinea, and Sierra Leone. It was not long after the Duncan debacle that it was realized that Ebola could get to Western countries. After all, it had taken an infected passenger from Liberia to Lagos, Nigeria, to spread the disease to Nigeria. On July 20, 2014, a traveler from Liberia, who had been infected with the Ebola virus, arrived at the Murtala Mohammed Airport in Lagos, Nigeria, where he was admitted to a private hospital in Lagos, after he became sick. The infected passenger had inadvertently exposed fellow passengers on the flight, the airport personnel, and many others, to the disease when he was confirmed to have the Ebola virus.

According to the Federal Ministry of Health in Nigeria, Nigeria became one of the countries in sub-Saharan Africa to be infected with the disease, following the arrival of the Liberian who had brought the disease to Nigeria. Following the strict guidelines adopted by the Nigeria Center for Disease Control (NCDC), the known 72 people who had been in direct contact with the Ebola infected patient from Liberia, were immediately put on observation and 21 day incubation period for the symptoms of the virus. The immediate problem was to contain the disease from spreading in Lagos, a commercial city with an overpopulation of estimated 21 million people. Allowing the disease to spread in Lagos would be catastrophic. An Ebola infected Nigeria (whose population was over 170 million) would mean a global epidemic whose impact would be akin to the Black Death that had killed millions of Europeans from 1346-53.

The Black Death was caused by Yersinia pestis . Like Ebola is fast becoming, if not contained, yersinia pestis had had its symptoms, and those symptoms included pneumonia that eventually became an epidemic that wiped out millions of Europeans in the 14th century. The Black Death had at first been underestimated before it became a plague.

It was urgent for the Jonathan administration in Nigeria (renowned for ineffectuality and inefficiency) to contain the disease or face a catastrophe that was similar to the Black Death. Had Nigeria's outbreak not been quickly contained, it would have spread to neighboring countries like Ghana, Benin Republic, Togo, Chad, amongst others. The surprised rapid response of the Nigerian government, under President Goodluck Jonathan, who is often fondly referred to as bad-luck Jonathan by many Nigerians, that included using the resources and assets at its disposal to fight the disease; and making the disease a top priority, helped contain and eliminate the disease in Nigeria. That quick response eventually made the World Health Organization to declare Nigeria free of the disease, barely three months the infected traveler from Liberia flew to Murtala Mohammed Airport, in Lagos, with the disease.

While Ebola has definitely been a scourge and a curse, it has also been a blessing. As aforementioned, every tragedy has its own blessing or advantage. Prosperity usually follows the aftermath of any war. The Ebola epidemic was a war, according to health experts. The outbreak of every war often results in many deaths; but prosperity usually follows wars because of the reconstruction booms, in the aftermath. In the aftermath of the Second World War, which lasted 10 years, from 1935-1945, the world knew a new form of economic prosperity that quickly erased the pains and bitterness of the decade-long war.

Prior to the Second World War, in the 1930s, the stock market had crashed, which lasted to the end of the war. In the economic downturn of that era, the crash of the stock market which started on September 4, 1929, wiped out individual retirement savings and wealth of most Americans. The ripple effect of the stock market crash in the U.S. would affect the world, resulting in the Great Depression which resulted in the plunging and plummeting of international trade. Unemployment soared to as much as 50% as businesses and corporations virtually went belly-up. As businesses failed and savings wiped out, crop prices fell by as much as 60%.

The Second World War would end the bitterness of the Great Depression, if only to be replaced with conflicts and the tragedies of war. The prosperity that ensued when the war ended brought new wealth that, for some, erased the ugly memories of the Great Depression and the war.

For sub-Saharan Africa, especially the affected countries of Liberia, Sierra Leone and Guinea, the disguised blessings and advantages of Ebola outbreak may be the infusion of foreign aids and medical infrastructures that are sprouting up in Monrovia in Liberia, Conakry in Guinea and Freetown in Sierra Leone. Along with the new medical facilities and infrastructures will be the training of medical personnel in the three countries on how to respond to disease outbreaks. Several countries in Africa, especially in West Africa, do not have effective emergency response systems. Hopefully the Ebola scare will create effective emergency response systems and units, akin to the 911 in the U.S. that will help West Africans with medical emergencies.

United Kingdom, Australia, United States, China, and even cash strapped Cuba and many other countries are pouring in their resources to ensure that Ebola is not only contained in West Africa but also eliminated. While the efforts of Western and other countries are laudable, critics opined that it may be a little too late. The disease has already infected many citizens in the United States, Spain, United Kingdom and Mali. In Mali, a two year old girl had died of the disease. The two year old girl had been infected when she had traveled by bus with her grandmother from Guinea through Mali to the western town of Kayes.

To contain the disease in Mali, efforts were made to find the passengers in the bus so that they could be tested for the symptoms, and put under observation. But in Africa, especially in West Africa, finding the passengers who had traveled in the same bus as the infected two year old girl would be difficult. On January 19, 2015, the government of Mali declared that it was Ebola free, that there had not been new infections in over 42 days.

Chapter 4

The Influence of Belgian Nuns and Dr. Peter Piot

The outbreak of Ebola in West Africa, in 1976, may have been caused, in part, by Belgian nuns who had used unsterilized needles to inject vitamins to poor pregnant African women. Researchers like Dr. Peter Piot had quickly recognized the source of the epidemic and had immediately put an end to the practice. Was the action of the Belgian nuns deliberate or out of ignorance? For most Africans, it was a Western conspiracy to further degrade and marginalize Africans especially sub-Saharan Africans. For Belgian nuns to have used unsterilized needles to inject vitamins (if they were vitamins) into the bodies of pregnant women, makes one shudder with apprehension and fear. According to a health expert with the World Health Organization, the actions of the Belgian nuns were an inadvertent omission. If the intentions were inadvertent, what was then done to correct the deadly mistake? Though Dr. Piot was dispatched to the region at the outset of the outbreak, no further actions were taken to develop a vaccine to make sure Ebola did not reoccur in sub-Saharan Africa.

Dr. Peter Piot who was a 27 years old virologist when he was dispatched to sub-Saharan Africa to track the deadly virus that would later be known as Ebola felt a thirst for adventure and was purpose driven. Sub-Saharan Africa was just the place for his medical adventure when he found his niche in the form of the discovery of the virus, Ebola. Working on discovering the virus in his laboratory in Antwerp, Belgium, and using the blood samples he had taken from those infected, the journey to identify and track Ebola was then in the offing.

According to a healthcare expert interviewed for this book, Dr. Piot had received the blood sample from a nun who had contracted the then mysterious virus and who had suffered a tremendous loss of blood. With the blood sample in two glass tubes in a plastic cooler, collected from an infected nun in Zaire, Dr. Piot would relentlessly embark on the onerous task of identifying the virus which was first thought to be malaria.

Though the disease was first thought to be yellow fever, which is a common ailment in West Africa, it would take further and more rigorous tests to identify the virus as Ebola. Though Dr. Piot's laboratory at the Institute of Tropical Medicine had the resources to detect tropical diseases such as yellow fever and malaria, it took several blood analyses to understand the nature of the virus that bore a resemblance to the symptoms of influenza. What first baffled Dr. Piot and his fellow researchers was that the symptoms were fever, weakness, severe aches and pains and breathing problems, which were symptoms of influenza, a common sickness that is often caused by the genus influenza virus.

According to the World Health Organization, as part of the experiment to detect Ebola, Dr. Piot embarked on using the blood samples taken from a Flemish nun who had been infected; and injected the blood into cells grown in the laboratory. Some of the blood samples were also used for tests of microbes like microscopic living things such as the brains of mice. Viruses like the Lassa fever that causes mouth ulcers, muscle pains; small hemorrhages under the skin, heart and kidney failures were first identified. Other viruses like the Marburg that causes fatal hemorrhage was also identified, including dengue that is usually transmitted by aedes mosquitoes that causes severe joint pain.

Having exhausted testing known and unknown infectious viruses, Dr. Piot was still unable to identify the virus that had infected the Flemish nun. With additional efforts and determination, the experimental mice that were injected with the infected nun's blood were put on observation for possible results.

With all the tests and confirmations carried out by Dr. Peter Piot, one would have thought that Western countries would have used the results obtained by the virologist to create a vaccine to prevent future outbreaks. But that wasn't the case. Since the outbreak was limited to sub-Saharan Africa, rich Western countries neglected to fund a drug or vaccine that would prevent future outbreaks.

Chapter 5

Africa Flu and Western Ebola

In sub-Saharan Africa, there is no seasonal flu as often seen in Western countries. What sub-Saharan Africa has is the perennial malaria and yellow fever, which according to scientists and healthcare experts with the World Health Organization and CDC, has symptoms similar to the flu virus. Malaria is generally caused by the bite of mosquitoes and is often passed from one person to another. Though the malaria disease is a treatable disease, it is a serious disease that is known to kill thousands of Africans annually, according to the World Health Organization.

The malaria disease is also caused by sporozoan parasites (genus Plasmodium) in the red blood cells. The transmission of it is by the bite of anopheline mosquitoes. The symptoms usually include chills and fever. With malaria, the air can be infected with a noxious substance which can also cause a disease such as malaria, whose known symptom is fever.

When the Ebola disease became a West African scourge, the West at first chose to ignore it, likening it to the flu virus. There were lots of reasons for likening Ebola to the flu virus. One of the reasons was that Ebola and the flu virus share similar symptoms. The Ebola virus belongs in the categorized filoviruses group called genus Ebolavirus which causes fatal hemorrhagic fever. Recall that the malaria disease also causes fever.

The known symptoms of Ebola, according to CDC and World Health Organization, include fever, severe headache, muscle pain, weakness, fatigue, diarrhea, vomiting, abdominal pain and hemorrhagic bleeding. Comparing flu with Ebola, it can be seen that the two viruses share similar symptoms, except for the hemorrhagic bleeding and abdominal pain. Hemorrhagic bleeding and abdominal pain seldom occurs with a flu virus infection.

The similarity between the symptoms of the flu virus and Ebola virus was what made several Western countries to conclude that the Ebola virus was the Africa equivalent of the Western flu virus. The name Zaire ebolavirus of African origin emerged as a disease peculiar to sub-Saharan Africa, just as the malaria virus had been categorized as a virus common in sub-Saharan Africa.

The yellow fever which often causes the yellowing of the skin of an infected person is another sub-Saharan Africa disease caused by the bite of African mosquitoes. According to the World Health Organization, the yellow fever is a prevalent infection that usually occurs in warm tropical weather conditions. The symptoms of the yellow fever include some of the symptoms of Ebola and malaria which are fever, headache, prostration and albuminuria. Albuminuria is often present in the urine of an infected individual and is symptomatic of the kidney disease.

Other known symptoms of the yellow fever include jaundice which is a yellowish pigmentation of the skin, body tissues, and body fluids; which is caused by the deposition of bile pigments. Jaundice can result in satiety, distaste and hostility. Other known symptoms of the yellow fever include hemorrhage. The Ebola virus also causes hemorrhage. The difference is that the yellow fever is caused by a flavivirus of the genus flavivirus. The yellow fever is transmitted through mosquito bites.

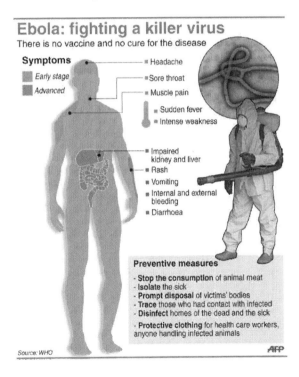

When the symptoms of Ebola, malaria and yellow fever are compared and examined, the similarities in the symptoms become very narrow. Little wonders healthcare experts in western countries had at first called the Ebola virus an African version of the western flu virus.

Chapter 6

Can the flu vaccine be used as an Ebola vaccine?

If the symptoms of the Ebola virus are almost similar to known symptoms like malaria and the flu, why can't the vaccine that is used for the flu virus be used for Ebola virus? The answer lies in the deadliness of Ebola because of the quickness with which Ebola kills compared with the flu virus. According to a recent poll, over forty percent of Americans view Ebola as a major threat, compared to less than ten percent that viewed the flu virus as a moderate threat to public health. Enterovirus, on the other hand was viewed by less than one percent as a threat to public health. According to the poll fewer than one percent even knew about enterovirus compared to over seventy percent that knew of the Ebola virus.

Enterovirus is a genus of picornaviruses that often occurs in the gastrointestinal tract, which has been linked to deadly respiratory infections among children in some parts of the U.S. In some cases, infected children often experience muscle paralysis, according to the CDC. Enterovirus has affected children in forty-five U.S. states, with five fatalities. If enterovirus had emanated from sub-Saharan Africa, it would have been publicized as a plague in the media, an African scientist opined.

Some experts with both the CDC and the World Health Organizations asserted that enterovirus will likely have more deadly consequences among children in the U.S. than the flu and Ebola viruses combined. Though the flu virus kills thousands of Americans every flu season, and send thousands more to hospitals, panic level is minimal compared to the panic level associated with Ebola.

The unanswered question among panicky Americans and Westerners was: what scares more – Ebola or the flu? Judging by the recent hue and cry and the clamor of alarm caused by Ebola, it would be safe to say Ebola.

From February 2014 through November 2014, Ebola claimed over 5,300 lives in West Africa. In that same period, the flu virus will claim ten times more lives during the flu season. Though there is no vaccine for Ebola, except for the experimental drug, Zmapp, the flu virus has a vaccine, including numerous drugs to combat it; yet the death toll is far higher than the Ebola virus.

According to the New Yorker, the media pays less attention and hardly raises alarm about the fatalities caused by the flu virus, compared to the panicky alarm raised about the threat of Ebola to public health. The overblown coverage of the Ebola virus made hospitals across the U.S. to reexamine their preparedness for the Ebola virus. While the panic caused by the media hype helped hospitals and healthcare facilities to increase their preparedness for disease outbreaks such as Ebola, it did nothing else other than to increase the stigma associated with Ebola.

That stigma included outright discrimination of sub-Saharan Africans who live in the U.S. and Europe, or had traveled within the time of the outbreak to their native countries in West Africa. The stigma also temporarily crippled the economies of the three affected countries whose borders and schools were closed, to avoid further transmission and spread of the disease.

In Liberia, foreign investors and contractors abandoned the projects they were already working on, and hurriedly left, from the country when the outbreak occurred in 2014. Roads that were being constructed were quickly abandoned, leaving the roads in poor dilapidated conditions with potholes and waterlog.

With foreign investments gone, foreign businesses and corporations closed their businesses, thereby increasing the already worsened unemployment in a country barely recovering from the devastation of a crippling war.

Some African countries like Morocco that was scheduled to host the African Cup of Nations said it would not host the game or commit to the schedule to host the game because of Ebola scare, according to BBC News Africa. Morocco worries that Ebola could spread to the country through the anticipated thousands of West African football supporters that would travel to that country for the three week African Cup of nations.

According to the Wall Street Journal, Morocco was thrown out of the 2015 African Cup of Nations and stripped of its hosting rights for not abiding by the scheduled dates, for early 2015. Morocco, a country that often considers itself an Arab country rather than a North African country, has often fallen out with the rest of the continent. Morocco has also, reportedly, refused to be part of the African Union because it did not consider itself an African country even though it is geographically an African country.

Though Morocco has, in fairness, requested to postpone hosting the African Cup to 2016, the attitude of its citizens during recent games in that country in which players from West Africa were called Ebola, had already created a bad impression. When Morocco had requested to postpone hosting the game to 2016; and had refused to commit to hosting it in early 2015, it was all that the Confederation of African Football could take. Morocco had already done enough damage to the African psyche, for an African country!

Chapter 7

<u>Thomas Eric Duncan</u>

Thomas Eric Duncan who became the face of Ebola in the U.S. had traveled to the Promised Land, or what most immigrants called the land of the Golden Fleece where opportunities abound and dreams are realized and achieved. Little did he know that coming to America, for him, would be a clarion call that would summon him to the doorsteps of hell and death, in the land of greener pastures, flowing with milk and honey; where freedom is almost guaranteed, albeit to a chosen few! He had not known that his poor country of Liberia was his destiny and not the purported land that flows with milk and honey.

He had come to America, whether for a wedding or graduation, he had come. He had come with high hopes and pent-up dreams. Dreams held in ambience. Little did he know that the dream would die with him upon entry, through the prejudiced gates, to the land of milk and honey!

He had gleefully and hopefully boarded that plane that would take him from Liberia, through Brussels and Washington to Dallas. Exhausted after the long journey, he was happy. Exhaustion was a small price to pay for finally making it to the land of the Golden Fleece. It has been a long wait, too long already. It was a dream that finally came true for Duncan. But that dream would be short-lived!

Arriving and probably jetlagged from that long flight that took him to three distant cities, he was probably worn with fatigue, with his immune system reduced by the change of environment, weather and scenes, not to mention the meager foods he was fed in the confined airplanes he took to get to his destination.

Already weary from the long journey, he probably underestimated the extent of his exhaustion from the long trip and assumed the worst. Perhaps he had caught the plague that had bedeviled his country. Unbeknownst to him he was walking into a devil's trap he followed his first thought and went to the hospital near him. After all, this was the white man's land where help was at the snap of the finger and at the beck and call of every American. How mistaken he was! Little did he know that without insurance the paradise he found could easily be his doomsday! He walked into that Texas Presbyterian Hospital, expecting the kindness and goodness he has heard so much about the white man's hospitality.

Not knowing what was really wrong with him, since nothing was wrong with him; the nurse had given him some antibiotics and sent him home. Wrong diagnosis it seems; or maybe not! Days later, Duncan would return in an ambulance, still unwell. With fever at a 103 body temperature, and from the Ebola plagued Liberia, the information was enough to quarantine the unsuspecting Duncan.

Quarantined, unfed, untreated, sedated and on a ventilator, death would be a matter of days. Rather than treat the misdiagnosed patient, hospital authorities would shift blames from the nurse that first saw Duncan to the doctors on duty when Duncan had first visited the hospital. In the meantime Duncan lay dying. "Why didn't anyone ask Duncan if he was from Liberia?" Authorities asked, as if coming from Liberia was a death knell. For Duncan, the death knell was already ringing, unbeknownst to him.

Quarantined and untreated, Duncan's condition would gradually get worse. Whatever ailment he had at the time of admission took a turn for the worse. The irony was that the day he was reported to be in a stable condition was the day he would die! How can a hospital tell the media that Duncan was improving and getting better and then the very next day announce that he was dead? Doesn't make sense, does it?

The most astonishing aspect of the whole saga was the illogical deduction that beats the deductive reasoning about the Duncan sad story. If Duncan had been sick with Ebola, how come his fiancée, Louise Troh and her children never got sick with Ebola? Deductive reasoning: perhaps he never had it in the first place. If Duncan never had Ebola how and where did Nina Pham and Amber Vinson, the nurses who took care of Duncan, contract the virus? Deductive reasoning: perhaps both Nina Pham and Amber Vinson never had the Ebola virus either. The illogical deduction about the Duncan story is that the Texas Presbyterian Hospital had, along with CDC, declared that both nurses had symptoms of the virus, which was attributed to a body temperature that was over 103, in both nurses.

Having a body temperature of 103° has never, before Duncan's arrival, been a qualification for the Ebola virus. Though a 103° often means a patient was feverish, it has never been a dangerous medical situation. What had qualified both nurses to be Ebola infected may have been that they had body temperatures that hovered around 95° and above. Because both nurses had attended to Duncan before his death, it was prematurely assumed the nurses had the Ebola virus.

To further buttress these assertions, the CDC evidentially informed Amber Vinson that it was alright for her to travel when the nurse had informed the agency that she was having a body temperature of 95°. When she had self monitored herself, fearful that she might have contracted the Ebola symptoms, she had rightfully reported her situation. Arriving from Cleveland Ohio where she had gone to make a wedding arrangement for her upcoming marriage, she would later be quarantined when her condition did not improve. The reason for her quarantine was that she was assumed to have contracted the Ebola symptoms because she was one of the nurses who had "treated" Duncan.

The Texas Presbyterian Hospital had admitted that it did not know how to handle the Ebola virus because it did not have the equipment or the training to identify and handle Ebola infection. The hospital's admission of its ignorance about the Ebola virus explains why Duncan was not treated, unless of course Duncan was not treated because he did not have health insurance – another deductive reasoning. Hospitals are often reluctant to treat patients without medical insurance even though they are required by law to treat all patients.

On Nina Pham's and Amber Vinson's "Ebola" symptoms, it can be safe to assume they probably had the flu virus since we were in the flu season when Duncan had supposedly brought Ebola to the U.S. from Liberia. Suspecting that the nurses probably had the flu virus rather than Ebola would be a safe assumption as both the Ebola and the flu virus share similar symptoms.

When asked how she got Ebola, Amber Vinson, according to the CNN said "it is a mystery to me." If the nurse felt it was a mystery to her, even after she had attended to Duncan who supposedly had the virus, then it was probably as she said – a mystery, as she did not expect to have the virus, having taken all the necessary precautions when she had attended to Duncan.

Another illogical deduction about those who had directly and indirectly been in contact with Duncan is that none had contracted the virus save the two nurses, Nina Pham and Amber Vinson. And the two nurses had recovered within days, another reason to believe that they never had the Ebola virus to begin with.

The U.S. doctors who had contracted the virus had taken much longer to recover. Kent Brantly, who according to the AP had contracted the virus while "treating a steady stream of patients with Ebola in Liberia," had taken much longer than Vinson and Pham to survive the virus. He had been flown to the U.S. when his condition had worsened in an isolation unit where he had been quarantined in Monrovia while receiving treatment.

Dr. Brantly's coworker, Nancy Writebol, had also reportedly fallen ill of the virus. Brantly and Writebol had been separately flown to the U.S. for treatments. AP reported that Dr. Brantley's "prognosis is grave and efforts to evacuate him to Europe for treatment have been thwarted because of concerns expressed by countries he would have to fly over en route to any European destination." Arriving in an Atlanta hospital, in the U.S., Brantly's condition would remain grave and critical for days, before gradually improving. According to the AP, Dr. Brantly had spent three weeks at the Emory University Hospital, where he had received treatment for Ebola, before being discharged, free of the virus.

Nancy Writebol, an American missionary, and aid worker, had, according to CBS News, been infected with the virus on July 22, 2014, when she had first thought she was sick with malaria, before being diagnosed and confirmed to have the Ebola virus. Recall that the malaria virus has similar symptoms as the Ebola virus. She had been immediately isolated when she had tested positive for the Ebola virus. Like Dr. Brantly, she had also been flown to the Emory University Hospital in Atlanta, where she had received treatment before being discharged. Both Brantly and Writebol had, according to the CBS News, received the "experimental drug treatment called Zmapp."

Thomas Eric Duncan had reportedly tested positive while already on U.S. soil and had not been flown to the Emory University Hospital like Brantly and Writebol; and had not received the Zmapp drug treatment or any experimental drug treatment. Texas Presbyterian Hospital was reportedly not equipped to handle and treat Ebola and did not transfer Thomas Eric Duncan to a hospital that was equipped to do so. Deductive reasoning: Duncan was black and couldn't afford the treatment.

Duncan's nephew, Josephus Weeks, would rightly echo the racial sentiments already felt by most West Africans when he said: "Had he been another color, he probably would be living today, he would have survived it. And that's what's really hurting me the most: … They treated him the way they did because of the color of his skin. You stand a chance if you're white, but not if you're black." Weeks comment would make a case for deductive reasoning when the treatments received by Dr. Branktly and Writebol are compared with the "treatment" received by Thomas Eric Duncan. Another American doctor, Dr. Rick Sacra, a medical missionary, was flown to Omaha's Medical Center to be treated for the Ebola virus. According to CNN, Rick Sacra was the third American who had contracted the Ebola virus in Liberia and had been flown to the U.S. for the Ebola treatment. Dr. Rick Sacra was reportedly infected at a general hospital in Monrovia where he had been delivering babies. He had survived the disease having been treated and cured by the Omaha Medical Center.

Another deductive reasoning is why the CDC did not authorize Thomas Eric Duncan to be flown to Emory University Hospital or Omaha Medical Center for treatment. These hospitals, according to CNN, were equipped with qualified doctors and nurses to handle Ebola virus. The logical conclusion is racism!

A new Ebola filter that fights Ebola was reportedly used to cure an Ebola patient in Germany. The Filter, Hemopurifier, according to Time Magazine, was developed by Aethlon Medical and has been in use since the recent outbreak of Ebola in March 2014. The filter "can pump out enough copies of itself to overtake the immune system." This method of curing Ebola, according to Aethlon Medical, reported by Time, was a specially designed cartridge that is attached to a dialysis machine which can effectively tip the balance to favor the body of an infected patient. The way it works is relatively simple and intriguing. The lectin in the filter attracts Ebola viruses "and sucks them from the blood as it flows through," the blood stream. Why the filter was not used on Thomas Eric Duncan and Dr. Salia Martin, both Africans, is baffling.

Specialized planes were used to transport Americans who had contracted Ebola to the U.S. for further treatment at the Emory University Hospital, and lately, at the Omaha's Nebraska Medical Center. Why wasn't Duncan flown to Emory University Hospital or Nebraska Medical Center? After all two Americans with Ebola had been successfully treated at the Emory University hospital, even before Duncan arrived in the U.S. on September 20, 2014. Duncan had tested positive on September 28, 2014, a few days after he arrived from Liberia.

What criteria did the Texas Presbyterian Hospital use to determine that Duncan had Ebola other than the fact that he had recently traveled from Liberia to the U.S.? Apart from reportedly having a body temperature of 103°, and showing signs of weakness, which are both symptoms of both the malaria and the Ebola viruses, what further proof did the hospital garner before quarantining Duncan? Information was not given that Duncan was hemorrhaging and vomiting blood. Information was also not given that Duncan had had abdominal pains. The only information given was that Duncan had tested positive for Ebola by virtue of his having a body temperature of 103 degree Fahrenheit. For a hospital that does not know anything about Ebola, how was that determination made? Would the hospital have recognized Ebola if it had been presented with the disease?

What is known is that Duncan had been sedated and put on a ventilator; and then left alone to languish and enervate in the name of containment. Amber Vinson best presented a case of doubt about being infected. She had contacted the CDC when she first suspected that she might have the disease, when her body temperature had read 95 degree Fahrenheit. The CDC had told her there was no cause for alarm that she could travel. The CDC believed then that Amber Vinson did not have the virus. Vinson herself told the media that getting the virus was a mystery to her, when she had reportedly tested positive for the disease.

Nina Pham who had shot to a 15-minute fame in the media when she had reportedly tested positive for the Ebola virus had been shown on television having fun in her quarantined isolation unit, smiling and telling her friends that she loves them. Her demeanor hardly bespoke of someone ridden with the Ebola virus. Her new heroic image would be further enhanced with her meeting with President Obama, an opportunity that was not presented or granted to Amber Vinson when the latter had been released from the hospital; when she had been declared free of Ebola. Though she was reportedly said to have received a call from President Obama, it was hardly the same as meeting with the president in the White House.

The treatment of Nina Pham in the media was remarkably different from the treatment Amber Vinson had received. "Though not white, Pham had been treated a whole lot better than Vinson, both in the media and in isolation," says a nurse, at the same Texas Presbyterian hospital, who did not want to be named. According to ABC News, Dr. Brantly "flew to Dallas on Sunday, one day after Pham tested positive for the virus. He donated his blood, packed with antibodies that should fight the disease." Why didn't Duncan receive the same blood that was "packed with antibodies" from Dr. Brantly who had been infected and cured, long before Duncan came to the U.S with Ebola? The words of Josephus Weeks reechoes here that Duncan was discriminated against because of the color of his skin. According to ABC News, Pham was "doing well, she's being treated very well, and she feels comfortable," a feeling Duncan could not have expressed since he was not even given the opportunity to get well. Daily News (Nov. 1, 2014) reported that Pham's dog, Bentley, a King Charles spaniel, had reunited with Pham when the latter was discharged from the hospital, free of Ebola. Daily News reported that Bentley never tested positive for Ebola but had been put on a 21 day "precautionary quarantine."

On the contrary, Duncan's belongings that were never even tested for Ebola were destroyed. Duncan's fiancée, Louise Troh's properties, according to Mail Online (November 2014), including the family car, were reportedly destroyed when her home was sanitized. Troh and her children never tested positive for Ebola. On the other hand, Pham's belongings were untouched. She was able to return to her life and properties. Duncan's fiancée had her properties, including the only family vehicle, destroyed. Pham had tested positive in the same hospital that Duncan had tested positive. Why were Troh's properties destroyed and Pham's properties left intact? A case of racism can be made with the difference in the treatments received by both parties.

Louise Troh was released from her forced isolation unit, to homelessness. Mail Online reported that she had lost her residence and belongings after they were sanitized. She was "left homeless and with nowhere to go after her apartment was taken away from her when it was decontaminated. Many of the family's possessions were seized and incinerated to destroy all viruses and pathogens." She was living at a Church conference center after losing her home. Recall that Troh did not test positive for Ebola. Pham had tested positive for Ebola and was able to reunite with her dog, Bentley, and her properties. All that Troh would be allowed to keep were "a few plastic bins filled with personal documents, photographs, trophies and a Bible, the Dallas apartment was stripped down to the carpeting and the contents were destroyed."

Another incidence of discrimination and racism is the manner Troh and her family was treated. When Duncan was diagnosed and reportedly tested positive for Ebola, according to ABC News and Mail Online, a Dallas court ordered the family to remain in the apartment, along with the contaminated linens Duncan had used. There was utter disregard for the safety of, and total disregard, for the family's health. The fact that Duncan had reportedly tested positive should have been enough for the court to immediately remove the family from the environment, and the contaminated linens Duncan had used incinerated. Rather, the family was quarantined in the apartment, with Duncan's used linens and personal belongings, while under house arrest, guarded by heavily armed police to make sure they did not leave the apartment.

It would be five days before they were moved to a four bedroom home owned by the Catholic Diocese of Dallas. The city and the court did not show any concern for the welfare of the children in the apartment. Sources close to the family said the city never expected the family to be uncontaminated with Ebola. They had thought the entire family would be infected. The initial idea was to incinerate them along with Duncan's and Troh's belongings. It was a shock to the city of Dallas that, according to the unnamed sources, Troh and her family were uninfected and even survived beyond the 21 day incubation period, without Ebola.

Amber Vinson, on the other hand, was able to return to her life as she had left it, even though she had reportedly tested positive for Ebola. "I have no idea," she told CNN. "I go through it almost daily in my mind: what happened, what went wrong. Because I was covered completely every time; I followed the CDC protocol. ... I never strayed. It is a mystery to me," she reportedly told the media. Recall that Duncan did not have or displayed the Ebola symptoms when he had left Liberia on September 19, 2014. It will be days before Duncan would experience high body temperature which was reportedly confirmed to be Ebola because his body temperature had read over 103 degree Fahrenheit.

When criticized for boarding a flight to travel home to Cleveland, Vinson, according to CNN would retort that "I'm a nurse. I care. I care for me; I would not put myself in danger. First, I would not take Ebola to my family and my best girlfriends. I would not endanger families across the nation, potentially exposing them to anything," she said. "I had no symptoms. There was no way, at that time -- I could not transmit it."

In a similar circumstance, Duncan would be criticized harshly, even threatened with prosecution, for knowingly traveling to the U.S. with Ebola. Recall that Duncan had passed through several airports and had been tested and screened before boarding the various planes he took, before and after he disembarked, in Dallas, Texas. During those tests, he never tested positive or showed signs of the symptoms. It would be days, after his arrival, before reportedly testing positive for Ebola, if he actually tested positive. Remember that his fiancée, Troh, her children, and family, with whom Duncan stayed, in the apartment, did not contract the virus. They were even subjected to the linens Duncan had used when he had reportedly been contaminated, for five days before they were transferred to a house provided by the Catholic Diocese of Dallas.

A CDC director, Dr. Tom Frieden, according to CNN, told the media that Vinson "shouldn't have taken the flights," to go home to Cleveland and back to Dallas. She had earlier been instructed by the same CDC that she should take the flights. "I did what I was supposed to do," Vinson retorted, CNN reported.

Vinson would later add, according to CNN: "I did what I was supposed to do, and now you're saying I should not have flown. You know, I checked multiple times before I even left Dallas to see if it was OK to go."

The difference between Vinson and Duncan is that the former was treated, even though she was black like Duncan, but she was an American, which makes a big difference. Duncan, who was blamed to his grave for bringing Ebola to the U.S., never got treated. He never had the opportunity of being given an antibodies blood transfusion that Nina Pham received, courtesy of Dr. Brantly. Why didn't Brantly donate his blood to Duncan like he did with Pham? He flew in a day after Pham tested positive and donated his blood to save the nurse. Why did Thomas Eric Duncan not get the same blood donation from one of the survivors? The only logical explanation is because he was black.

Unlike Duncan's fiancée, Louise Troh, the only thing that Vinson will lose would be her engagement ring and wedding binder she had used to plan her upcoming wedding, which were destroyed by the cleanup crew after the nurse had tested positive for Ebola. Though her fellow passengers on the flight to Cleveland and on the flight back to Dallas were located and put on voluntary incubation for 21 days, none contracted the virus. Louise Troh did not have the same voluntary 21 day incubation. Troh was confined in one place with armed guard, in a house arrest.

There is no doubting the difference in the treatment of Louise Troh, Duncan, and the two Dallas nurses. There was a noticeable shabby and ignoble treatment of the infected Duncan and the uninfected Louise Troh, in the hands of Dallas authorities. Would Duncan have received a better treatment if he had been a different color? Josephus Weeks, Duncan's nephew, thinks so. And the whole world thinks so. Everyone, save Duncan, his fiancée and her family, were treated with respect and dignity. Duncan's fiancée, Troh, would be subjected to house arrest while being allowed to languish in confinement with the linens Duncan had used when he had reportedly tested positive for Ebola. The linens did not get incinerated as Vinson's engagement ring and wedding binder, to prevent the family from getting infected. It was assumed they were already infected and were waiting their turn to die and be cremated like Duncan!

Chapter 8

Was Duncan a Villain or a Hero?

To millions of Americans in the U.S., Duncan was a villain who knowingly brought Ebola to the U.S. with intent to spread the disease. No one had stopped, during the saga and unfolding events, to think that it would have been impossible for Duncan to have intentionally traveled to the U.S. with Ebola. Duncan was tested in every airport he transverse. The argument was that Duncan had lied on the form he had filled regarding having been in contact with someone with the disease. Did Duncan know that the pregnant woman he helped in Liberia had Ebola? Probably not, as Duncan could not have been able to come close to an Ebola infected person in Liberia at the time, since infected individuals were being quarantined by Liberian health officials and taken to isolated units and places. Who determined that the pregnant woman Duncan had helped in Liberia really had Ebola? Was it possible she may have died from complications related to her pregnancy, like the convulsion she had suffered from? As far as everyone was concerned the death of the pregnant woman was Ebola related. After all, she was a Liberian and every death occurring in Liberia during the summer of 2014, was Ebola related!

The Huffington Post reported that Duncan showed the first signs of Ebola on September 25, 2014, five days after he had arrived in the U.S. According to the Huffington Post, Duncan was screened before getting on the plane in Liberia where Liberian healthcare workers reportedly took his temperature which was at 97.3 degree Fahrenheit. The 97.3 degree temperature indicated that Duncan did not have fever or any other symptom of Ebola.

The Associated Press reported that Duncan filled out a form in which he was asked if he had been in contact with, or been exposed to anyone with Ebola, to which Duncan had answered no. Duncan may have been telling the truth as he would not have knowingly helped an infected person, knowing the consequences of helping an infected person unprotected; especially when he was due to travel in the next few days, to the U.S.

The New York Times reported that four days before Duncan traveled to the U.S. he had helped his neighbors to transport Marthalene Williams, who was pregnant and sick, to and from the hospital. The New York Times also reported that Marthalene

Williams had been refused treatment and admission at the hospital she was transported to, because there was no space; and the pregnant woman had been brought back home, with Duncan assisting, where the woman had died in the wee hours of the following morning.

In a detailed investigative report conducted by the New York Times, the paper found that Duncan may not have known he was exposed to Ebola. According to the Times, those who had helped the pregnant woman, including Duncan, on 72nd SKD Boulevard, in Monrovia, Liberia, believed the pregnant woman's convulsions were related to her seven month pregnancy. Duncan had been asked if he had been exposed to anyone with Ebola and he had rightly answered no; because he assumed, like everyone in his neighborhood on 72nd SKD Boulevard in Monrovia, that he had helped a pregnant woman with pregnancy complications. In the U.S., Duncan would have been a hero, not a villain as he had been painted by all and sundry.

The false assumption that Duncan knowingly got on a plane to seek medical help in the U.S. is fraught with ignorance, says a family member who knew Duncan very well. First, it is not easy to just get a visa and jump on the plane to the U.S. It takes months, sometimes years, to procure a U.S. visa, especially coming from West Africa. And coming from West Africa, one does not just buy a ticket to come to the U.S. Duncan had had his tickets purchased long before his heroic encounter with the pregnant woman, Ms. Williams. With four days before he would travel, it would have been virtually impossible for Duncan to make travel arrangements, within days of helping the pregnant woman. In the U.S. where things work more efficiently, it would have even been impossible to conclude a travel arrangement for another country within four days, let alone in West Africa where things move at a snail pace.

Duncan had heroically used his instinct to help a dying woman, something that most good Samaritans would do, even here in the U.S. But was helping a sick pregnant woman something he shouldn't have done? Ebola is not the only disease killing Liberians. Suppose the pregnant woman had died of other ailments other than Ebola? Who was there to determine that the woman had died of Ebola?

In Liberia, President Ellen Johnson Sirleaf, the 24th and current president of Liberia reportedly said Duncan would be prosecuted if he returned to Liberia, for bringing Ebola to the U.S. and for lying on the questionnaire he filled. The Associated Press reported that

"Liberian officials say they will prosecute Thomas Eric Duncan, the man infected with Ebola at a Dallas hospital, because he lied at the airport about having been in contact with anyone with the disease when he left Liberia." The irony of it was that Duncan did not lie when he said he hadn't been in contact with anyone with the disease as he did not know that the pregnant woman he had heroically helped had the disease. If she did have the disease!

It was not even determined that the pregnant woman Duncan had helped had the disease; because the woman did not get to see a doctor at the hospital; because the hospital had been full, with no space for the pregnant woman. The woman had died the next morning, and it had been assumed, according to CNN and AP, that the woman had died of Ebola, because Ebola was at the time, the leading cause of deaths in Liberia.

As Duncan lay dying in a Dallas hospital, his country's president, Ellen Johnson Sirleaf, and health officials in that country were busy castigating him, and threatening to prosecute him when he returns to Liberia. Rather than show the dying man some sympathy, and even some empathy, some Liberian politicians, including the president of Liberia were prejudging and criticizing a man who had, days before, heroically helped a pregnant woman suffering from pregnancy related convulsions. Duncan and those in his neighborhood who had also helped the pregnant woman did not know the woman had Ebola nor was it ever confirmed that she did.

In a civilized society like the U.S., Duncan would have been a hero rather than a villain. He would have been a hero for going the extra mile for another human being. Instead of being celebrated as a hero, he became a villain and a victim who had suffered death for his heroism. Meanwhile, in the U.S. Nina Pham would be hailed a hero and even able to visit the president of the United States, in the White House for having survived Ebola; that she had mysteriously contracted while taking care of Duncan. Pham would be toasted by all and sundry while Duncan would be castigated a villain by his own country's president.

Duncan had helped to transport a pregnant woman to and from the hospital in Liberia, four days before he would travel to the U.S. and was, according to the AP, screened at the airport in Liberia for the symptoms of Ebola, which he did not have. And for not knowing he had Ebola; and for truthfully answering he had not been in contact with anyone with Ebola on a form he filled out at the airport, "he would be prosecuted," says Binyah Kesselly, chairman of the board of directors of the Liberia Airport Authority. Kesselly reportedly said Duncan brought a stigma to Liberians living in the U.S and abroad, as if Liberia was not already stigmatized with Ebola, before Duncan came into the picture.

In the U.S., Dallas County District Attorney, Craig Watkins, according to NBCDFW.com, said his office was considering charges against Duncan for bringing Ebola to the U.S.! The announcement was not unexpected, considering that Duncan's own country of Liberia had earlier castigated him as a villain who would be prosecuted if he ever returns to Liberia. Craig reportedly said: "We are actively having discussions as to whether or not we need to look into this as relates to a criminal matter. If it warrants a Dallas County prosecution then we will pursue it. But it may be more of a federal issue," Watkins reportedly told NBC5's 'Lone Star Politics.

Rather than the District Attorney's office pursuing the Texas Presbyterian Hospital for misdiagnosing Duncan and sending him home with antibiotics, the DA's office would attempt to make a scapegoat out of Duncan. Was Duncan targeted because he was black? No. Duncan was targeted for prosecution because his country had initiated the idea to prosecute him for something he did not cause.

Nina Pham and Amber Vinson became heroines for surviving Ebola while Duncan became a villain. Why? Not because Duncan was black but because he was a sub-Saharan African from Liberia. Duncan may have been untreated at the Texas Presbyterian Hospital because he was a poor black Liberian with no medical insurance and money, but he was first marginalized and degraded by his own country of Liberia, before Dallas picked up on it. In fairness, Texas Presbyterian Hospital and the D.A.'s office may have also reacted to the attitude of Liberian authorities that threatened to prosecute and imprison Duncan when he returns to Liberia, as he lay dying.

"If President Ellen Johnson Sirleaf and her office had shown some empathy rather than castigation, the D.A.'s office and Texas Presbyterian Hospital would have followed suit," says a hospital insider who preferred to be anonymous. Though there is no doubt the actions and inactions of the Texas Presbyterian Hospital smacks of racism, the ignoble manner Liberia treated its own citizen was largely responsible for Duncan's death!

Chapter 9

Why Africa Continues to Suffer Degradation

For centuries, Africa has been degraded and marginalized for reasons other than the color of the skin of Africans. It had all started when Africa was subdivided by several European countries in the Berlin Conference of 1884. With the then German Chancellor Otto von Bismarck presiding, the foreign ministers of 14 European countries and the United States had met to create the rules for the future exploitation of the multifarious and numerous natural resources that abound in what the Europeans called the Dark Continent. In the meeting to divide Africa, there were no representatives from Africa to decide its future. The decisions were made, signed, sealed and delivered by Westerners!

To partition the Dark Continent, the 14 foreign ministers from European countries and the United States felt there was the need to lay a ground rule in the partitioning of Africa, so as to avoid conflicts among the European countries and the United States. During the conference, Germany had sought more advantages that would boost its influence and opportunities against its major competitors like Great Britain, France, Portugal, Spain, amongst others. To avoid conflicts of interests, it was felt that the groundwork be laid down to create a geopolitical map of Africa that would serve the interests of the major players at the conference.

To ensure a level playing field that would benefit the stakeholders at the conference, the Dark Continent was subdivided on the basis of affluence, influence and economic significance of the stakeholders. With Germany seeking more influence and opportunities, negotiations were made, and agreement reached, to ensure that each country gets its own share of the abundant natural resources in Africa. The basis of the conference was to weigh the amount of natural resources available and how the resources were to be exploited to each member country's advantage.

With Africa divided among the nations in attendance, to ensure that the numerous natural resources were exploited to the maximum, the colonial masters (as they were called), formed a government in each divided territory to ensure that Africans were restrained and controlled. It was feared that inadequate control could spark ethnic and tribal violence that would torpedo, and destroy the interests of the colonial masters. To ensure that each country was safe and protected, the colonial masters gave each territory a name that best suits their geopolitical interests.

Critics of the colonial master's intention in Africa opined that the 1884-85 conference degraded Africa and fostered ethnic and tribal violence that would later become the hallmark of Africa. Rather than ensure that Africa was divided to benefit Africa, the continent was divided to benefit the colonial masters who had years before, sent explorers to explore the mineral resources that abounded in the Dark Continent. Though African countries would, in the early part of the 20th century, regain a semblance of the independence the African freedom fighters had sought, Africa's problems would only deepened with a new unending post-independence warfare.

To further create a lasting divide, the colonial masters imposed their languages on the territories each country controls, which was another form of control and restraint. With the French imposing the French language in the colonies it controls, the British would also impose the English Language in its territories. The Portuguese imposed the Portuguese language in its territories; while the French imposed its language in the territories it controlled. With each colony speaking a different language, imposed by the colonial masters, it would be a matter of time before Africa would permanently become foreigners to each other, in their own continent; and would forever be alienated from each other with different tongues and languages.

As each colonial master sought to expand its influence, greed would define the interests of countries like the French which dominated a sizable portion of West Africa. The British would also control a number of West African territories including East and South Africa. Belgium was apportioned a section of central Africa such as the Congo. Each European country was given territories that best suited its finances and influence. Portugal was apportioned a few territories in West Africa and Southern Africa. Acquisitions and territories were based on the finances available to each European country.

To reassess the African continent, a new ground rule would be created under the auspices of the new League of Nations, created after the First World War. With the formation of the League of Nations, countries involved in the negotiation in the Berlin Conference of 1884-85 would have their territories reassigned. Germany, because of its role in the war, would have its territories placed under the control of the new international body – League of

Nations, which created a new ground rule for colonizing and managing the African territories.

With the League of Nations formed, it was felt that Africans should be introduced to science, civilizations and Christianity. With the African indigenes subjected to what the Europeans and the League of Nations called civilization, leaders like King Leopold II of Belgium would enjoy greater influence and enrichment through the infrastructural development, and sale of lands, in the name of bringing science to the indigenes. Critics observed that the actions of Belgium's King Leopold II introduced some of the corruptions that became endemic in the African continent because of his scandalous business practices that became prevalent in the region at the time, and in the years thereafter.

Belgium's King Leopold II plundered the African territories held by Belgium and other territories he was involved with, by transferring most of the wealth he unscrupulously acquired to Belgium, and converting them, to his personal coffer and use. According to the BBC (February, 2004), "While the Great Powers competed for territory elsewhere, the king of one of Europe's smallest countries carved his own private colony out of 100 km2 of Central African rainforest. He claimed he was doing it to protect the natives from Arab slavers, and to open the heart of Africa to Christian missionaries, and Western capitalists." The excuse was a smokescreen designed by King Leopold II, to exploit Africa to the fullest for his own personal gains and enrichment.

King Leopold II was also said to have been responsible for the death of millions of Africans, while leaving the territories broke, and in poverty, with the raw materials plundered to benefit the factories in his country and Europe. King Leopold II unleashed untold misery, poverty and grief in Africa, especially in what is now known as the Democratic Republic of Congo, then Zaire.

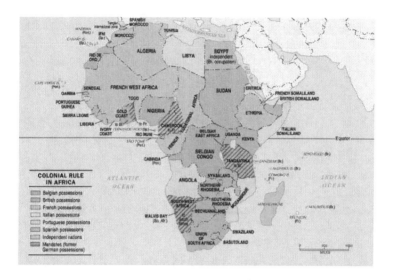

The violence that continues to plague and bedevil Africa was first started by King Leopold 11, who at the time, according to BBC News Africa, turned the country that is now Congo, into a labor camp, using the indigenes to cultivate and harvest his expansive rubber plantation in Africa. King Leopold II's action and unscrupulous dealings in Africa directly contributed to the deaths of millions of innocent Africans, in West Africa, especially in Congo. The legacy of violence established by King Leopold II continues to resonate and endure, in Congo and the rest of Africa. Coercion, tormenting, chopping off of limbs and raping of women, that were started a century ago, during the evil colonial rule of King Leopold II, continues to be the lots of Africans, especially in Congo and West Africa in general.

Chapter 10

Africa's Economic Mobility and Setbacks

African countries continue to strive for economic greatness in the 21st century. The economic growth rates of most African countries continue to surpass most European countries that were once their colonial masters. In Ebola stricken Liberia, the economic growth rate was 5.8, prior to the advent of Ebola, according to the Central Bank of Liberia. When Ebola struck, Liberia's economy tremendously slowed down because of the scare of Ebola, which drove away investors, especially foreign investors. Another reason for the slowdown, according to Wall Street Journal, was the travel ban, border and school closures, imposed by the Liberian government; a step that was taken to contain Ebola.

According to the World Bank, Liberia is one of the poorest countries in the world with a low per capita income; and a GDP per capita of $299.45. The standard of living is extremely low, with an acute shortage of basic infrastructure such as pipe borne water, and electricity. Civil wars and corruption had largely been responsible for the enduring low per capita income and poor standard of living. Though the country has had successive inept and corrupt leaders, coupled with a devastating civil war, there has been a remarkable economic recovery in the last few years, prior to the Ebola outbreak, according to the United Nations. With increased efforts in tapping the country's natural resources, and expansion in the mining and rubber industries, economic growth had steadily been expanding. Economic experts believe part of the reason for the economic growth has been the campaign to stem out corruption and eradicate red tape and unnecessary bureaucracy in the government psyche.

Though poor, Liberia has been on the upward mobility, economically, in the last few years, since the dawn of the millennia. The economic growth rate of Liberia has been at a steady pace, a pace that was good enough to attract envy from Western countries that would prefer to see Africa remain a begging and subservient nation than a self-sufficient nation with economic significance.

Other Ebola stricken countries like Sierra Leone and Guinea have also been striving economically with steady growth rates prior to the Ebola scare and impact. Sierra Leone, for instance was one of the countries that had been doing very well, economically, before the Ebola epidemic. Sierra Leone's steady economic growth rate, along with other African economic growth rates, was one of the reasons World Bank predicted that the 21st century would be Africa's century. Countries like Kenya, Ethiopia, Ghana, Nigeria, amongst others, have been growing steadily, economically, that economic experts predicted that Africa was on the verge of surpassing many Western countries in economic growth.

Sierra Leone's economic growth rate was also the envy of most countries, as the country's economy continues to grow at a steady pace. According to the reports released by World Bank: "Real Gross Domestic Product (GDP) increased to 15.2% in 2012, after expanding by 6% in 2011 due to the commencement of iron ore production in Sierra Leone while non-iron ore GDP growth was 5.3%." The country's envious growth rate was spurred by the country's reinvestment and expansion in the agricultural sector of the economy, while also increasing the construction of its infrastructures. Refocusing on the country's iron ore projects, along with increased spending, added needed boost to the economy. Increased government spending also added to consumer confidence and spending, which boosted economic growth in the country. Increase in efficiency in the services provided by both government and private sectors had, also largely been responsible for the steady increase in economic growth, according to the World Bank.

Though Sierra Leone experienced a temporary setback with a less than expected growth rate in 2012, due to the problems at its Tonkolili iron ore mine, the economy still maintained a 15% economic growth in 2012. Though the growth rate fell by 2% to 13% in 2013, the forecast, according to The International Monetary Fund (IMF), for 2014, had looked good and had been expected to exceed 14%. IMF said "the current account deficit of the balance of payments is projected to narrow to 10.5% (19.1% in 2013), while reserve coverage would improve to 3.4 months of imports." With the scare and impact of Ebola, those gains will be stymied. With Ebola creating a gridlock, Sierra Leone's prospects of becoming a self-sufficient nation has been temporarily derailed and hampered.

With the Ebola gridlock, World Bank forecasted that Ebola has hampered economic growth in large numbers. The setback caused by Ebola threatened to erase the upward economic mobility that Africa has enjoyed up to the point of the Ebola outbreak.

EBOLA HITS ECONOMIC GROWTH

West African economies were growing fast, but the World Bank now estimates the outbreak will deprive the region of more than $2 billion in growth

■ Pre-crisis estimate ■ October estimate ▨ December estimate

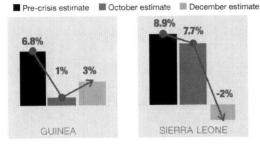

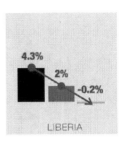

SOURCE: World Bank

Why would Sierra Leone that had a good economic prospect be derailed by Ebola? And was the virus deliberately spread by Western countries to derail Africa's economic rise? Many Africans, who were hopeful of Africa's economic rise, continue to ponder the question. Recall that a group of Belgian nuns had used unsterilized syringes to spread Ebola in sub-Saharan Africa, in 1976, under the pretext of giving vitamins to pregnant women? How did the virus resurface and who is responsible for its newest outbreak?

In its most recent report, the World Health Organization reported that Ebola reoccurred in Guinea in 2014, spreading to Liberia and Sierra Leone because of the proximity of those countries; and also due to the way of life of Sub-Saharan Africans. The consumption of bush meats and the spread of the disease through fruit-bats were some of the reasons advanced for the latest Ebola spread.

It would seem plausible that if the latest Ebola spread had been as a result of a conspiracy that the three poor countries most affected by the Ebola outbreak would be the ideal countries to spread the virus. There are also those who contend that the virus was deliberately spread through poor countries that lacked the resources to combat and contain the disease.

In Guinea and Congo, the legacy of King Leopold II endures as West Africa was once again plunged into misery, poverty and sicknesses. It was as King Leopold II would expect West Africa to be, many years after the crooked and notorious Belgian King plundered Congo and its environ of its resources; and led many innocent Africans to their untimely deaths. It was in the same sub-

Saharan Africa that Belgian nuns had surreptitiously injected pregnant women with vitamins with unsterilized syringes during an Ebola outbreak in 1976.

Despite all the obvious setbacks, in sub-Saharan Africa, economic growth continues to increase. Impediments and economic setbacks like civil wars, terrorism, graft and corruptions notwithstanding, World Bank forecasted that sub-Sahara Africa was on the move to taking its rightful place in economic significance, in the millennial. In 2013 alone, "GDP growth in the region strengthened to 4.7 percent in 2013, up from 3.7 percent in 2012, supported by robust investments in the resource sectors and public infrastructure. However, domestic constraints and a tightening global environment will moderate growth in the medium term."

Though the economic outlook for sub-Saharan Africa has been robust, several challenges, besides the sudden reoccurrence of Ebola, had started to hamper economic growth. Though still sustainable, most countries that had been predicted to achieve continuous economic growth had initiated bold moves that had started to limit the growth achieved in the short term. With fiscal and current deficits widening across the region, due to ambitious public expenditure and overambitious investments, coupled with unsustainable increment in wages, uncertainty has started to set in. In addition, increased transfers, subsides and declining revenues due to declining commodity prices, and deterioration of fiscal obligation, had started to surface among several countries in the region, before the Ebola epidemic. Apart from the expected economic problems caused by Ebola, another problem has surfaced in the Ebola stricken zones.

According to Margaret Chan of the WHO "the Ebola epidemic has set back political stability and economic recovery in the afflicted countries of Sierra Leone, Guinea and Liberia, with heavy toll on frontline domestic medical staff." With scanty medical personnel which compute to two doctors for every 100,000 people, in places like Sierra Leone and other African countries, adequate healthcare provision has become a luxury in sub-Saharan Africa. The outbreak of Ebola reined in the ugly reality of life in Africa, especially in West Africa. Compared to the U.S. where there are about 240 doctors for 100,000 patients, life in Africa is still coated and shrouded in misery and high mortality rate.

Not all countries in the region have embarked on economic programs that can sustain continuous growth. Some African countries like Zambia had used its fragile economic growth and bubble, to increase the wages of its public servants in excesses of 45% of its GDP in 2013. Though Zambia's growth had been fragile, the government felt its civil servants should be rewarded, possibly in an attempt to boost dedication and loyalty in the workforce. It was felt that a satisfied workforce would boost productivity and create workplace satisfaction. It was a good move except that the economy was not buoyantly strong enough for such wage increments. According to the World Bank, the country quickly found out that its public finances were unsustainable.

The unsustainable path of fiscal mismanagement for several African countries had to be corrected in order for the continent, especially West Africa, to continue to meet its fiscal responsibility. A fragile economy, it was discovered by Zambian leaders, could not carry the burden of excessive spending. It was a path that was not sustainable under the bubble growth. For most countries in sub-Saharan Africa, rising fiscal deficits, and debt to GDP ratio, had steadily increased, despite the recorded growth. Unrestrained government borrowing had systemically risen to unsustainable level among low income generating countries to 43.3% of GDP in countries such as Mozambique. The same was true of Gambia which rose to 82.1% of its GDP in 2013.

Middle income generating countries in sub-Saharan Africa with systemic rise in borrowing and public debts, in comparison with their GDP ratios, include countries like Senegal with 45.9 percent debt to GDP ratio. Ghana whose growth has been widely reported as one of the beacons of hope for the rest of the region had a 60.1 percent debt to GDP ratio. Cape Verde or the Republic of Cabo Verde, an island country, in the coast of West Africa, had a 95.0% debt to GDP ratio. The increasing debt to GDP ratio in some of these countries compelled the World Bank and IMF to advise the leaders of these West African countries about fiscal responsibility and consolidation; in order for the countries to rebuild fiscal buffers.

Economists predicted that the expected move by the U.S. Federal Reserve to taper its assets purchasing program would further set back some of the gains most sub-Saharan African countries had achieved between 2012 and 2013, before the advent of the Ebola epidemic in the region. Tied to the asset purchasing program of the U.S. Federal Reserve System, is the currencies of frontier economies like Nigeria, South Africa, Ghana and Zambia. According to the World Bank, investor sentiment also hampered growth, partly due to the scare of Ebola and terrorism in the region. In Nigeria for example, Boko Haram has unleashed untold violence in the Northeast of the country, in cities/states and towns like Maiduguri, Yobe, Kano, Kaduna, and even the capital, Abuja; areas considered the commercial hub of the country.

With the exception of Lagos, which is considered the commercial capital of the country, the rest of the country is under siege as a result of unrests in the Niger Delta and terrorism in the northeast. Added to that is the fiscal irresponsibility of the government of President Goodluck Jonathan, whose continuous increment in the salaries and wages of politicians and a select cadre of public servant, has led to unsustainable public expenses. Nigeria and Zambia have been under heavy scrutiny and pressure from the World Bank and the IMF to curtail their expenditures and fiscal irresponsibility. There have been pressures on both countries to consolidate their finances in order to allow room for economic growth and fiscal sustenance.

As investor sentiment has led to low investment in West Africa, so has short term capital flows to the region, coupled with low commodity prices and, in the case of Nigeria, declining oil prices in the global market. With the outbreak of Ebola on July 23, 2014 that caused a few Nigerians to lose their lives, economists believe that Ebola scare, though short-lived in Nigeria, had changed investor sentiments and interests in the country. Though Nigeria became Ebola free in October 2014, following the precautions taken to contain the disease by the country's leaders, investors are still slow returning to the country, which has significantly contributed to low capital flow, according to the World Bank.

In the case of Zambia, which was the first to use its debt to raise over $1 billion through the sale of "10 year dollar-dominated bonds priced at 8.6 percent, compared with 5.3 percent on its maiden bond issuance in 2012," ambitious increase in the wages of public servants and unprecedented investment in undue infrastructures has somewhat systemically set back the gains achieved through the issuance of debt-related-bonds and iron ore projects, says the World Bank. The resultant budget deficit and investor demands for debt-related bonds have also reduced growth albeit by a small margin. Though Zambia was not affected by the Ebola scare, investors are still worried about the ravaging disease in countries like Sierra

Leone, Liberia and Guinea where over 11,000 Ebola patients have died and over 30,000 have been infected.

African nations with full National Income Accounts							
'00-09 (a)	2010	2011	2012	2013e	2014f	2015f	2016f
GDP at market prices (b)	4.5	5.2	4.5	3.7 4.7	4.7 5.1		5.1
(Sub-region totals - countries with full National Income Accounts + BOP data) (c)							
GDP at market prices (c)	4.5	5.2	4.5	3.7 4.7	4.7 5.1		5.1
GDP per capita (units in US$)	2.2	2.6	1.9	1.1 2.1	2.1 2.5		2.6
PPP GDP (c)	4.7	5.7	4.9	4.0 5.3	5.2 5.4		5.3
Private consumption	5.4	2.2	4.0	0.6 4.8	4.6 4.3		4.4
Public consumption	5.9	7.0	13.3	2.7 5.8	5.2 4.9		4.8
Fixed investment	7.8	6.6	8.6	7.2 5.1	4.4 5.3		4.8
Exports, GNFS (d)	3.9	20.6	16.6	0.4 4.7	4.9 5.8		5.7
Imports, GNFS (d)	7.0	10.0	15.7	-2.4 4.7	4.3 4.4		3.9
Net exports, contribution to growth	-0.7	3.1	0.5	1.1 0.1	0.3 0.7		0.8
Current Account Balance, % of GDP	-0.1	-1.0	-0.7	-2.7 -3.4	-3.6 -4.3		-4.4
GDP deflator, median in LCU	6.5	7.2	6.9	5.3 4.4	6.1 5.5		-5.7
Fiscal Balance, % of GDP	-0.4	-3.7	-1.3	-2.8 -3.0	-2.7 -2.5		-2.5
Memo items: GDP							
SSA excluding South Africa	5.2	6.1	5.0	4.2 6.0	5.8 5.9		5.7
Broader geographic region (including high income countries) (e)	4.6	5.1	4.5	3.6 4.6	4.6 5.0		5.0
Oil Exporters (f)	5.7	6.0	4.0	3.0 6.2	6.0 6.0		5.7
CFA countries (g)	3.8	4.9	2.5	5.3 3.9	5.0 5.0		4.5
South Africa	3.2	3.1	3.5	2.5 1.9	2.0 3.0		3.5
Nigeria	5.7	7.8	6.8	6.5 7.0	6.7 6.5		6.1
Angola		10.9	3.4	3.9	6.8 4.1	5.2 6.5	6.8

Listed in the table above are, according to the World Bank, the economic growth rates of most African countries in the last few years. The steady growth rate was what led most economists and the World Bank to predict that Africa was on the verge of becoming economically self-reliant and significant in the millennial.

Chapter 11

<u>Western Ebola Patients versus African Ebola Patients</u>

Since the Ebola outbreak in Guinea and its spread to neighboring Sierra Leone and Liberia, several sub-Saharan Africans have died from the disease, including 11 African doctors like Dr. Godfrey George who was the medical superintendent of Kambia Government Hospital in northern Sierra Leone, before he died of Ebola. Dr. Martin Salia, who contracted Ebola in Sierra Leone, became the second Ebola victim in the U.S., and the second African, according to CNN, to die of the disease in the U.S. The first patient was Thomas Eric Duncan, an African who had arrived from Liberia to marry his longtime fiancée, Louise Troh, when he contracted and died of the disease. The second was Dr. Salia, a surgeon who had contracted the disease in Sierra Leone where he had been working to save lives.

In contrast, Dr. Kent Brantly, 33 years of age, who had been working for Samaritan's Purse in Liberia since October 2013, as part of his post residency program, had been the group's medical director at the Ebola center in Monrovia when he had contracted Ebola. Sick with Ebola, Brantly had been "in very serious condition," says Ken Isaacs, the vice president of Samaritan's Purse. Dr. Brantly had been successfully treated in the U.S. and had recovered. The same had been the case with Nancy Writebol of Charlotte, N.C. who had contracted the Ebola disease and was successfully treated in the U.S. Both patients had at first been in critical but stable conditions just like Dr. Martin Salia. Writebol and Dr. Brantly had contracted the same Ebola disease and had survived the virus after they had both received treatments in the U.S.

Dr. Salia who had been flown to the U.S., had paid his way to Nebraska Medical Center, on a chartered flight from Sierra Leone, that he had paid for, had died the following Monday, having arrived the Saturday before, according to Reuters. This was a sharp contrast to Dr. Brantly and Nancy Writebol who had both been successfully treated and had lived to tell the story of their ordeal with Ebola. The excuse given by the Nebraska Medical Center as to why Dr. Salia didn't survive was that his Ebola infection was already at an advanced stage before he was brought to the hospital. Dr. Salia had tested negative for Ebola on November 6, 2014, just days before. How did the virus get to an advanced stage when he did not test positive days before? Dr. Brantly and Writebol had contracted Ebola in the same amount of time and they had survived without the excuse that their infections had reached advanced stages.

Why is it that when it comes to Africans being successfully treated as their American counterparts that the Africans never survive? Long before Duncan came to the U.S. and tested positive for the Ebola virus, Dr. Brantly and Writebol had been infected with Ebola and were successfully treated in the U.S. How did Duncan who did not have Ebola when he arrived in the U.S. on September 20, 2014 die of Ebola when Dr. Brantly and Writebol who had contracted Ebola in Africa before being flown to the Emory Hospital in Atlanta survived the disease? The words of Josephus Weeks reechoes again that it all boils down to the color of the skin.

Another reason may also lie in the CNN and BBC News Africa reports that Dr. Martin Salia had paid his way to get treated in the U.S. while Dr. Brantly and Writebol had been funded by their group. The BBC News Africa had also reported that the arrival of Dr. Salia had been subdued, with only one police escort. On the other hand, the arrival of Dr. Brantly had been marked with high media coverage, fire trucks, police vehicles and motorcycles. Same disease infections, different treatments! The differences in the treatment would reflect in the survival of the American healthcare workers and the death of the African healthcare worker, and Duncan. It didn't matter that Dr. Salia was a permanent resident in the U.S. who had gone to Sierra Leone to provide needed healthcare to his people under the auspices of the United Methodist Kissy Hospital in Freetown, Sierra Leone. He was still an African!

Another American doctor, Dr. Craig Spencer, 33, who had been infected with Ebola in Guinea, West Africa, had also been flown to the U.S. where he had been successfully treated at the Nebraska Medical Center. According to the Daily News, Dr. Spencer's condition had "worsened," and had "entered the next phase of his illness," after he had been diagnosed with the disease and suffered from gastrointestinal symptoms. NBC News had also reported that Spencer had been given the experimental drug called Brincidofovir, in addition to being given plasma transfusion by Nancy Writebol. Dr. Martin Salia did not have the privilege of being given the Brincidofovir drug or a plasma transfusion.

When Nina Pham had been infected Dr. Brantly had donated his blood which contained antibodies as part of her recovery. Writebol had given plasma transfusion to Dr. Spencer. How come none of these former Ebola patients had donated antibody and plasma transfusion to help Dr. Salia and Duncan? All the ten American healthcare workers, including doctors and nurses, who had been infected with Ebola in West Africa had survived. Two Africans had died of the disease in the U.S.! Dr. Martin Salia and Thomas Eric Duncan had been Africans. Dr. Salia had been a Sierra Leonean national while Duncan had been a Liberian – both died of the disease on U.S soil where help was readily available. That help was never rendered to them!

Dr. Rick Sacca, 51, became the third American infected with Ebola while delivering babies at a general hospital in Monrovia, Liberia. Like Dr. Spencer, Dr. Sacca had been successfully treated at the Nebraska Medical Center, the same hospital that Dr. Salia had died of Ebola.

Successful treatment of Ebola infected Africans had been nonexistent while it has been remarkably successful amongst non-Africans. In the U.S., only Africans had died from Ebola, while other races who had been infected had survived. In Europe, like the U.S., those infected with Ebola had also survived!

In France, a French citizen working for The International Medical Humanitarian Organization – Medecins Sans Frontieres (MSF), who had been a healthcare volunteer in Liberia had developed the Ebola symptoms and had been flown to France on September 18, 2014, for treatment. Unlike Africans who had been infected with the disease and hadn't survived, the French citizen had been successfully treated at the Begin Military Teaching Hospital and had been discharged less than a month later. The fate of a non-French citizen who had been infected with Ebola and who had been flown to France from Sierra Leone had been remarkably different.

Unlike in the U.S. where Africans infected with Ebola had not made it, the first recorded African doctor of a Senegalese descent, an epidemiologist working for WHO in Sierra Leone, had contracted the disease on August 27, 2014, and had been flown to a hospital in Hamburg, Germany, that specializes in the treatment of highly contagious diseases. Though transported in a specially equipped plane to the northern city of Hamburg, the patient was able to walk off the plane to receive treatment, according to Yahoo News, and was successfully treated and declared Ebola free on October 4, 2014. The resultant stigma associated with Ebola had made the epidemiologist to request that his name and personal information be made confidential and undisclosed. Hard to blame the Senegalese doctor considering the stigma associated with the disease.

German doctors had been holistically optimistic enough to believe that by gradually reducing the infected patient's fever and pain, and keeping the patient's body hydrated, that the disease can be eliminated in a patient. Those simple measures, according to a Hamburg health department spokesperson, Rico Schmidt, can help stabilize the patient. Another optimist German, Stefan

Schmiedel, who specializes in tropical diseases, said such simple measures can also reduce the mortality rate of Ebola. Though the measure had not worked for another African healthcare worker who had died while receiving treatment at the hospital in July, it had however been successful enough to save the life of the Senegalese epidemiologist.

Unlike in the U.S. where Africans infected with Ebola have not been successfully treated, a Ugandan doctor who had been working in Sierra Leone when he had been infected with Ebola, on October 4, 2014, had been flown to the Frankfurt University Hospital, where he had received several experimental drugs and had recovered. According to Reuters and the Huffington Post, the patient had been a physician working for the Italian NGO in Sierra Leone. At the behest of the World Health Organization who had asked Germany for help to treat the Ugandan physician infected with Ebola, the patient had been flown to Germany where he had been treated in an isolation unit of the Frankfurt's University Hospital.

A third patient, according to the New York Times, a 56 year old Sudanese, Abdel Fadeel Mohammed Basheer, a laboratory technician working with the United Nations Mission in Liberia would however die on October 9, 2014, at the St. Georg Hospital in Leipzig, Germany, of the Ebola virus. Though St. Georg Hospital in Leipzig was one of the oldest hospitals in Germany and was said to specialize in highly contagious tropical diseases, it would be unable to treat its first Ebola patient, thereby recording the first Ebola patient to die of the disease on German soil.

In Norway, a female doctor with Doctors without Borders, a Norwegian volunteer, was confirmed infected with the Ebola virus on October 6, 2014, while working with Ebola patients in Sierra Leone. The patient, Silje Lehne Michalsen, was reportedly flown to the isolation unit of the Oslo University Hospital for treatment. Less than two weeks later, on October 20, 2014, the patient, according to YAHOO News, whose condition had been critical but stable, had recovered and was discharged.

A Cuban doctor, Feliz Sarria, an internal medicine specialist, working at the Kerry Town Ebola Treatment Center, according to Bloomberg News, who had been part of the Cuban healthcare workers sent to West Africa to help combat Ebola, by that country's government, had had a fever and had tested positive for Ebola on November 17, 2014, in Sierra Leone, where he had been treating Ebola patients, and was flown to Switzerland for treatment, at the behest of, and under the auspices of, the World Health Organization.

In England and in August 2014, a British volunteer nurse working at the Kenema Government Hospital in Sierra Leone, had tested positive for Ebola and was flown by the Royal Air Force, with a specially equipped C-17 plane, to England. The nurse was cured and had later returned to Sierra Leone, a few months later, to continue the work of treating and caring for Ebola patients.

In Spain, a nurse's assistant, Teresa Romero, a 44 year old hospital worker, who had volunteered to help when two missionaries were flown from West Africa, had tested positive for the Ebola virus. She became the first person to contract the virus in Spain and in Europe, on October 6, 2014. According to the Economist, she had touched her face with a gloved hand after she had helped Ebola victims, and had thereafter caught the disease herself.

CNN reported that she had helped treat two Spanish missionaries who had contracted the virus in West Africa. One of the missionaries had contracted the disease in Liberia while the other had contracted it in Sierra Leone. The two missionaries had died upon returning to Spain. Though she was accused of not wearing the appropriate protective clothing and taking enough precautions, she would rebut that argument that she had taken the necessary precautions, albeit touching her face, which was against the safety protocols established by the World Health Organization. She said she wore protective clothing and followed the protocols. Over 50 people who had been in contact with her were carefully monitored for a 21 day incubation period.

Chapter 12

West African Countries Infected with Ebola Virus

Guinea, formerly known as French Guinea and now the Republic of Guinea, is distinctively different from neighboring Guinea-Bissau and the Republic of Equatorial Guinea. Guinea has a population of 10.5 million, and occupies a land area of 245,860 square kilometers. The capital is Conakry. The country gained its independence from France in October 2, 1958. Following the country's independence from France, its first president was Sekou Toure (1922-1984). With its independence, Guinea became the first French colony in West Africa to gain its freedom from French colonial rule.

Having helped fight for his country's independence, Sekou Toure would become anti-imperialist and a nationalist who fiercely believed Africa should be left to Africans. With bitterness and anger aimed at imperialist nations like Great Britain, France and the United States, Toure would work with other freedom fighters in South Africa and West Africa to fight for their countries' independence. Under Toure, the country became self reliant albeit having to depend on the Soviet Union for economic aids, a move made to fend off Great Britain and the United States.

The Republic of Guinea experienced the Ebola outbreak, according to the CDC and WHO, on March 25, 2014, with initial 86 suspected cases and 59 deaths from the disease. A report published in the New England Journal of Medicine indicated that a two year old child, Emile Ouamouno, had died of Ebola in Guinea on December 2013. The two year old boy was reportedly a native of the village of Meliandou, in Gueckedou, in the Nzerekore Region of southern Guinea. The boy's sister, mother and grandmother, were also infected with Ebola. The source of the Ebola virus had been fruit bats.

The disease would later spread like wildfire to the villages of Dandou Pombo and Dawa, also in Gueckedou. The midwife who attended to the initial patients had unknowingly spread the disease to the other villages by not wearing protective clothing. The disease had, as a result, spread to the Baladou district and on to Macenta town, with a population of 88,376; and on to the city of Kissidougou in southern Guinea, with a population of 102,675.

The ravaging virus that continued to wreak havoc would compel the new president of Guinea, President Alpha Conde, to declare a national health emergency in the country. To contain the disease, President Conde made concerted efforts to quarantine the affected areas. Those in the affected areas of the country were implored to stay in their homes to stop the disease from spreading. The border was heavily controlled to limit movements to and from other countries. Travel bans and restrictions were put in place. Infected individuals, suspected family and friends of those infected, were hospitalized and quarantined until they were cleared of the disease. An unspecified incubation period was in effect to mitigate the spread of the disease.

Part of the precautions taken by President Conde included preventing those who died from the Ebola virus from being transported between villages, cities and towns. The precautionary policy of President Conde was reminiscent of the precautions taken by President Mobutu Sese Seko Kuku Nbendu Wa Za Banga, who in 1976, had quarantined the region affected, including the capital of Zaire, Kinshasa, to prevent the spread of the disease.

Even with the precautions taken by President Conde, Ebola continues to ravage the citizenry of Guinea. The epidemic has reached an alarming proportion, prompting CDC to issue the following warning, on November 16, 2014: "CDC recommends that US residents avoid nonessential travel to Guinea. If you must travel, such as for humanitarian aid work in response to the outbreak, protect yourself by following CDC's advice for avoiding contact with the blood and body fluids of people who are sick with Ebola." As the disease continues to take lives and hamper economic activities in the region, CDC , WHO and other stakeholders have for the first time, in decades since the first outbreak of Ebola, started focusing on eradicating the disease from West Africa. It became known to all and sundry that Ebola can infect anyone, including the once invincible westerners, one African diplomat quipped.

Recognizing the need to take action before Ebola traverses West African frontiers to Western frontiers, international organizations such as Medecins San Frontieres (MSF) quickly launched an emergency response to combat the deadly virus, in March 2014. Over 24 doctors, logisticians, hygiene and sanitation experts were mobilized and dispatched to Guinea, setting up isolation units in suspected areas like Gueckedou, Macenta and the Nzerekore region in southern Guinea. According to Dr. Esther Sterk with MSF, "Isolation units are essential to prevent the spread of the disease, which is highly contagious."

In Sierra Leone, 6,802 cases of Ebola were reported with 1,453 deaths at the end of summer of 2014. This was an alarming number for a country where the tenth doctor, Dr. Aiah Solomon Konoyeima, recently died of the disease. Doctor Tom Rogers and Dr. Dauda Koroma had died of the disease, and were buried, a day before Dr. Konoyeima died of the disease.

Sierra Leone is a republic and a former British colony, often referred to as the Republic of Sierra Leone, in West Africa. The Ebola virus had also struck like a lightning, bringing socioeconomic activities to a screeching halt. Sharing a border with Guinea in the northeast, and Liberia in the southeast and the Atlantic Ocean in the southwest, becoming infected with Ebola scourge would be inevitable in Sierra Leone. With a tropical climate where tropical fruits and fruit bats are prevalent and with a diverse environment that ranges from savannah to rainforests, Ebola outbreak would become a predictable disease in Sierra Leone and sub-Sahara Africa. With a total land area of 71,740 kilometers and a population of six million, the Ebola virus would hit the country with a vengeance.

Unlike Guinea that was colonized by France, Sierra Leone had Portuguese and British influences. The name Sierra Leone was derived from the Portuguese word Serra Leoa. In early times, in the 1700s, in the 18th century, Sierra Leone was a hub of slave trade transactions and activities because of its proximity to the Atlantic Ocean, in the southwest of its border. Its capital city, Freetown was founded in 1787 for enslaved and exploited Africans who had fought for, and with the British, in the American war of independence. In that war, also called the American Revolutionary War, in the latter part of the 18th century between 1775-1783 Africans were used to fight in a war that had nothing to do with them. Many Africans had died in that war and those that survived were confined, relocated, and remained in what is now called Freetown.

The American War of Independence was the military wing of the American Revolution which was fought between Great Britain and the revolutionaries in the 13 British colonies in North America who wanted independence from Great Britain. The 13 British colonies declared their independence from Great Britain; with the declaration of independence as a nation; that would later become the United

States of America. Not wanting to risk their own British citizens, the British had used African slaves who had been sold or captured as slaves, and guinea pigs for the war, since African slaves were seen as material properties rather than human beings. Though no reliable record of casualties is available on African dead slaves, it is said that untold number of African slaves were slaughtered in the war.

The war that had first started as a revolt against the harsh socioeconomic policies of the British Empire would culminate in a full-fledged war that would traverse British North America, with other countries such as Spain, France and Netherlands also joining and fighting against the British.

With the creation of Freetown, for enslaved and freed Africans who had been used in the war, and named as the capital of Sierra Leone, experts believed the economic future of the country was at that time defined and paved. The history of Sierra Leone goes back thousands of years, far beyond the enslavement of Africans. Historically, Sierra Leone has been home to many inhabitants who were mainly invaders who had been attracted to the country because of its rich cultural and mineral resources, dating back to the Portuguese invasion or 'visit' in 1460, towards the end of the 15th century. As earlier stated, the Portuguese named the country Serra Leoa, which the British would later change to Sierra Leone.

Freetown, the capital, in earlier times, was also a hub of commercial activities, especially for European traders, who used unscrupulous African rulers for protection and supply of slaves and ivory in exchange for European manufactured goods. With local African rulers selling out their subjects for inferior and cheap European goods, the slave trade would become more attractive than ever, ensuing in the Treat of Utrecht in 1713. With the treaty in place, and the end of the Spanish war of secession (1701-1714) in sight, in which Spain ceded territories like Gibraltar, Minorca and Nova Scotia to the British, it was agreed that Asiento would be given to the British. The fate of present and future African slaves would firmly be enshrined in the exclusive contract for the sea transportation of purchased African slaves to North America and the Caribbean Islands.

The so-called exclusive rights to the South Sea Company would change hands again as Queen Ann, the then Queen of England (1665 – 1714), whose country was strapped for cash, would sell it to cover the cost of the expensive war the Britain had engaged in.

The African slaves who had fought alongside the British during the American Revolutionary War of 1775-1783, were given freedom and allowed to return to Sierra Leone in 1787, to form their own country. Though the new settlement that was initially formed by the returning slaves from England and the United States had failed, it would be revived by the British through a commercial company that was sponsored by opponents of the slave trade. The name Freetown, as earlier mentioned, was coined by the returning slaves who had fought with the British against the United States during the American War of Independence. Freetown attracted other freed slaves from Jamaica, England and the United States, who arrived in 1800, at the outset of the 19th century. The freed slaves were only too happy to have their own country after years of enslavement. The new settlers from Jamaica were mainly English speaking settlers, having learned the language from their British masters.

The British kept its promise to end slavery especially for those who had dutifully fought alongside it against the 13 revolting colonies during the American War of Independence. In 1807, Great Britain formally outlawed slave trade. Another irony was that the British would once again repurchased the financially strapped South Sea Company, using the exclusive area as a naval base to fight slave trade, a trade it had profited tremendously from in times past. But Great Britain had made a promise and intended to keep it, and it was out of loyalty to the slaves who had fought with it during the war.

Sierra Leone would again become part of the British Protectorate from 1821 and onward to 1874, with the governor of Sierra Leone in charge of the British holdings in the Gold Coast or Ghana, while using Sierra Leone as the advisory and legislative base. It was just a matter of time before the British would once again take charge of the protectorate of Sierra Leone; and it did in 1896. The British thought it was necessary to assume responsibility for Sierra Leone in order to prevent the French from taking over the protectorate. The French at the time became overly ambitious in its quest to exploit and colonize the region. Since the British had already initiated a policy to stop slave trade in the region it felt the French would undo its program of ending slave trade in the region, if Sierra Leone was not protected.

The irony of British intentions became manifested when it assiduously and unremittingly fought against the indigenes who did not want western rule in the region. Some of the newcomers who had returned from Jamaica and the Caribbean as free slaves were tired and weary of being under western oppression and wanted to truly be free. Indigenous uprisings led by freedom fighters like Bai Bureh (1840 – 1908), a Sierra Leonean ruler and military strategist, would put the British on notice that its intentions were not unnoticed. Just like the French that the British were trying to forestall, the British had their own agenda and ambition to increase the size of its protectorate in order to have access to the abundant natural resources in the region. To finance the protectorate, the British would impose all sorts of taxes, including the notorious hut tax that was imposed on individual huts, which further incensed the indigenes.

The imposition of hut taxes and the forced labor imposed on Africans in the region, which was reminiscent of the slave trade, angered the indigenes who distrusted the British intentions. That distrust further increased the size of Bureh's uprising in the north as other uprisings would start in the south, led by Kai Londo, (1845-1896), a Kissi warrior. Londo's uprising would only last a couple of years as Bureh was captured and imprisoned; and eventually exiled in the Gold Coast, now Ghana. His fellow freedom fighters and comrades were imprisoned and hanged by the British.

But Londo's impact was felt in the region. Though he died at the age of 51, he was able to make an impact that included road construction.

Western double standard, as displayed by the British smokescreen effort to protect the Protectorate of Sierra Leone from French ambitions in the region, became obvious in the manner the colonial overlord suppressed and hanged those who dared to challenge its rule and taxation policy.

Though suppressed, intimidated, and eventually exiled to Gold Coast, Bureh's relentless effort for self rule in Africa would spread in the region. After his death at the age of 68, in the Gold Coast, emerging African warriors in the Gold Coast like Kwame Nkrumah (1909 – 1972), would carry on his legacy of fighting for Africa (Pan-Africanism). The latter would fight, like Bureh, for the independence of Gold Coast, and eventually become its first post independence Prime Minister in 1957, when Ghana became independent.

Bai Bureh with a guard

The independence movement in Sierra Leone, inspired earlier by freedom fighters like Bai Bureh and Kai Londo, would later pave the way for independence, later on in the 20th century. It had all started after the World War II, when a war weary Great Britain, gave in to nationalist demands in Sierra Leone. The World War II had significantly reduced British significance and influence as a superpower and as an empire, following Hitler's war. Emerging from an expensive war and with socioeconomic devastation at home, Britain was less protective, and according to historians, less interested in pursuing its colonial interests. With the shortage of cash to rebuild, it was not a big surprise that the British would give in to the nationalist demands of the indigenous freedom fighters in West Africa.

Seizing on the opportunity presented by the war, freedom fighters in Sierra Leone and other parts of Africa would relentlessly pursue their quests for independence by using tactics some of them had learned from their colonial masters. Guerilla wars like the Mau-Mau uprising and rebellion in Kenya, were prevalent in Africa. In Sierra Leone, freedom fighters kept up the pressure on their British colonial master. The freed slaves who had returned years before from overseas and their descendants did not want oppression and colonial rule. They wanted their own country where they were free to make their own choices and decisions.

On April 27, 1961, Sierra Leone became independent from British rule, albeit remaining part of the commonwealth, which was still an extended part of British overlord. But it was better than being a colony. The Commonwealth of Nations, formerly British Commonwealth, was an association of independent and sovereign states that were still loyal to the British Monarchy, and to which the British Monarchy remains as the symbolic head of state, as head of the commonwealth.

Post independent Sierra Leone was a prosperous nation with abundant mineral and natural resources like iron ore and diamonds, which the British had, hitherto, controlled and exploited. With Sierra Leoneans in charge of their economy and resources, a new dawn would arrive in the new country.

The freedom fighters who fought the British for independence became the country's new political leaders. With abundant revenue flowing in from the cultivation, mining of iron ore and diamonds, the country's leader would embark on national reconstruction. The British had not used the revenue they exploited from Sierra Leone to build the country; rather they had used the revenue to rebuild their country, Great Britain that had suffered tremendous devastation during the World War II. It was now left to the new political leaders to harness the available resources to develop their country.

The new leaders in Sierra Leone embarked on educational project of building schools and universities. It was felt that an educated Sierra Leone would pave the way for a successful Sierra Leone that would someday be significant in global socioeconomic affairs. Premier colleges like the Njala University College, founded in 1960, and later University of Sierra Leone, would be the initial beneficiary of the country's leaders' quest for an educated nation. But that would be short-lived, as corruption would gradually become endemic.

Sir Milton Margai (1895 – 1964), the post independent Prime Minister who was also the first African to hold a ministerial and cabinet position under the British rule and protectorate, was a pro-British successful politician who successfully built a coalition of both indigenous chiefs and modernist elites to create a political environment that was devoid of enmity and rancor. Though a conservative politician, he would use his education and influence as both a medical doctor and politician, to create a feasible and conducive political atmosphere.

The family background of Sir Milton Margai prepared him for his successful political future that would unfold immediately after he became a physician. As the privileged grandson of a paramount chief, he was able to get the type of education that was rare at the time for Africans. He became the first physician in the entire British Protectorate. He also became the minister of health, and later minister of agriculture, under the British rule. It was rare at that time for an African to hold a cabinet position under the colonial rule but he did. His education and family influence also gave him the opportunity to work as a doctor under the British colony, where he was helping to provide needed healthcare to Sierra Leoneans. Though conservative and elitist, he would build a political dynasty that would transfer power to his younger brother, Albert, when he died in April of 1964.

The Ebola epidemic would hit Sierra Leone in an unprecedented fashion, years later. The infection in Sierra Leone, according to the World Health Organization, was caused by traditional healers who had unknowingly been infected after treating Ebola patients in neighboring Guinea. According to the CDC, "An outbreak of Ebola has been ongoing in Sierra Leone since May 2014." The death of some of the traditional healers or herbalists and the subsequent exposure of their infected bodies also caused the disease to spread, according to the World Health Organization. The Ebola epidemic in Sierra Leone was unavoidable as its neighbor to the northeast, the nation of Guinea, was already infected.

The Ebola outbreak in Sierra Leone was inevitable because of the country's border with Guinea in the northeast, a country already being ravaged by Ebola. According to MSF (Doctors without Borders), reported by YAHOO news, "Ebola has wiped out whole villages in Sierra Leone and may have caused many more deaths than the nearly 5,000 official global toll." An official with the medical group said the Ebola infections and deaths in Sierra Leone, were underreported, that the figures in the media was far below the actual figures.

Health officials were reportedly overwhelmed while some were abandoning their jobs for fear of infection in the country. The country's leadership closed the schools and borders to prevent further infection, at the beginning of the outbreak. Though the situation was reportedly "catastrophic," the government of Sierra

Leone continued to implement the recommendations of the World Health Organization and the CDC, to contain the disease.

The United Nations reported that several villages and communities had been wiped out in Sierra Leone, many of which were not statistically accounted for, due to the remoteness of the areas infected. According to WHO, there is one nurse for every 10,000 people; and with the alarming deaths of the nurses in the field, nurses and healthcare workers were gradually becoming in short supply to help treat those infected with the Ebola virus in villages and communities in the country.

The outbreak of Ebola in Sierra Leone placed a heavy financial burden on the already economically beleaguered nation where 11 doctors had died of the disease. The existing healthcare in the country, according to the CDC, continues to face the challenges of dealing with new and existing infections of Ebola in the country.

In Liberia, where the outbreak was worse than Sierra Leone and Guinea, the Ebola outbreak had set the country back economically, and to a degree, socially. Historically, Liberia should have fared much better than its neighbors in Guinea, Sierra Leone and Ivory Coast, considering its historical background. Unlike Sierra Leoneans who were mainly freed slaves who were loyal to the British Crown, and who had fought with the British during the American war of independence, and freed slaves from England, Jamaica and the Caribbean, Liberia is a country that was founded by United States and its citizens (the American Colonization Society), for its former slaves, on July 26, 1847. The slaves, according to historians, were freed black Americans that some citizens (abolitionists), of the United States had felt should be settled elsewhere as freed slaves other than America.

These set of powerful Americans perceived themselves as abolitionists who opposed slavery but did not want to live side by side with their former slaves, in the same country. These powerful abolitionists had instead designed a program to return the slaves back to their roots. Since the slaves were mostly descendants of the original slaves that were sold into slavery by their African forefathers, majority of them could not find, nor trace their ancestral roots. That problem was solved for them by these powerful American citizens who felt a new African country was necessary to accommodate the slaves and their descendants.

Liberia, as a result, became the second country that was established to accommodate freed slaves, in 1847. The first, as stated above, was Sierra Leone which was established by the British for the same purpose. It can be safe to assume the Americans were imitating their former colonial master, Great Britain, in creating Liberia. In the case of Sierra Leone, it was mainly as a 'reward' to those slaves who had fought with the British during the American war of independence. For Liberia, the settlement was designed to keep freed slaves from America.

Geographically, Liberia is a republic, officially the Republic of Liberia. The Republic of Liberia shares a border with Sierra Leone in its western frontier while it shares a border with Guinea in the northern frontier. The land area is 111.369 square kilometers, with a population of 4 million people. Its official language, as expected, is English, since the original settlers were freed slaves, along with their descendants who had learned the English language from their former masters. Ethnically, indigenous dialects abound, with over 30 of such different dialects spoken in the country.

Though Liberia was founded by the citizens of the United States – the American Colonization Society, for former slaves who 'opted' to live in a different country, historians believe the history of Liberia goes further than that. It is believed, according to historians, that the reason for the different dialects is because of the original settlers who had migrated from other parts of Africa around the 12th century. The Portuguese were said to have first explored and established contacts with the original indigenous settlers and had named it Costa da Pimenta as early as 1461, long before it was settled in by freed slaves from the United States, in 1847.

The name Costa da Pimenta (or Pepper Coast), was due to melagueta Pepper, a sort of African pepper that is very spicy. Historians also opined that the Dutch had, in 1602, established a trading post at the Grand Cape Mount County, and had ditched it a year after it was established. The grand cape mount county is one of the 15 counties that form the administrative division of Liberia. The British, because of its power and influence and burgeoning empire, established its own trading post in the Pepper Coast, in 1663. The area would be free of Western influence until freed slaves started to arrive from the United States, in 1821.

As earlier stated, a few powerful Americans fashioned themselves as abolitionists who had owned slaves and were now opposed to slavery. Though opposed to slavery, they did not want to see former slaves living as equal citizens with them in the same country. To solve the problem, a colony was founded and established for freed African American slaves, starting in 1800. The ship, Mayflower (formerly named Elizabeth), was loaded with initial 86 freed slaves from the United States and settled in the colony now called Liberia. Freed slaves would continue to be shipped to Liberia between 1821 and 1838, when the American Colonization Society named the colony, Liberia. Independence would be declared by the freed slaves on July 26, 1847.

There are other historical perspectives that the freed slaves from the United States were sent out of the United States by some powerful Americans because many slaves had fought with the British against the United States, during the American war of Independence. These Americans who had owned slaves and who had turned abolitionists had fashioned themselves being against slavery as an excuse to send the freed slaves back to Africa.

Whether it was as a form of payback because some slaves had fought with the British against the Americans; or it was because some former slaveholders did not want to live as equal citizens with their former slaves, it was hard to tell. The freed slaves were only too glad to be returning to the land of their forefathers. A land they had been forcibly taken and sold from, by their own ancestors and traditional rulers, as commodities.

There were other historical perspectives that many of the freed slaves in the United States were incapable of surviving on their own as free people. It was felt by many white Americans that returning them to the jungle of Africa would benefit the slaves more, than in the American society. The opinion that the freed slaves were mentally and physically incapable of succeeding in the United States was also one of the driving reasons for the quest to send the freed slaves back to Africa where they had originated from. It did not matter to those white Americans who felt the freed slaves were physically incapable of surviving in America that the same slaves had labored for them, in their plantations for many years. The same slaves who had been enslaved and used in plantations and farms as laborers were suddenly incapable of succeeding in America, as freed slaves! It became clear that the former slave owners did not feel comfortable living in the same country with their former slaves, as equal citizens.

The price of a slave, during the heydays of slavery, was based on physicality. The stronger and tougher a slave looked the more money it brought in the slave trade. But when the slaves became free, it became a question of mental and physical ability for them to succeed in the United States. The same abolitionists were the same people who felt the free slaves could not succeed in making a living by themselves in America.

Other former slaveholders felt the freed slaves were too inferior to live among them as equal citizens. The same racist white Americans, who had subjugated the slaves to hard labor, for many years, now created a lasting obstacle that still endure to this day; that blacks were inferior to whites, and were incapable of competing in the American society. That polarization can still be seen in American streets where white police officers continue to use blacks as target practice.

Some of those conspiratorial white Americans who had owned slaves and did not want freed slaves living among them were highly placed political leaders like President Thomas Jefferson (1743 – 1826), the third president of the United States and one of the authors of the Declaration of Independence of 1776. Jefferson, like many powerful white Americans were bitter towards the slaves who had fought with the British, against the United States, during the revolt and rebellion against the British. Though Jefferson was antislavery, he had owned hundreds of slaves, and had only reportedly freed those who had gotten old and sick and weren't useful to him any longer.

Part of Jefferson's wealth included the hundreds of slaves he had owned as properties. Jefferson was also said to have had a romantic relationship with one of his female slaves, Sally Hemings, (1773 -1835), with whom he had fathered many children. Sally Hemings, was a slave that was owned and sexually used by Jefferson to partly keep his promise to his late wife, Martha Jefferson (1748 – 1782), that he will not remarry; and also because of her mixed complexion, which made her look more white than black. Jefferson was also one of the advocates for the relocation of freed slaves to Africa. He had proposed sending freed slaves to Liberia to prevent them from living in the new nation of the United States. As earlier stated, part of the reasons was to make sure the freed slaves did not become a public charge; and also the fear that the freed slaves might become a political force that would seek revenge against their former white slaveholders.

Apart from the legendary sociopolitical problems created by colonial masters in Liberia, the country had also created its own problems that pushed the beleaguered nation to the brink of abject poverty. The problems besetting Liberia, before Ebola, dates back to

1817 when the American Colonization Society (ACS) was founded. The goal of ACS was to help freed slaves to return to West Africa, mainly to Cape Mesurado, a rocky land that had been forcibly purchased or seized from an indigenous traditional ruler, King Peter. From the very beginning, Cape Mesurado had faced hunger, strife and poverty as the land was partially barren due to the rockiness of the terrain.

As if Liberia did not already have enough problems of tribal attacks and poverty in earlier times, in the early part of the 19th century, the freed slaves from the United States who fashioned themselves as Americo-Liberians would create a socioeconomic divide that would further plunge the country into a polarized nation. The Americo-Liberians, because of their racially mixed ethnicity distinguished themselves from the indigenous people. They saw themselves as being superior to the indigenous Liberians because of their racially mixed color and European influence. The differences in color of the settlers from the United States and Europe would create tribalism and indigenous discrimination among the settlers, in Liberia, that would endure for years, sometimes culminating in violence.

Another problem that Liberia had in the beginning, right from the time of independence, was the class differences between the mulattos of mixed racial color and the indigenous Liberians who had settled there long before the freed slaves were brought from the United States and Europe. Most of these mulattos were economically richer than the indigenous Liberians, partly because of the wealth some of them had accumulated overseas, in the United States and Europe, and partly because of their skill in commerce. A skill they may have learned from their masters in the United States and Europe.

The economic differences between the rich mulattos and the poor indigenous Liberians would often create clashes between the mulattos and the indigenous Liberians. Historians opined that the discrimination and segregation among the two classes of Liberians may have been inherited by the mulattos from their colonial masters. The irony, according to Historians, was that these mulattos or Americo-Liberians who had once been slaves, started a different type of enslavement of their own people; institutionalizing a divide, and the discrimination that they had escaped from, in the United States and Europe.

The sociopolitical factors that divided Liberia would further deepen after independence was declared in 1847. Historians would often say that ACS had helped institutionalized the segregation that created many of the problems that divided Liberia by asking Americo-Liberians to declare independence in 1847. By declaring independence at the behest of ACS, which was partly funded by the group, Americo-Liberians felt empowered to call the shots. The empowerment given to Americo-Liberians would indirectly give the mulattos the mandate to politically dominate Liberia right from independence. Though a minority group, Americo-Liberians would become the rich and powerful class that controlled the socioeconomic and political society of Liberia, for many years.

With an overwhelming socioeconomic and political power, Americo-Liberians would unleash their own brand of racial discrimination and segregation in their new settlement and independent nation of Liberia. To maintain political power, indigenous black Liberians were disenfranchised by the mulattos, from the electoral process. Part of the reasons for the disenfranchisement was to prevent the base of political power from shifting to the majority indigenous black Liberians.

Liberia was dominated by two political parties to prevent indigenous blacks from having political power. The mulattos feared that limiting the political process to two political parties that were controlled by rich and powerful mulattos in the Liberian Party and the True Whig Party, that power would continue to remain in the hands of the minority – the Americo-Liberians. Like their former slaveholders back in the United States and Europe, the Americo-Liberians would practice the sort of conservatism that was reminiscent of the Republican Party in the U.S. They would even change the party name from Liberian Party to Republican Party, to buttress the fact that the party was an extension of the Republican Party in the U.S. But it was not.

Though the True Whig Party was funded by rich indigenous blacks, it was obvious that the political influence and power rested in the Liberian Party. The first presidential election of 1847 in which the Liberian Party held political sway and dominance, clearly demonstrated how much the indigenous blacks had been segregated from the political process. Many of the indigenous blacks could not vote and did not even know what was going on in their own country, politically. The elections were held and participated in by the mulattos and a select number of rich blacks. The political divide would further be entrenched in disharmony as the Liberian Party used its power and influence to suppress its opposition in the True Whig Party.

True to their Americanization, the Liberian Party, which later became the Republican Party, represented conservatism that was mostly comprised of rich mulattos; while the True Whig Party represented liberalism that was comprised of a select number of rich blacks and poor mulattos. The True Whig Party would later, in 1869, registered enough votes among the disenfranchised indigenous Liberians to win the presidential elections, in which Edward James Roye, a descendant of the Igbo people in Nigeria, was elected president. The victory would be short lived as Roye would be deposed, barely two years after he was elected. Following the deposition of Roye, the Republican Party would return to power, albeit temporarily as the Whigs returned to power again, in 1878. It was the beginning of a political turmoil in Liberia. With the changing political landscape in Liberia in which Liberians could vote, the Whigs were able to maintain its political influence from that point onward.

The crisis that would constantly bedevil the economic and political progress of Liberia would continue with numerous rebellions. The devastating rebellion of 1850s, due to the insurgencies of the Grebo and the Kru people, in the new nation is an example. In 1920s, another rebellion would take place that would almost cripple the country. The rebellions were mostly caused by those who had long been marginalized and disenfranchised by the Liberian Party and the mulattos or the Americo-Liberians.

Prior to Ebola, Liberia was already experiencing political and economic upheavals and turmoil. The ingrained discrimination and segregation that had heralded the arrival of the freed slaves from the United States and Europe would endure, long after independence was declared in 1847. That discrimination was further nurtured by western stakeholders who had thrived in, and exploited the divide among Liberians.

At one point, Westerners would use, and incite, poor indigenous Liberians to revolt against the mulattos' suppression and oppression. At other times, Westerners would also use the mulattos to further increase the fiber of the already divided and segregated nation.

The same twofaced Western interests and standards would also encourage surrounding colonies to clash amongst each other. The creation of the Republic of Maryland or the independent state of

Maryland in 1854 was an attempt to create a separate country that was mostly composed of America-Liberians. It was a small state that existed for a short period between 1885 and 1857. It was an offshoot of the divide that freed slaves from the United States had created to separate themselves from indigenous black Liberians. They had first settled in the state, in 1834, in an effort to create a separate country that was totally made of freed African-American slaves and freeborn African Americans from the state of Maryland, in the United States.

The Republic of Maryland had been the handiwork of the Maryland State Colonization Society, sort of like the American Colonization Society. Under the auspices of the Maryland State Colonization Society, the freed African American slaves tried but failed to have a successful country that was fashioned after the state of Maryland in the U.S. Though the Republic of Maryland later merged with Liberia because of the insurgencies of the Grebo and the Kru people, the merger with Liberia would be the catalyst that made the settlement of the freed slaves from the United States, possible.

The Grebo people had their own language or dialect that was spoken within the subgroup that included the Kru group; where another dialect was also spoken, in what is now called the Maryland County and the Grand Kru County in the southeastern part of Liberia. The subgroup that includes Grebo and Kru had, in the middle of the 19th century, rebelled against the oppression and suppression of indigenous black Liberians, by mulattos (Americo-Liberians), in their own lands. That insurgency had led to a merger of coexistence that though was fragile, became the entity now called Liberia. The Grebo people can also be found in the River Gee County and the Sinoe County. The population of the Grebo people had also spread to Cote d'Ivoire in the southwestern part of the country. Historians have often said that the Grebo people had spread around like the Kurds in the Middle East because of their initial displacement that was created by the freed African American slaves who had arrived in their land in the 1800s.

After independence in 1847, and having merged with the Republic of Maryland, Liberia had sought an expansion of its territories. That ambitious move to expand the country led to clashes with neighboring countries like Guinea and Sierra Leone, where the ambitious mulattos had sought expansion. Political historians believed that the expansion and subsequent clashes had been enabled by, and due to, the protection offered by the United States Navy in West Africa, that used its military superiority to prevent threat to the new nation from neighboring French and British colonies in Guinea and Sierra Leone.

Though indirectly supported and aided by the United States, Liberia would enjoy fragile peace and economic development. Corrupt and tyrannical leaders would rule the country, one after the other, with such tyrannical governments often ending in coups, bloodsheds and upheavals. A case in point was the administration of Samuel Kanyon Doe (1951-1990), who had ruled Liberia from 1980 to 1990. Doe had ruled the country with iron fist. As a despot and a tyrant, he was the chairman of the People's Redemption Council, and had ruled the country with his handpicked henchmen and cronies, often using the latter to suppress and murder his opponents. As the de facto head of state, following a military coup in 1980, he had promised a return to civilian government, and had positioned himself to be elected in an election in which he was elected, thereby becoming the 21st President of Liberia in 1985.

The significance of Doe's administration was that he was the first indigenous head of state in Liberia. As a member of the Krahn tribe of the Kru people and language, Doe had sought to make up for the oppression and marginalization the Kru people had suffered in the hands of the mulattos, by focusing on developing the Krahn tribe. As a member of a minority ethnic group, Doe felt the need to develop the once neglected and marginalized indigenes of the land. The Grebo and Krahn people were supportive of Doe's administration; and appreciative of its effort to develop their lands. Having been faced with economic and political marginalization by the powerful America-Liberian elites, who had earlier disenfranchised them, the Kru and Grebo people saw a chance to partake in the national cake through Doe.

The mulattos created a viable and formidable opposition to the administration of Doe. But the support and aid from the United States, in large part, silenced the opposition to Doe's administration.

Doe, according to most historians, accomplished a tremendous economic growth for Liberia by increasing commerce with Canada, China and several European countries, who in turn created considerable amounts of foreign investments in Liberia. Under Doe, Liberia enjoyed a great deal of economic improvement but the endemic corruption would undermine most of the economic gains.

Doe's administration would weaken as the cold war came to a screeching halt. The first problem Doe faced, albeit the support from the United States, was the constitution of 1984, that his opponents opined were written to favor him, in the election of 1985. The claims that the election of 1985 was marred with electoral malpractices and rigging also increased disenchantment with his government, locally and internationally. The reduction of economic aids from the United States due to the latter's recession and fiscal austerity in 1981, coupled with the end of the cold war, gradually obstructed economic growth, and subsequently eroded support for Doe's administration.

With the United States waning support, and internal rebellion from the opposition, a civil war would ensue that would lead to the capturing and execution of Doe, who had himself seized power, in a violent coup, earlier from his predecessor, William R. Tolbert, Jr. (1913-1980), who had been killed in the coup, on April 12, 1980, when Doe had seized power.

The overthrow and subsequent death of President Samuel Doe had been orchestrated by Charles Taylor who became the 22nd President of Liberia in 1997 until his resignation in 2003. Taylor had studied in the United States and had returned to Liberia to hold a position in the government of President Samuel Doe. Following the fallout with Doe, and his subsequent removal from office for corruption and embezzlement, Taylor had moved to Libya where he had received training in Muammar Gaddafi's military as a guerilla fighter. That training had helped Taylor to organize an army of opposition which had been funded by Gaddafi. Forming the National Patriotic Front of Liberia, Taylor had organized pockets of guerrilla wars against Doe, until the fall of the latter and his subsequent execution. Taylor, according to historians, orchestrated the civil war that led to the deaths of thousands of Liberians and Sierra Leoneans.

As one of the prominent warlords in Africa, that was reminiscent of the days of Mau Mau uprising in Kenya, Taylor earned himself a place in history. Using his education in the United States and his guerilla training in Libya under Gaddafi, Taylor would easily win over the war weary electorates of Liberia to get himself elected the 22nd president of Liberia.

Taylor's regime was marred with corruption, nepotism, favoritism and brutalism which were reminiscent of Idi Amin's regime, the third president of Uganda (1971-1979), and Sekou

Toure's regime, the first president of Guinea (1958-1984). Unlike Doe who had belonged in the Krahn tribe with a humble background and an indigenous Liberian, Taylor was an Americo-Liberian, born in Arthington, in Montserrado County in the upper stratum of the Liberian society. His father was a teacher, a sharecropper, a lawyer and a judge and was an Americo-Liberian. Taylor's mother, on the other hand, was a member of the Gola ethnic group in western Liberia.

Montserrado County is one of the 15 counties that formed the first level of the administrative divisions in Liberia. Taylor committed several atrocities and war crimes that included masterminding the civil war in Sierra Leone that lasted from 1991 to 2002. Like Doe, who in the twilight of his regime had faced oppositions and rebellions against him, Taylor would have the table turned against him as opposition grew against him. Fearing that the end was at hand, and worried that the fate that befell Doe might befall him, he had resigned, having lost most of the country in the civil war.

Escaping to Nigeria to escape prosecution and to seek political asylum, he would be extradited from Nigeria in 2006, at the behest and extradition appeal of the new president, Ellen Johnson Sirleaf. Detained in Sierra Leone after his extradition, by the UN, he would be charged in The Hague, for crimes against humanity. Convicted, Taylor would be sentenced to 50 years in prison "for aiding and abetting as well as planning some of the most heinous and brutal crimes recorded in human history."

Under President Ellen Johnson Sirleaf, Liberia would once again be bedeviled by corruption that has become endemic and part of the national psyche. As if the problem of corruption wasn't enough, the country would be plunged into the Ebola epidemic in March of 2014. Swept by Ebola, and with only about 50 doctors in a population of 4.3 million, a new devastation would plunge the country further into more socioeconomic problems and upheavals. The country had barely recovered from a civil war that ended in 2003.

The Ebola outbreak in Liberia worsened the already bad economic situation in the country. As Ebola continues to spread throughout sub-Saharan Africa, Liberia would cry out to the U.S. for help. The U.S. under President Barack Obama sent troops and medical equipment to Liberia. The Ebola virus was reportedly a bio-safety level four pathogen which was an RNA virus whose outbreak first occurred in West Africa in 1976. Prior to late March 2014 when the Ebola outbreak first occurred in Liberia, the country had a little over 50 doctors in a population of 4.3 million. The population was already reduced by the devastating civil war that ended in 2003.

Apart from Ebola that has scared potential investors away from Liberia and other parts of West Africa, and Africa as a whole, corruption is also one of the problems besetting Liberia. According to USA Today, "Liberia and Mongolia are the two most corrupt countries in the world." In Liberia, according to a recent study, 86% of those surveyed blamed corruption in the public sector as the most destabilizing force in the country.

The Ebola epidemic that has killed over 9,000 sub-Saharan Africans in Liberia, Sierra Leone and Guinea, had also spread to other countries like Mali, Nigeria and Senegal. Mali was declared Ebola free in January 2015; while Nigeria and Senegal were declared Ebola free, a few months later, in October 2014. With over eight people confirmed with Ebola in the West African country of Mali, the country, according to the World Health Organization was likely to have more cases of Ebola, unless a concerted effort was made to contain it as happened in Nigeria and Senegal. Fox News reported on November 25, 2014 that "Six of Mali's eight Ebola patients had died," of the disease. As Ebola continue to spread in Mali, over 270 people were being monitored while several others were put on 21 day incubation period. Mali would become Ebola free on January 18, 2015, following a 42-day period without a new case of infection of Ebola.

The disease that has killed over 9,000 people in sub-Saharan Africa entered Mali, according to Fox News, through a 70 year old imam who had traveled from a neighboring Guinea to Mali. Ebola in a fragile country that was already bedeviled by terrorism, coups, strife and poverty, was likely to become another Liberia because of the country's poor healthcare system and struggling economy, according to the World Health Organization.

The history of Mali and its attendant sociopolitical problems goes back to its origin and independence. Geographically, Mali is an enclosed land, located away from the ocean in a land-lock. As the eighth largest country in Africa and occupying a land area of 1,240,000 square kilometers, which is an equivalent of 480,000 square miles, the country has a population of 14.5 million, a population that is the equivalent of Liberia and Sierra Leone combined.

Mali was a French colony that officially became a republic after independence, in 1960. The post independence President was, President Modibo Keita, who ruled the country as its first president from 1960 to 1968. Keita was a trained teacher who had ventured into politics in the then French Sudan where he became the secretary general of the Sudanese Union – an organization he had cofounded. Having reportedly fought against colonial rule, Keita would merge his Sudanese Union with the African Democratic Party, to consolidate power. His political ambition and the quest to end colonial rule would land him, temporarily in prison, by the French, in 1946. The imprisonment consolidated his power and influence as a freedom fighter; and endeared him to the people in French Sudan.

After his release, and buoyed by the popularity he had gained with the imprisonment, Keita would win himself a seat in the territorial parliament of French Sudan. The political future of Keita would get brighter as he rose to the position of a deputy in the French National Assembly, and as the territory's first vice president.

Soon, that surging popularity he had earned would further land him in a higher position as the mayor of Bamako (now the capital of Mali). With the political gains he had won as a political prisoner, and as a freedom fighter, Keita won overwhelmingly big in the elections of 1957; and in a referendum of 1958, to determine the future of the territories in French West Africa. Keita would fight once again with a strong political campaign for sovereignty and self-rule in French Sudan. Having successfully campaigned for independence, Keita would seek, and settle for an autonomous state that culminated in the Mali federation that was comprised of Senegal and Sudan.

With the success of the campaign, Keita would easily become the first president of the new federation of Senegal and Sudan. The federation was however short-lived as the countries in the federation became agitated with disagreements, and wanted independence from the federation. In August of 1960, following disagreements among the countries involved in the federation, the split in the federation would further deepen. Though Keita remained president of the now weakened federation, the ruling party, headed by Keita would declare Mali a separate entity with the independence and Republic of Mali in September of 1960, a month after the federation essentially fell apart.

Historians believe Keita's Marxist and communist political stance paved the way for the future political and ethnic conflicts that brought chaos to the country. His one party system and cling to power, and his belief in the Marxist political and economic philosophy, in which the elimination of classes in society was paramount, defined his legacy. The Karl Marx political and economic philosophy that he adopted would further create a political divide that alienated him from the free market economies in the West, according to historians.

Though strategically and geographically placed in the commercial hub of Africa's commerce, Mali would remain economically poor.

The Republic of Mali shares borders with Guinea, Senegal, Mauritania, Algeria, Niger, Burkina Faso and Cote d'Ivoire. A large expanse of the country is barren with only the south having a fertile land area. For agrarian farming, the country derives its water from the Niger and Senegal rivers.

The Republic of Mali is comprised of eight regions with most of its regions covered by the Sahara desert. The Sahara desert is the third largest desert after Antarctica (earth's southernmost continent comprising the South Pole); and the Arctic (in the northernmost part of the earth). The economic mainstay of the country is agriculture and fishing. The farming is sustained by the water from the Niger and Senegal River where fishing is also supported. Though Mali is mostly an agrarian country, it is endowed with enormous natural resources like gold and salt. Mali is the third largest producer of gold and salt in Africa.

Even with enormous natural resources of gold and salt, the country is, according to the United Nations, one of the poorest countries in the world, with more than half of its citizens living below the international poverty standard of $1.25 a day. Part of the reasons for the poverty in Mali is mostly due to its religious clashes. With over half of the population nondenominational Muslims and with a constitution and legislation guided by Sharia Law, the country's political system is, according to observers, set on a trajectory that is on a periphery of exploding into religious violence.

Mali was once an important West African empire that was a part of burgeoning empires that controlled most of the trades in sub-Saharan Africa such as the trans-Saharan trade. As part of the Ghana, and Songhai Empire, Mali enjoyed a tremendous amount of significance and prosperity. The Mali Empire, in its heydays, flourished in the arts, mathematics, astronomy and literature. According to historians, in the 1300s, the Mali Empire was bigger than most European countries such as its former colonial master, France. The Mali Empire was so significant and humongous that it covered most of the West African coast.

Mali became a victim of Western greed and conspiracy in the 19th century, during the Berlin conference of 1884-85, during the scramble for Africa's riches and natural resources. France was apportioned the control of Mali, among others, combining it with French Sudan. France was also apportioned other African territories like Senegal. With Sudan and Senegal fighting for, and obtaining independence, Mali would become a federation.

With the Mali Empire totally disintegrated, the once flourishing center of arts and culture would become susceptible to internal greed, political struggle, strife and lust for power. After independence in 1960, Mali had an enduring one party rule that ended when the military intervened in a coup that led to the enactment of a new constitution that subsequently established Mali as a democratic and multiparty system, albeit with a Sharia Law.

Mali has had more than its fair share of political violence and turmoil, since independence. After a long period of autocratic rule that brought temporary peace to the country, the military coup of 1991 would pave the way for future upheavals that continue to beset the country to this day. That political upheaval reared again in 2012 when there were clashes in northern Mali which resulted in the temporary secession of the Tuareg rebels or militants and the declaration of the short-lived Azawad state.

The Azawad National Liberation Movement, often called the National Movement for the Liberation of Azawad, is a militant and political movement that is comprised of militants who had been trained, armed and funded by Muammar Gaddafi, the late Libyan leader who had secretly maintained the grand ambition of destabilizing Africa in order to recreate the United States of Africa; out of the ruins and destabilization that would ensue. The Azawad-based militant organization is entirely composed of the Tuareg people who historically live in the Sahara desert that traverses both West and North Africa.

The Berber speaking people of Tuareg has an estimated population of 1.2 million people. Most of the 1.2 million Berber speaking Tuareg live in the Sahara portion of Niger, Mali and Algeria. The Tuareg people are historically nomads who move from place to place. And because of the nomadic nature of the people, they can also be found in southeastern Algeria, and in southwestern part of Libya, including some who live in the northern part of Burkina Faso. A small portion of the Tuareg people live in northern Nigeria, where some have been rumored to have enlisted with Boko Haram, the Islamist-terrorist militants terrorizing Nigeria and Cameron, that is responsible for the deaths of thousands of Nigerians since its formation in 2002, by Mohammed Yusuf. Yusuf was killed by the Nigerian military in 2009.

Unlike the nomadic Fulani people who are a mixture of sub-Saharan and North African people, with a population of over 40 million, scattered in several West African countries (mostly in the Sahel areas) like Nigeria, Guinea, Cameron, Senegal, Mali, Niger, Burkina Faso, Sudan, Chad, Gabon, Ghana, Liberia, Egypt, Morocco, Algeria, Libya and Angola, the Tuareg people are small in number with a population of just over 1.4 million people.

Mali would find itself once again in a destabilizing conflict in January of 2012 when the Tuareg militants tried to form their own state of Azawad. The attendant chaos led to a military coup when the army fashioned itself as trying to bring peace and order to the country. The military interference soon culminated in a state of anarchy that allowed Islamist rebels to wade in, in the chaos, resulting in a conflict between the Tuareg people and Islamic Jihadists.

Though some of the Tuareg militants had been trained by Muammar Gaddafi and had even fought in the Libyan revolution, in a futile effort to keep their benefactor, Gaddafi, in power, they could not withstand the Jihadists who easily overwhelmed them. Mali had been further plunged into a state of anarchy as both the Tuareg and Islamist militants fought for control of the country. Fearing that the country was near disintegration and in a state of anarchy, the former colonial master, France, would send in troops in an operation called Operation Serval in January 2013, to restore order. Bolstered by the French troops, the overwhelmed Mali military would together with French troops, recapture most of the areas in the north the jihadists had taken over during the conflict.

A semblance of peace had temporarily returned to the country with the return to civilian rule, with the presidential elections that was held on July 28, 2013. The presidential election would be marred by accusations of electoral malpractices. The foreign-supervised election would end up in a runoff a month later, in August of 2013. A parliamentary election was also held in November 2013, in an attempt to create a power sharing apparatus that would involve all and sundry, in the war weary nation. Economically, Mali is a very poor nation, one of the poorest in the world. If the Ebola epidemic had not been quickly contained, Mali would have found itself overwhelmed and unable to stop the spread of the disease. The country's healthcare system is currently challenged with the shortage of qualified healthcare professionals such as doctors and nurses. In its present economic state in which its GDP hovers around $6 billion with a pre-Ebola growth rate of 3.5%, according to the International Monetary Fund, the country's economy was already strapped for cash, prior to the outbreak. Terrorist activities, corruptions and maladministration were already factors impeding the country's economic growth. The Ebola epidemic had threatened to make an already bad situation worse.

Though Mali had made a strong effort to revitalize its economy decades earlier by reaching an agreement with the World Bank and the International Monetary Fund, to help manage its fiscal responsibilities, the country has struggled in reforming its public enterprises. With the agreement reached from 1988 to 1996 with IMF, the government of Mali was able to cut back its public expenditures in order to balance its budget.

To increase revenue in order to generate needed funds, the government had to privatize most of the enterprises it controls. At that time, it was felt that privatizing most of the public enterprises would increase efficiencies, and generate profits. The public enterprises had, before the austerity and economic reforms, been operating at losses due to huge overheads and bloated payrolls. Several of the unmanageable enterprises were liquidated to settle public and private debts, and to streamline the economy to be more productive.

According to the Central Bank of West African States, and the IMF, a total of sixteen enterprises were privatized, twelve of which were partially privatized, with some other twenty of the enterprises liquidated. Unprofitable and poorly managed enterprises like the railroad was taken over by organizations like the Savage Corporation. Other public enterprises that were performing poorly like the Cotton Ginning Company and the Societe de Telecommunications du Mali had gone through numerous economic restructures to reduce inefficiency and corruption.

Historically, governments across the world have never been good managers of public enterprises. Enterprises providing public utilities like electricity, water, sewage and other essential services often perform better when left with the private sector to mange, for better efficiencies. According to the World Bank, the rural areas of Mali barely have electricity with only about 13% of the population having access to electricity. The absence of adequate electricity, according to the report, could hinder economic growth, as has been the case in most underdeveloped countries in Africa, and in Mali.

With the help of the International Development Association (IDA), in collaboration with the government of Mali, efforts are being made to ensure that the rural and urban areas of Mali have adequate electricity in order to bolster its dwindling economic development. The goal of the joint project is to increase grid connections of electrical wires and equipment to cover more homes and businesses. In 2010, for example, World Bank reported that "43,311 grid connections covering about 650,000 people had been made by indigenous private operators. In addition, the project has connected 803 public institutions, including 172 schools and 139 health centers."

To ensure continuous economic growth and progress in Mali, the World Bank had, in partnership with donor countries and banks in Europe, initiated a new renewable energy technology mix that would provide solar home systems photovoltaic (semiconductors), that will further provide renewable energy to households and businesses in both rural and urban areas. The projects will be funded through "IDA Credit of US$35.7 million and a Global Environment Facility (GEF) trust fund of US$3.5 million." Upon "satisfactory performance of the project," more funds were to be made available for additional projects.

Countries that had agreed, prior to the Ebola outbreak, to provide additional financing for the projects included Russia and the Netherlands. The Netherlands had also embarked on a plan to promote the productive use of the renewable energy in order for the people of Mali to continue to realize, and benefit from, the usefulness of having adequate electricity.

The outbreak of Ebola had threatened to setback these projects as had happened in Liberia and Sierra Leone where public and private constructions, and foreign investments and programs were abandoned, for scare of Ebola. The Ebola threat, according to economists and officials with the World Health Organization, will likely hamper the economic adjustment programs that have created economic growth and had reduced fiscal irresponsibility, in sub-Sahara Africa. If the disease had not been contained as was the case with Nigeria and Senegal, the progress made by Mali in reducing its deficits and increasing its GDP would have hit a gridlock.

The laudable move to join the World Trade Organization on May 31, 1995, helped to create a pathway for Mali to finally revitalize its economy and increase growth, but that, according to economists will not be able to withstand the scourge of Ebola if the government had not taken a drastic step to contain the disease.

The only silver-lining is that Mali is part of the French Zone, a connection that has been in effect since 1962, a few years after the country declared independence. Membership in the zone allows Mali access to French aids and assistance. Part of that economic assistance is Mail's connection to French Central Bank, a connection that helps with loan guarantees and finances. Though the creation of the Euro-zone in 1999 has been a drawback for Mali, according to observers, Mali still maintains its connection, along with seven other countries in the French zone.

The question that critics continue to ask is whether France can still maintain its financial connection and obligations with the seven countries in the French zone. That question was answered in January 2013, when French troops joined the Malian troops to rescue the country from Islamic jihadists who had taken control of the country, in a military operation called Operation Serval. That military operation indicated that France intended to maintain its obligation to Mali.

Mali can survive, economically, if it can effectively utilize its natural resources. For example, agriculture has always been the bedrock of Mail's economy. Cotton is one of the country's foreign exchange-earners and is exported to countries like Senegal and Ivory Coast, amongst others. Mali also produces staple foods like rice, millet, corn, vegetables, tobacco, and assorted tree crops. The combination of Mali's agricultural produce, including gold, amounts to over 80% of the country's total export.

The agricultural sector employs over 80% of Malian workers. In comparison, only 15% of Malians are employed in the service sector. Though the vagaries of inclement weather often disrupt employment in the agrarian sector, it essentially holds steady throughout the year. The mining sector in Mail is also a viable employer of labor. With capital infusion and assistance from the International Development Association, foreign investment in the mining sector continues to grow. Mali, because of renewed foreign investment and capital infusion, continues to maintain its position as the third largest producer of gold in Africa, behind South Africa and Ghana. The advent of terrorism had threatened to undermine the socioeconomic progress Mali has made in the past few years. As if the threat of terrorism, which has bedeviled progress in most West African countries like Nigeria, was not enough, the advent of Ebola had threatened to take away whatever modicum of prospect the country had achieved.

With the threat of Ebola and the ongoing terrorist activities in the northern part of the country, foreign investments and economic activities are likely to be disrupted. Thankfully, Ebola was contained in January 2015, in Mali, according to the World Health Organization.

Prior to Mali containing Ebola in January 2015, several countries, including the U.S., had warned their citizens to stay away from Mali, in part because of terrorism, and in particular, because of the northern part of Mali, along the border with Mauritania, where violence and religious clashes were most palpable. A warning posted on the website of the U.S. Department of State, Bureau of Consular Affairs, read:

> We strongly warn against travel to the northern parts of the country and along the border with Mauritania, particularly in areas that are not patrolled and where there is little to no security presence. There remains ongoing conflict in northern Mali and continuing threats of attacks on and kidnappings of Westerners and others.

With the threat of kidnapping and death, potential foreign investors were already wary of traveling to Mali. The ongoing energy development that has attracted assistance from Western countries and international banks would have come to a halt for fear of Ebola, as had happened in Liberia, Sierra Leone and Guinea, if the disease had not been quickly contained.

Terrorism continues to be a major scourge in Africa, especially in West Africa. Like Nigeria where Boko Haram controls the northeast of the country, Mali's northern parts are controlled by Islamic-jihadists. Though the 2013 presidential election that was anticipated would bring peace to the country through an all inclusive democratic process has not met expectations, political observers see the high voter turnout and near-peaceful election that was almost devoid of violence, save for minimal reports of conflicts, as a beacon of hope for future peace. The high voter turnout notwithstanding, ongoing Islamic terrorism and jihad threatened to plunge the country into a state of anarchy and a failed state. But there is still hope as French and African troops continue to combat Islamic jihadists in northern Mali.

Islamic terrorists aside, extremists and militants who had been trained by the late Libyan leader, Muammar Gaddafi, continue to create unrests and clashes in the northern part of Mali. The al-Qaeda-linked jihadists which include al-Qaeda in the Lands of Islamic Maghreb (AQIM); Ansar al-Dine – which fashions itself as the helpers of the Islamic religion that is led by Iyad Ag Ghaly that wants to impose strict Sharia law in Mali; and the Movement for Oneness and Jihad (MUJAO), are part of the terrorist activities besetting Mali. With Ebola joining the fray, the future of Mali had looked bleak unless the combination of the African Union and French troops can dislodge these various terrorist and destabilizing groups from the country.

The African Union (AU), whose membership consists of 54 African states continue to face several challenges of its own that makes it less effective in the region. The African Union, according to observers, faces financial and organizational problems. Contributions to the coffers of the union and the unanimity of some of its members have often been a problem in its effectiveness. The other problem the union faces is that most of its members have their own terrorist issues that they are unable to contain. For example, Nigeria, the most populous country in the union, has its own terrorist problem with Boko Haram. Unlike the pockets of extremists in northern Mali, Boko Haram is a major terrorist organization that is responsible for the weekly deaths of hundreds of Nigerian Muslims and Christians, in Nigeria's northeast.

The African Union was established on May 26, 2001, in Addis Ababa, and launched a year later in 2002, in South Africa, to replace the ineffective and the heavily criticized inefficient Organization of African Unity (OAU). The AU members are heads of state and government of its member states; and they meet twice a year.

The failure of AU to solve Mali's terrorist problems has largely been due to lack of funds and poor management of the Union. Like OAU before it, the organization lacked unity of purpose and strength. Though the AU is credited with getting the new transitional military leaders in Burkina Faso to agree to return the country to civilian rule, it remains to be seen if the Burkinabe military will keep to its promise to return the country back to civilian administration. In Mali, for example, the success achieved in that country has reportedly been due to the assistance rendered by the French troops who had collaborated with the Malian troops to dislodge the jihadists, and the militant extremists who had taken over the northern part of the country. While the AU troops have stayed to ensure peace in the north, the poorly equipped AU troops whose military hardware and weapons are inferior to the superior weapons of the well funded militants and jihadists, will hardly be effective without the French troops. There are daily reports of casualties on the part of AU troops due to the inferior and inadequate weapons at the disposal of the troops, which is hardly surprising, considering as mentioned earlier, the poor financial state of the Union.

Nigeria, the giant of Africa is said to be Ebola free, after the country's first misadventure with the disease which resulted in 19 infections and seven deaths. The Ebola virus had been brought to Nigeria by an Ebola patient, Patrick Sawyer, who had arrived from Liberia and had denied having had any contact with anyone with the disease before his travel to Nigeria. Sawyer had infected the doctor who had treated him and many others, resulting in seven deaths while 19 others were infected, according to the Wall Street Journal.

Dr. Ada Igonoh, a 28 year-old physician, who had treated the Ebola patient, Sawyer, in July 2014, later became infected with the disease. Dr. Igonoh had used common sense to continuously rehydrate herself, knowing she was losing body fluids by the seconds, during her quarantine in an isolation ward "in an old building, with rats and mosquitoes," where she had learned to survive without having the benefits of the experimental drug, Zmapp or blood transfusion (from survivors) for antibodies "that have been given to U.S. and European patients and that scientists and doctors believe may help." She had survived by following the simple procedure of rehydration, along with the determination to survive the deadly disease.

In her forced quarantine in the isolation ward "in an old building," Dr. Igonoh said she was on her own as no one came to check the levels of potassium and electrolytes in her body to make sure the chemical imbalance in her body did not lead to organ failure and arrhythmia. The absence of the various substances in the body fluids that control how the body processes waste and absorbs vitamins and minerals can lead to organ failure, such as kidney, liver and heart failures. Thomas Eric Duncan and Dr. Martin Salia had both experienced organ failures because of the inadequate level of potassium and electrolytes in their bodies which created imbalance in the body fluids; that control the processes of the body functions. When Duncan, as was the case with Salia, had had organ failure, they had suffered from dehydration as their bodies did not have enough body fluids to enable their organs to properly function. The organ failures had resulted in their deaths. If there had been rehydration as Dr. Igonoh had done for herself, their body fluids would have had enough substances to enable their organs to function.

Dr. Igonoh, according to the Wall Street Journal, was told that "90% of the treatment was dependent on me," which means her consciousness enabled her to maintain enough determination to survive and rehydrate herself, in the absence of anyone to monitor the level of potassium and electrolyte in her body. Dr. Salia and Duncan were both sedated to where they could not help themselves to the level of being able to maintain that 90% determination that was required to survive.

In her determination to survive in her conscious state of mind she had maintained that "even if it's just a 1% survival rate, I will be part of that 1%," a luxury that Duncan and Salia did not have as they were both sedated and put on a ventilator. Dr. Igonoh yet again proved that Ebola can be successfully self-combated without being made unconscious through sedation and ventilator.

The heroic survival of Dr. Igonoh made her ability to fight the Ebola disease as the byproduct of a miracle, and the will to survive. Another Nigerian doctor, a senior doctor who had treated Patrick Sawyer, had died of the disease. According to PM news (a Nigerian tabloid), the doctor was "the most senior who participated in the management of the (first Ebola) patient" during the first outbreak in Nigeria when Sawyer had arrived in Lagos.

Nigeria's success in containing the Ebola virus was surprisingly unexpected of a country whose lukewarm attitude toward issues of national significance is legendary. The country's lack of effort to combat poliomyelitis, a highly infectious disease that is caused by a virus, is another example of the government's inability to contain an infectious disease. According to the World Health Organization, Nigeria is one of three countries still battling poliomyelitis. The other countries in the same situation are Afghanistan and Pakistan, both developing countries like Nigeria. In 1988 there were 125 countries with poliomyelitis. Out of that alarming number of countries with the virus, only Nigeria, Afghanistan and Pakistan are unable to totally eradicate the disease. In Nigeria, poliomyelitis has, according to WHO, remained "polio-endemic," because the Nigerian government has failed to take the necessary steps towards ending the disease.

Unlike Ebola, poliomyelitis usually affects children under 5 years of age. The World Health Organization indicated that one in 200 infections can lead to irreversible paralysis in children, with the disease. Children infected with the disease often have high mortality rate. Among the infected, "5% to 10% die when their breathing muscles become immobilized."

While infections have decreased in 122 countries, Nigeria remains one of the countries whose efforts to combat the disease is abysmal. Since 1988, poliomyelitis has decreased by as much as 99% from "an estimated 350,000 cases." Currently in 2013, there are 416 cases of new infections in Nigeria, Afghanistan and Pakistan. The reduction of the disease is, according to the World Health Organization, due to the global efforts to eradicate the disease from every country in the world.

Though Nigeria, Afghanistan and Pakistan continue to lag behind in eradicating poliomyelitis, there has been a remarkable reduction in the number of infections in the countries where the disease is most prevalent. Like Ebola, poliomyelitis is very contagious. Unlike Ebola, poliomyelitis is mostly contracted through the air. Children are often at risk of contracting the disease when they play with their peers. Unlike poliomyelitis, Ebola can only be contracted through body fluids and blood.

For a disease that mostly affects children under the age of 5, one would think Nigeria will be interested in making the same effort it made with Ebola to eradicate the disease. After all, the children are the future. And if children under 5 years of age are constantly being infected, that means Nigerian children under 5, who are the future of Nigeria, face the possibility of death, in the ratio of 5% to 10%. According to the World Health Organization, the failure of countries like Nigeria, Afghanistan and Pakistan to eradicate poliomyelitis will likely result in 200,000 new infections every year.

Poliomyelitis is as deadly as the Ebola virus, if not deadlier, according to the World Health Organization. The disease often invades the nervous system and can cause total paralysis within a few hours. The virus is usually transmitted "by person-to-person," that is mainly spread through the contamination of food and water. The virus can also spread through the mouth. The most common symptoms of poliomyelitis include fever, fatigue, headache, vomiting, stiffness in the neck, and severe pains in the limbs. Unlike the Ebola virus whose cure has been effective with Zmapp, poliomyelitis has no cure but it can be prevented through a vaccine.

Nigeria's geopolitical landscape has had its challenges right from independence from the British, in 1960. With an estimated population of 175 million, Nigeria has a land size of 356,669 square miles or 923,768 kilometers. Ethnic and tribal clashes have often defined Nigeria's landscape because of the uniqueness of its people and culture. When the British had ruled Nigeria, the issue of tribal clashes and ethnical distrusts had often threatened to disintegrate the country. Critics believe the British knew that it would be impossible for Nigeria to maintain its sovereignty without breaking apart. Rather than fix the problem, the British had left the issue for the new indigenous leaders who had fought the British for independence.

Nigeria's history goes as far back as 11,000 B.C. before the European invaders and settlers. Around the 11,000BC, Nigeria was the cradle of civilization in Africa. The region or territory that became Nigeria was the cradle of ancient African civilizations that attracted settlers from all over the world. The Igbo subgroup or the people of the Nri Kingdom were among the original settlers in the region. The kingdom had flourished while creating a landscape for religious and social tolerance. The various tribes and ethnic groups had learned to live in peace, save for rare clashes.

The Songhai Empire and Nigeria had both occupied the same region. Around the same time, in the 11,000BC, Islam made its way to the northern part of Nigeria – Hausa States. The arrival of Islam in the 11th century heralded new problems for the northerners in the northern part of Nigeria. That new problem was the religious clashes that Islam brought to the region. The practitioners of Islam brought their own interpretation of the Koran, along with its conflicts and frictions. For a while, in earlier times, the Muslims felt people of other faiths were unbelievers that should be converted by force. The use of force as a method of converting people of other faiths led to jihad, which Prophet Muhammad made popular as its earlier crusader. To appease the Muslims in the north, the Nigerian government quietly allowed the use of Sharia Law and Sharia courts in some parts of the region, as well as allowing Muslims to self-govern themselves at the local level. Critics believe that was a mistake that eventually led to the creation of Boko Haram.

The unsettled ethnic and religious problems that were left behind by the British engulfed into a full-fledged civil war (1967-1970); that resulted in the deaths of over 1 million Nigerians from starvation and war, a few years later.

The southeastern region of the Igbo speaking people had wanted to secede from Nigeria to form their own separate country called Biafra. The Nigerian government had refused the secession. A civil war had occurred due to economic, ethnic, cultural and religious tensions between the Hausas in the north and the Igbo people in the southeast of Nigeria.

The Igbo people felt marginalized and left out of the political process and had wanted their own country. Since the country's natural resources were mostly in the southeast, the Nigerian government had fought back against the self-proclaimed Biafra, declaring its leader, Odumegwu Ojukwu (1933 – 2011), an enemy of Nigeria. Ojukwu had served as the Nigerian military's governor of the then Eastern Region in 1966, following the military coup of 1966 that had toppled the post-independence civilian administration of Abubakar Tafawa Balewa (1912-1966), Prime Minister (1960-1966), and Benjamin Nnamdi Azikiwe, head of state (1960-1963), and governor-general of Nigeria, and also Nigeria's first president when the country became a republic in 1963, from 1963-1966.

It didn't matter to the then "power lustful Ojukwu" that Azikiwe was from the southeast and of the Igbo tribe. Ojukwu felt marginalized, considering the part he had played in the 1966 coup, and also the fact that the Igbo people were the original settlers in the country. A region, he believed, controls most of the country's economic mainstay of mineral and natural resources. "The dissatisfaction of being a governor instead of a head of state led him to lead the secession to form a new country called Biafra," a Western observer opined. But Nigerian historians believe the assassination of Johnson Aguiyi-Ironsi who toppled and seized power from the civilian administration prompted Ojukwu's angst and ambition to secede.

Another big bone of contention was the assassination of Ojuwku's fellow countryman, Johnson Aguiyi-Ironsi (1924-1966), who had first seized power from the civilian government of Tafawa Balewa and Nnamdi Azikiwe, in a military coup. Ironsi had seized power from the civilian government of Balewa, to bring peace to the political chaos that was then threatening to destabilize the country. Some northern military officers had accused Ironsi of tribalism and had revolted against what they perceived as his Igbo-people-favored government or tribalism. Some other Nigerian historians also believe Ojukwu may have been incensed by the assassination of Ironsi on July 29th 1966, and felt the need to secede to form a separate country for the Igbo people. Another school of thought contended that Ojukwu had himself felt marginalized in the power sharing of the time.

The troubled Nigeria's political landscape would struggled on, after the bloody civil war that took over 1 million lives. The emergent military government of General Yakubu Gowon in August 1966, in which Ironsi had been deposed and assassinated, would strive to maintain a reconciliatory government by declaring a no-victor-no-vanquished truce. A temporary peace would return to the country with amnesty and forgiveness extended to Ojukwu who was in exile, until Gowon himself was deposed on July 29, 1975, by another northerner, General Murtala Muhammed (1938-1976).

The military government of Muhammed (1975-1976), had been short-lived as his government was also toppled; when he was assassinated at the age of 37, by another northerner, Colonel Buka Suka Dimka, a lieutenant colonel in the Nigerian army in the physical training division. The abortive coup that resulted in the assassination of Muhammed made Dimka a villain, and Muhammed a hero. The poorly organized and unpopular coup did not receive the blessing of the coup-weary nation, and was immediately crushed hours later by forces loyal to the government of Muhammed. Though Dimka fled, he was later arrested and executed in a firing squad, for treason.

The legacies of military governments and coups would follow years later. Immediately after the air was cleared with Dimka's arrest and subsequent execution, a new military leader, this time, a Yoruba soldier, from the western part of Nigeria, took over. General Olusegun Obasanjo became the military head of state, in 1976. He ruled Nigeria until 1979 when he handed over to a civilian government, as he had promised he would. It was rare to see a military leader that kept his word but Obasanjo did. An election was held and a new civilian government came to power, under President Shehu Shagari. The civilian government of President Shehu Shagari was marred by corruption, chaos and near-anarchy that were reminiscent of the post-independence political chaos that had heralded the first military coup of 1966. President Shehu Usman Aliyu Shagari became the second civilian president following the numerous coups in Nigeria. As the president of Nigeria's second republic (1979-1983), Shagari governed an unruly class of political thugs whose lust for power was reminiscent of the first republic's political unrest and unhealthy, violent rivalry and disquiet quest for office.

Though a northerner of the Fulani descent, he was considered weak and unable to reconcile political differences among the politicians within his own party and in the opposition. The political chaos and violent rivalries among the northern and southern politicians was another catalyst for military intervention. The near-anarchy and political violence of President Shagari's tenure in office, attracted the military, once again, to intervene to bring peace to the volatile political atmosphere, and to the country.

As if there were not already enough coups, another northerner, General Muhammadu Buhari, took over, in a military coup, on December 31, 1983, to supposedly restore peace to the country. But Buhari would be deposed shortly after taking office on August 27, 1985, barely two years later. Buhari had only ruled for less than two years when he was deposed in a military coup. Like Shagari before him, Buhari was also considered weak as he could not end the corruption among the military's rank and file. General Buhari was succeeded by Ibrahim Badamasi Babangida, who took over from Buhari, in a bloodless military coup, on August 27, 1985, to become head of state. Unlike Buhari who was considered weak, Babangida was a dictator and a blood thirsty tyrant, who was mostly hated for his extrajudicial killing and suppression of Nigerians, especially the press.

Babangida was known for his brutality and suppression of the media and press freedom. He was accused of murdering the late Dele Giwa (1947-1986), founder and editor of Newswatch magazine, on October 19, 1986, in a letter bomb that was sent to the editor's home as he ate breakfast with his family, on a Sunday morning. The assassination of Giwa had occurred two days after he was questioned by Babangida's state security service officials. According to Amnesty International, there was evidence of severe human rights violation and abuses during Babangida's regime. Babangida was corrupt and accused of embezzling and looting Nigeria's treasury to enrich himself.

Under the military administration of General Ibrahim Babangida, Nigeria's economy suffered as the country's capital, public and private expenditure exceeded both its GDP and GNP. The country had resorted to borrowing which further worsened the already beleaguered economy. The oil glut of the late 1980s and subsequent OPEC embargo of production restrictions did not help matters as Nigeria continually struggle to meet its fiscal obligations. To meet the guidelines lenders and banks had set, including the IMF and other international banks, austerity measures were imposed to cut back on spending.

The military government went on the airwaves to encourage the masses to curtail their spending habits. But the slogan should have been directed at Babangida's administration that was known for its extravagant spending. It was not long after, that the country's currency, Naira, started to weaken against international currencies like the U.S. Dollar. Since money was needed as the country was strapped for foreign currency, the administration had to devalue the country's currency to increase export. So to boost export and to increase revenue, Nigeria had to devalue its currency to what it gradually became today.

The public outcry against Babangida's brutality and suppression of press freedom became unbearable as the years unfolded. Foreign and international investors were beginning to lose faith in Nigeria's stability, as coups after coups continued to plague the country. To restore hope, Babangida promised to return the nation to a civilian administration. An election date was set. But the outcome of the election did not please the military junta of Babangida and the election results were cancelled and annulled, immediately after the election results were announced.

After the controversial annulment of the general election of 1993, the country was further plunged into unrests and violent protests. The unceremoniously and controversially annulled election by General Babangida, did not please the electorates who felt robbed of their constitutional mandate to appoint a civilian leader. The country was plunged into another chaos. It was felt by the electorate that their chosen leader, Moshood Abiola of the Social Democratic Party, was unjustly denied the mandate to rule. The general election had brought a sigh of relief that was ended by the annulment, after several intermittent military coups had bedeviled the country's growth and economy.

The annulment was a blow to Nigerians who had already suffered enough injustice and extrajudicial killings, under the brutal regime of Babangida and previous military juntas. Since the election was the first since the 1983 military coup that ousted President Shehu Shagari, the country had been plagued by one form of unrest after another. A country that was once Africa's beacon of hope became doomed and stalled with unending military coups.

To assuage an angry nation that was upset about the denial of their rights to choose a leader, a palace coup occurred in which another northerner, General Sani Abacha, took over, in a bloodless coup. Abacha's regime made the brutal Babangida's regime looked like a child's play, in comparison. Abacha essentially became the Nigeria's replica of the late Idi Amin of Uganda for his brutality and abuse of human rights. Abacha did not only plundered Nigeria's treasury and rendered the country broke, but also, by default, rendered the currency, Naira, more worthless. National borrowing became endemic as the country's expenditures and spending soared and was over 160% of its GDP. Abacha's administration lasted five years, from 1993 to 1998, in which Nigerians both at home and abroad were subjected to inhuman treatment, imprisonments, deaths by firing squad, and the most extreme brutality and oppression only similar to Mobutu Sese Seko's and Idi Amin's regimes.

Though Abacha was credited with economic improvement that mainly resulted from the additional devaluation of the country's currency, Naira, to increase export; and the coincidental upsurge in the international oil price due to the lifting of embargo by OPEC; the unnecessary devaluation of Nigeria's currency further reduced the country's economic significance as borrowing continued amid the increased oil revenue. With burgeoning external debts and rising unemployment, Abacha would set the stage for discontent and pockets of armed robberies and kidnappings by mostly unemployed college graduates who could not find jobs. The growing insurgencies in the south, in the Niger Delta, also resulted from Abacha's negligence to develop the oil producing areas that had been continually affected by oil spill, in the Niger Delta. Critics believe that the Abacha's administration set the stage for the insurgencies in the Niger Delta and the formation of Boko Haram, years later, in the northeast.

Abacha's regime was so formidable and awe inspiring that the labor union was silenced. The few Nigerians that took to the streets to protest the high unemployment rate were quickly suppressed.

Extrajudicial killings became commonplace, and a norm, during the brutal regime of Abacha. As if God had been listening to the wailings and cries of Nigerians, one summer day of June 8, 1998, Abacha collapsed and died, and Nigerians felt their prayers had been answered! Nigerians were overjoyed; and celebrated the death of the tyrant and dictator. A transitional government was quickly installed to set the stage for an election.

Nigerians were all too happy to embrace the transitional government of Abdulsalami Abubakar who ruled from 1998 until the election of 1999 that ushered in President Olusegun Obasanjo. For Nigerians, Abacha was a bad omen that had signaled the dawn of terrorism and mayhem. The terrorism that started during the regime of Abacha, according to critics, still endures till today, with Boko Haram in the center stage and the major player.

In a nutshell, Abacha's death heralded the beginning of a new Nigeria that was chaotic and ungovernable. Though that new beginning came in a snail pace and at a huge price that Nigeria could barely afford, it didn't bring the anticipated peace. It ushered in Boko Haram, in the northeast. Following Abacha's death and the installation of a transitional government of General Abdulsalami Abubakar, Nigeria would gradually begin to see the pathway to a civilian government. In 1999, that pathway toward a democratic process was made possible when a new constitution was written that signaled the end of military rule in the country.

The successful election of 1999 ushered in the civilian government of President Olusegun Obasanjo who ruled for eight years before reluctantly relinquishing power when his term ended. His quest to elongate the two-term presidential term to a third-term was met with resistance and bitterness from Nigerians. Left with no choice, he had handpicked a successor in Umaru Musa Yar'Adua, who eventually succeeded him, and who died in office, before he could finish his first term in office.

A lot of critics would say President Obasanjo selfishly created the turmoil that would transcend his handpicked successor's short-lived administration, to the administration of Goodluck Jonathan.

Boko Haram, the civilian government's nemesis since 2002, intensified its Islamic extremism in 2009. As Boko Haram continues its exploits and destructions, of bombings and raiding, of villages and cities in the northeast of Nigeria unchallenged, it became clear that the chaotic and sometimes rivalrous Nigerian politicians would be helpless in dealing with the Islamic jihadists. With Boko Haram establishing its own caliphate in some parts of northeast Nigeria, the country would be plunged further into a state of anarchy. The already marginalized and economically sidetracked Nigerians in the northeast of the country became subjected to the violent whims and caprices of Boko Haram, in the absence of an effective government in the area.

Those who offered any modicum of resistance to Boko Haram's caliphate were either beheaded or forcibly recruited into the group. Kidnapped women and children were often used as decoys and suicide-bombers, for suicide bombings of government and military installations, government infrastructure, including market places, mosques and police stations.

Though oil boom brought enormous revenues to Nigeria, downtrodden Nigerians seldom see or feel the impact of the revenue from the oil; as politicians and their cronies often make it impossible for the money to spread to the poor in Nigeria. As the world celebrated the economic coming of age of Nigeria, the world also decried the country's inability to solve its terrorist and poverty problems.

Nigeria's terrorist problem reached its crescendo and height, when over 200 Nigerian secondary school girls were kidnapped in Chibok, on April 14, 2014. Months later, over 2000 Nigerians were slaughtered in Baga by Boko Haram, on January 9-10, 2015. The 200 kidnapped girls were never found. Boko Haram said the girls were converted to Islam and married off to its soldiers and militants.

As of December 2014, Boko Haram has kidnapped additional secondary school girls from secondary schools in the northeast; and had converted hundreds of kidnapped women into sex slaves and suicide bombers, including girls as young as 10 and 12 years of age. As Boko Haram increases its violence and jihad, so did the Nigerian military became weak. It was hard to believe the Nigerian military could not overwhelm a bunch of untrained thugs and militants fighting for Boko Haram. Reports abound of Nigerian soldiers running at the sight of Boko Haram militants!

The government of President Goodluck Jonathan looked on, helplessly, as Boko Haram declares the northeast a caliphate. The Nigerian government couldn't do anything if it wanted to as the country's military lacked the courage and weaponry to face the well funded and well equipped militants, BBC News Africa reported.

A few Nigerian soldiers who dared to challenge the Nigerian military for not providing superior and modern weaponry to fight the jihadist Islamists were charged with mutiny and put in prison, to face a possible death sentence. Amid the chaos and turmoil that has become the lot of Nigerians, is still the thriving economy in the country, spurred by the oil boom in the economically neglected south, in the Niger Delta.

Nigeria's economic growth and significance has continuously been bedeviled and marred by selfishness, greed; lust for power, corruption, embezzlement, tribalism, favoritism, and nepotism. Chaotic civilian governments that were often roiled by political violence and killings have been grounds for past military takeovers. Economists believe Nigeria's potentials were diminished by the incessant coups and bad governments. Thieving national and state governments have also been the hallmark of civilian administrations. James Ibori of Delta State was reported to have stolen millions of dollars meant for the development of his state while the former governor of Bayelsa state, Diepreye Alamieyeseigha was also reported to have stolen millions of dollars meant to develop his state's infrastructures, and to pay workers' salaries.

BBC News Africa reported that Alamieyeseigha was detained in London for money laundering in 2005, following a tipoff from one of the governor's confidants. At the time of his detention and subsequent arrest, Alamieyeseigha was in possession of looted £1m in cash that had been stolen from his state's treasury in Beyelsa state. Additional search would net more stolen cash that amounted to over £1.8m ($3.2m). The governor was also reported to have stolen six years of federal oil allocations to his state, which amounted to over £32 million. He had reportedly used some of the stolen money to purchase properties in the excess of £10 million in London.

The federal allocation money he stole had been funds meant to develop his state and to pay workers' salaries. Meanwhile in his state, workers were owed salaries for upward of six months while roads were unrepaired and unpaved. Constructions were in uncompleted stages while major projects were abandoned for lack of funds – because the funds had been stolen by the governor.

While on bail in London, Alamieyeseigha had infamously and shamelessly jumped bail. Dressed like a woman, he had shamelessly escaped from London, under a disguise; and had boarded a plane to Nigeria. Another crooked governor of the lost generation genre was, James Ibori, the former governor of Delta State who, like Alamieyeseigha, had notoriously plundered his state's treasury to enrich his bank accounts overseas, and to buy personal properties in

South Africa and in Europe. Ibori stole millions of dollars that belonged to his state, including several years of federal allocation to his state. Ibori was apprehended while on the run in the Middle East and was convicted of corruption, with the help of the British authorities.

With crooked government figures like James Ibori and Alamieyeseigha, Nigeria's development has been on a perpetual setback, falling behind other developing countries with similar natural resources. Nigeria appears to have found itself in a gridlock where progress becomes almost impossible, an official with the World Bank opined. Aside from having declared itself free of Ebola, the country is still facing insurgencies in the Niger Delta where foreigners continue to be kidnapped in the oil fields and where oil pipelines continue to be sabotaged. And in the northeast, Boko Haram appears to have taken over the northeast, having declared an Islamic state that is similar to the Islamic State in Iraq and Syria (ISIS), led by Abu Bakr al Baghdadi.

Nigeria's volatile political landscape has largely made it possible for insurgencies to continue in the Niger Delta and for terrorism to continue to prevail in the northeast of the country, observers said. Corrupt politicians have often been accused of aiding and abetting destabilizations and insurgencies in the Niger Delta for political gains and personal enrichment. In the north, the same is true of Boko Haram, with northern politicians being accused of complicity with the Islamic jihadists.

There are other factors responsible for the insurgencies in the oil rich Niger Delta which the Nigerian government have overlooked for decades, and which succeeding governments have allowed to degenerate into chaos. One of such factors is negligence of the oil producing areas of the country, according to a former militant called General Boyloaf who now goes by a different name and title: Dr. Ebikabowei Victor Ben. The issue of insurgencies in the Niger Delta will always remain if the government does not develop and compensate the people in the area, the ex-militant said. In a report published in the Vanguard Newspaper of September 7, 2013, Boyloaf said oil theft has continued because the owners of the land where oil facilities are located "did not feel any sense of belonging after many decade of oil production."

Other factors have been the complicity of unscrupulous businessmen and women, including the police, the army, and several government functionaries and stakeholders, who continue to illicitly benefit from the illegal oil bunkering and theft, critics observed. There are also the politicians in the Niger Delta who have often used proceeds from such illegal oil bunkering to finance their political ambitions and campaigns. Reports abound that some influential members of the Nigerian business community have illegally benefited from such oil bunkering. Critics have often blamed the Nigerian government for not building enough refineries in the area; to create employment for the youths in the creeks in the Niger Delta who have resorted to oil bunkering because of unemployment. Some of the unemployed youths are also involved in the many militant groups and insurgencies in the area, CNN reported.

The inability of the Nigerian government to build refineries is also one of the factors that had encouraged oil bunkering and insurgencies in the Niger Delta. If the nation's politicians had kept their promises to build refineries, the country would not have any need to import its own oil back to the country for domestic consumption. According to Bloomberg Business Week – Global Economics, "More than 90 percent of Nigeria's budget comes from oil and gas; until recently, the country was Africa's leading exporter of oil. And yet Nigeria refines less than one-fifth of its own output—so little, in fact, that it has to re-import its own oil, refined elsewhere, at a higher cost."

The most compelling reasons for Nigeria's problems with unrests in both the Niger Delta and the northeast has been due, largely to youth unemployment, that successive Nigerian governments failed to address. Lack of meaningful investments in manufacturing, and organizational development had, according to economists and the International Monetary Fund, contributed to the high youth unemployment in the country. High youth unemployment, critics also observed, is the reason for the existence of Boko Haram and increased kidnapping and armed robberies in the country.

Instability in the government, corrupt politicians and endemic illicit gains by graft, incessant coups, political intolerance and killings, continue to hamper economic growth and development in the country. Nigeria's refusal to address its social and economic problems had also been a contributing factor to the social and political instability in the country. In a recent poll, Nigerians believe their problem is the politicians who continue to loot and plunder the oil revenues in the country's coffer.

While Boko Haram has been a major scourge in Nigeria's northeast, 60% of Nigerians overwhelmingly blamed the politicians for the problems besetting the country. Less than 20% blamed Boko Haram while fewer than 5% blamed armed robberies and the insurgents in the Niger Delta, for Nigeria's problems. Nigerian politicians, starting with the country's so-called fourth republic, which commenced in 1999, have abysmally added to the growing unrests and tribulations in Nigeria. Political violence created by politicians had added to political and economic turbulence in the country. The fourth republic constitution is often seen by most Nigerians as a meaningless constitution that politicians themselves do not abide by. The government's inability to seriously prosecute corrupt politicians who often return to office after being accused of embezzlement and theft, is one of the reasons most Nigerians do not believe the government is there to protect their interests.

The civilian administration of President Olusegun Obasanjo brought back the political violence of the 1960s in which political opponents were wantonly murdered by their fellow politicians, and in which thuggery defined the political landscape. For example, the murderers or assassins of the former minister of Justice, Bola Ige, in December 2001, were never brought to justice, despite government's claim that it was following solid leads. The investigation and subsequent reports, on the assassination, never materialized. Other widely publicized assassinations had also gone uninvestigated and unprosecuted.

While the Obasanjo administration is credited with reducing the nation's debts and streamlining the economy; and also with helping to bolster the country's GDP, most of the problems that had, and continue to, bedevil the country were also created by the Obasanjo administration. Critics blamed Obasanjo for the emergence of Boko Haram. Obasanjo was excoriated for not honoring his party's zoning system that allows the rotation of the presidency between the north and the south, which in large part, paved the way for the formation of Boko Haram in the north. Obasanjo's usurpation of, and violation of, his party's zoning system and futile attempt to create a third term, created disagreements and disgruntlement that eventually led to the formation of Boko Haram, in 2002, and heightened the group's deadly activities in 2009 and onward.

Immediately after Obasanjo left office at the end of his 2nd term, and following the public outcry of his attempt to change the constitution to allow room for a third term, things had started to turn for the worse in Nigeria. President Umaru Musa Yar'Adua won the presidential election and became president, in 2007. But an enmity was already created in Atiku Abubakar, Obasanjo's former vice president, who felt it should have been his turn to be president. It was the same period that Boko Haram had started to increase its violent activities in the northeast, with some northern politicians reportedly aiding and abetting the Islamic jihadists.

The same political intolerance continued under President Yar'Adua with endemic corruption and embezzlement. President Yar"Adua died before he could complete his first term in office, on May 5, 2010. At the time of Yar'Adua's death, Boko Haram had gained a foothold in the northeast, and had started small scale terrorism, targeting mostly Christians in the area.

The ascension of Goodluck Jonathan to the presidency, following Yar'Adua's death, intensified Boko Haram's activities in the northeast, with increased beheadings, suicide-bombings and killings of Christians and moderate Muslims in the region. As President Jonathan rules the country, it became apparent that some northerners were angry that they had been left out of the political process. To appease the situation, some party stalwarts advised President Jonathan not to run for president, when he completes the term of the late President Yar'Adua. But Jonathan was adamant and said he would run. Some northern politicians had raised the issue of the zoning system that had been part of the party's constitution since its formation, but Jonathan and his supporters had refused to abide by the zoning system of the party and had chosen to run. Disgruntled northern politicians who had once been military leaders during past military regimes, like General Muhammadu Buhari and General Ibrahim Badamasi Babangida, had reportedly sworn to make the country ungovernable.

True to their words, the country has been largely ungovernable, especially the northeast, thanks to Boko Haram's terrorist activities in the area. As Boko Haram increases its weekly violent terrorist activities in the northeast and in the capital city of Abuja, so has uncertainty in Nigeria. Since 2009, Boko Haram has reportedly killed, and maimed thousands of Nigerians, and has displaced millions in the northeast of Nigeria and Abuja, the capital. The country has indeed been made ungovernable with Boko Haram controlling most towns and cities in the northeast, with its own caliphate and Islamic state.

The state of emergency declared in the northeast, by President Goodluck Jonathan, has been as infective as the administration, to combat terrorism in the region. Millions of northern Nigerians have been displaced while several millions have fled their homes. The army that was supposed to provide security in the northeast have been reportedly overwhelmed and subdued by Boko Haram. Reports abound of Nigerian soldiers running at the sight of the Islamic jihadists, BBC News Africa reported. Some northerners said Nigerian soldiers often run at the sight of Boko Haram! The soldiers claimed Boko Haram militants have better weapons than they do!

Nigeria remains, in large part, ungovernable and abysmally a failed state. The country remains in a perpetual state of anarchy as President Jonathan prepares for reelection, against national outcry that he should step down, in 2016. Critics blamed President Jonathan for the increased terrorist activities in the northeast. President Jonathan has also been blamed for the increased graft and corruption, including the reported mysterious disappearance of over $20 billion from the nation's coffer. For some Nigerians, President Jonathan brought bad luck to Nigeria hence he is nicknamed Bad-luck Jonathan by many Nigerians.

Nigeria continues to lag behind several other African countries in economic development. In corruption, Nigeria maintains its position as the 39th most corrupt nation in the world, and the 3rd most corrupt nation in West Africa, according to Transparency International. ThisDay tabloid reported that "the 2014 Transparency International Corruption Perception Index ranked 174 countries it surveyed based on how corrupt their public sector is presumed to be."

USA Today reported that "In Nigeria, 94% of people claimed their political parties were corrupt, the most in the world." Corruption in Nigeria has become endemic; and successive national governments have been unable to, or unwilling to, do anything about it. Economists believe that corruption is one of the reasons Nigeria has not achieved its economic potential in the world.

In Senegal, another West African country of 13.5 million people caught in the Ebola epidemic and blitz, was able to contain the Ebola disease due to that country's government efforts to contain and prevent the disease. According to the World Health Organization, "Senegal's response is a good example of what to do when faced with an imported case of Ebola." Part of the government initiative in containing the disease included immediately identifying the 74 people the patient who had contracted the disease had been in close contact with and quickly testing all the reported cases. Part of the government's processes of containing the disease also included stepping up "surveillance at the country's many entry points and nationwide public awareness campaigns." The Ebola outbreak had occurred, and confirmed in Senegal, on August 29, 2014, when according to Huffington Post, a young man who had arrived in Dakar by road from Guinea had contracted the disease "where he had direct contact with an Ebola patient."

The outbreak in Senegal has been minimal compared to the cases in Liberia, Sierra Leone and Guinea, where the outbreaks had been horrific and deadly. The infected young man in Senegal had quickly recovered by September 5, 2014, barely a week after he had been confirmed to have the virus. The miraculous recovery had made it possible for the young man to return to Guinea after laboratory samples "from the patient tested negative, indicating that he had recovered from Ebola."

The Huffington Post further reported that the World Health Organization had declared Senegal free of Ebola because the country successfully "made it past the 42-day mark, which is twice the maximum incubation period for Ebola, without detecting more such cases." Though Senegal remains vulnerable to the disease because of its geographical proximity to Guinea and Mali, the country has remained watchful and vigilante of travelers traveling from neighboring countries by road and by air, and also by complying with the guidelines provided by the World Health Organization.

The history of Senegal made it possible for that country to successfully contain the Ebola outbreak. Senegal is one of the very few countries in Africa that has not been bedeviled by incessant coups and political upheavals and turmoil that had beset other sub-Saharan African countries like Nigeria, Ghana, Liberia, amongst others. Senegal is a former French colony with an estimated population of 13 million.

The country's name, Senegal, was, according to historians, derived from the Senegal River that lies in the border between Senegal and Mauritania. The land area of Senegal is estimated at 197,000 square kilometers or 76,000 square miles.

Senegal obtained its independence from France in 1960, almost three centuries after France first took control of the region in 1677, in the 17th century. During the period of 17th and 18th centuries, the coast of Senegal was used as a trading post by several European colonial masters, for slave trade and other commercial activities. Like most sub-Saharan African countries, Senegal has a tropical climate with dry and rainy seasons.

Compared with other countries with oil, Senegal is mostly an agrarian economy and is dependent on its fishing, sugarcane, peanuts, cotton, green beans, tomatoes, melon, mango and crucial cash crops. Other sectors in the economy that generates revenue include phosphate mining, fertilizer production, oil refinery, and construction.

The history of Senegal goes beyond the 17th century when the French first took control of the country in 1677. According to historians, the area now called Senegal had been home to several invaders around the 7th century. Some of the kingdoms that were established during the 7th century gave way to empires like the Takrur Empire that existed around the lower Senegal River, two centuries later, in the 9th century. Subsequent empires that are worthy of note included the Namandiru and the Jolof (also called Wolof) empire between the 13th and 14th centuries. These empires essentially went through transitions that later became what is today called Senegal. But prior to that, the eastern part of Senegal was also part of the Ghana Empire.

Long before the advent of colonialism, several West African, and African countries were interconnected through tribal and ethnic affiliations. For example, what is Senegal today had once belonged to another empire that included Mali; and then there was also the Ghana Empire connection, not to mention Guinea and Sierra Leone. When the French landed in the region and took over Senegal in 1677, there was already a confederacy of several smaller empires that were affiliated by ethnic and tribal connections.

The presence of countries like France, Portugal, the Netherlands, Spain, and Great Britain, among others, further created a divide that permanently segmented the various cultures and tribes that were once united. The introduction of foreign languages into the colonial territories by the colonial masters spurred distrusts and language barriers that further divided and bedeviled Africa's socioeconomic development.

Though Senegal has a strong Muslim population, with Islam being introduced by Toucouleur and Soninke, in conjunction with the Almoravid dynasty in earlier centuries, Senegal is still able to maintain religious tolerance among the different religious groups that include Christians and pagans. Unlike Nigeria and Mali where there is religious intolerance and clashes between the different faiths, Senegal maintains a peaceful coexistence among the different religions in the country.

Though Senegal is not as economically buoyant as Nigeria and Ghana, the country has been able to maintain a stable government that was devoid of political upheaval and intolerance. Such political stability has been the envy of most countries in West Africa where terrorism and religious frictions have become endemic. Nigeria, Mali, and a few countries in West Africa have had to constantly deal with terrorism.

In North Africa, countries like Libya, Algeria, Egypt and Tunisia continue to have sociopolitical upheavals, in addition to religious violence and terrorism. Unlike these North African, and West African countries, Senegal has been able to create a peaceful coexistence between the Christians and Muslims in the country.

It was not surprising that Senegal was able to contain the Ebola virus immediately it hit its shores. The same cannot be said of Sierra Leone where 11 indigenous doctors who had been treating Ebola patients had died of the disease. According to the Voice of America, the 11th Sierra Leonean doctor had died of the Ebola virus. The government of Sierra Leone has, according to the WHO, not done enough to contain the disease. A recent survey indicated that 70% of the Ebola infections "did not come from either the country's Ebola holding centers or treatment facilities." Majority of the infections have come from direct contacts with infected patients, according to the WHO.

Though countries like Nigeria and Senegal are currently Ebola free, the disease is still ravaging lives in Sierra Leone, Liberia and Guinea. According to the World Health Organization, the governments of the infected countries have not done enough to contain the disease. In order to reduce the rate of infection, the World Health Organization opined that, "it's critical to handle patients and victims properly to stamp out the outbreak." The diagram below portrays the percentage of the efforts being made by the governments of the infected countries to reduce the rate of Ebola infections in West Africa.

WHO'S MEETING TARGETS?

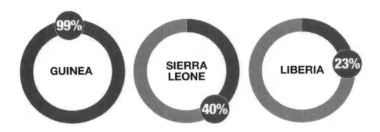

Guinea is exceeding U.N. goals, but Liberia and Sierra Leone are far from meeting them

■ Ebola patients isolated

GUINEA 99%

SIERRA LEONE 40%

LIBERIA 23%

SOURCE: World Health Organization, Nov. 26, 2014

Chapter 13

The unimportance Africans/Blacks in the U.S

The unnecessary death of Thomas Eric Duncan from Ebola once again manifested the utter unimportance of the lives of Africans and blacks in the United States. Could the life of Thomas Eric Duncan have been saved? Unequivocally yes! Duncan had been neglected, and denied the Ebola medication that could have saved his life, Duncan's nephew, Josephus Weeks said. That is if Duncan had actually been sick of the disease in the first place. Could Duncan have been misdiagnosed? Probably yes. After all, his fiancée, Louise Troh, and her children, and family who were in the apartment with Duncan when he supposedly became sick of Ebola, never got the disease.

For a disease that purportedly and supposedly infects others through body fluids, saliva, blood, amongst others, one would have thought that one of the occupants in the apartment with Duncan when he got the disease would have contracted the disease. That is if Duncan actually had it.

There is no doubt that he probably kissed his fiancée, Louise Troh or even became intimate with her on the first night of his arrival from Liberia, to the U.S. It wouldn't be inconceivable for him to have been intimate with a woman he hadn't seen in years. If he already had the symptoms when he arrived, chances were that he would have spread the symptoms and disease to his fiancée and the other occupants in that apartment in Dallas, where he had stayed prior to his hospitalization and eventual death. But he did not spread the disease because he probably did not have it? And eventually no one in the apartment, save Duncan, "contracted the disease."

Assuming he had it, he had gone to the Texas Presbyterian Hospital for treatment and was given antibiotics on his first visit. When he was reportedly confirmed with Ebola, why didn't the hospital transfer him to Emory University Hospital in Atlanta, for treatment? After all, the hospital had previously and successfully treated two U.S. healthcare workers who had contracted Ebola in Liberia, long before Duncan arrived in the U.S. If the Texas Presbyterian Hospital was not equipped to treat an Ebola patient, why was Duncan put in a ventilator and sedated without treatment? The World Health Organization said 90% depended on a patient's will to survive. Why was Duncan not allowed to exercise that 90%

chance or some of it? Being put on a ventilator and sedated robs a patient the opportunity to exercise a free will. Was it because he was black, and didn't have insurance; and didn't have any money and was an African? Josephus Weeks, Duncan's nephew, thinks so.

The same situation bespeaks the case of Dr. Martin Salia, who had been working in his native Sierra Leone as a surgeon, where he had contracted the Ebola virus. Dr. Salia had paid his way for a medical emergency flight to the U.S. and had been quietly received and taken to the Nebraska Medical Center where he had died, of "advanced Ebola." Dr. Salia's organs had reportedly failed due to the "advanced Ebola infection." It didn't matter that on November 6, 2014, Dr. Salia had tested negative for Ebola. Less than two weeks later, on Monday November 17, 2014, he had died of the disease! Dr. Salia was the third Ebola patient treated at the Nebraska Medical Center, and the only one to die!

How did Dr. Salia's Ebola disease become suddenly advanced when he had tested negative just November 6, 2014? Previous survivors had had the disease longer and did not die from it. Dr. Kent Brantly had had the disease longer than Dr. Salia; but the former lived to tell the story! Why? Because Dr. Brantly is an American and white while Dr. Salia was a mere resident and an African! A Sierra Leonean living in Houston said.

The lame excuse the hospital gave was that Dr. Salia "had advanced symptoms when he arrived at the hospital Saturday, November 15, 2015, which included kidney and respiratory failure." Recall that the World Health Organization reported that Dr. Salia had tested negative for the disease on November 6, 2014! So, within two weeks, the disease went from being negative to being advanced? A Sierra Leonean health official asked. Dr. Kent Brantly had the disease longer than Dr. Salia and his infection did not progress to an advanced stage to where his organs failed! Dr. Salia had been working as a general surgeon at Kissy United Methodist Hospital in Freetown, Sierra Leone, when he contracted the disease.

The question is why Dr. Salia did not receive the same treatment that Dr. Kent Brantly and other infected Americans had received? Why wasn't Dr. Salia or Duncan given the antibody or the experimental drug Zmapp? Were they not deserving of the drugs or that the drugs wouldn't work for Ebola infected Africans? For Africans, being denied treatment for Ebola and not having access to available experimental drugs, "is akin to blacks being systemically oppressed and brutalized by white police officers,"one black activist said. The history of blacks in the United States and their mortality rate, in the hands of white police officers, tend to be unimportant to white Americans as a whole, a recent poll indicated. Just like with Africans who have continually faced different types of stigmatizations, and lately being stigmatized with Ebola, blacks in the U.S. continue to face a different sort of stigma. The Ebola epidemic and the consequences of being a West African, and being tarred with stigma, continues to bedevil the lots of Africans in the United States and in Europe. The Ebola virus continues to put Africans in an unbridled position of being stigmatized and marginalized.

For centuries, Africans have often suffered, forsaken and marginalized because of the color of their skin. Everything evil and bad is often associated with black. For example, aids is said to have sprung from Africa, even though proofs abound of Europeans traveling to Morocco to practice their homosexuality at a time when it was illegal to be homosexual in Europe and the United States. Aids/HIV has, according to World Health Organization, been linked to homosexuality and unprotected sex.

In England, those found to be gay were ostracized in medieval periods till the end of the 19th century when it simmered down, towards mild acceptance in some parts. Although homosexuality was still considered sodomy, and punishable by death in the latter part of the 19th century and up to the middle of the 20th century, society became more tolerant of male homosexuals than with female homosexuals toward the end of the 20th century. And because of the stigma associated with being gay, most Europeans chose Morocco, in Africa, to practice their homosexuality. Some historians believe aids crept into Africa through the homosexuality that was practiced in places like Morocco at the time, and also the fondness of some Europeans with their animals whom they often slept, and sometimes intimate with, at the time.

It is ironical for Africans to continually be forsaken and stigmatized for a disease that was brought to the African continent by Europeans. And with history as a narrative of how aids crept into Africa, Africans continue to face untoward discrimination. Africa continues to wallow in the dark due to circumstances created by early European invaders in Africa

In 21st century America where an African American is elected president of the United States, discrimination and marginalization of blacks continues to be on the rise. If it is not police brutality it is an unjust slaying of a black man by a white man, as happened when a white man, Michael Dunn, 45, shot and killed a black teen, Jordan Davis, 17, in Jacksonville, Florida, in November 2012. Dunn had walked up to a group of black teens sitting in their car at a gas station and rudely asked them to "turn down the loud music blaring from their car and, after an exchange of words, opened fire on the vehicle," killing Davis, The Daily News had reported. The failure of the justice system to indict and punish trigger happy white police officers who often target poor blacks, further reaffirmed the age-old racism that continues to be prevalent in many parts of the U.S

Added to the already legendary police brutality are the numerous reports of black males being lynched in several small towns and cities across the country, in the U.S.! According to CNN, a 17 year old boy, Lennon Lacy, who was dating a 31 year old white woman, in Bladenboro, North Carolina, was found hanging from a tree after he had gone for a leisurely walk, on August 28, 2014. The police had concluded that the 17-year-old had committed suicide because he was found hanging from a tree. The fact that the teen had been dating a 31 year old white woman in a predominantly white town, that was a stronghold of Ku Klux Klan, and also the fact that the clan had been burning crosses and espousing hatred for blacks, days before the hanging, did not trigger any reason for an investigation. The fact that one of the former lovers of the 31 year-old white woman was a member of the clan was not enough for the police to start investigating the obvious lynching that was reminiscent of clan's modus operandi of the early part of the 20th century.

The police had, as usual, rushed to judgment that the teen had committed suicide. What would be the motive for suicide for a star athlete who had played lineman position for the West Bladen High School Knights, and who was focused on his education and football? How could the boy have committed suicide when he had just packed a gym bag for the gym, and had just washed his ankle brace and had hung it on the clothesline to dry?

The deceased's older brother, Pierre Lacy, according to CNN, said "he may have either been strangled somewhere else or been placed there or he was hanged there while people were around watching him die." North Carolina's Chief Medical Examiner reportedly declared the teen's death a suicide, because of the way he died. The teen had been focused on college and football. There was no reason for him to take his own life when everything was going very well for him, his mother reportedly said. What the police overlooked was the fact that the teen had been dating a 31 year-old white woman who was also a neighbor and whose former lover was a member of the clan. And besides the obvious, a lot of small towns still frown on interracial relationships, in the U.S. According to CNN, "Some people in their small, southern town did not like that the two were together." The deceased teen's mother had disapproved of the age difference between her son and the 31 year-old white woman.

Several residents in the town reportedly wondered if "Lennon had been killed because he was in an interracial relationship." But the obvious facts were that there was a heavy presence of the clan in the town, and that the 31 year-old white woman, had had a relationship with a man thought to be a clan's member. To further confirmed racial implication, a week after Lennon Lacy was buried, a local white teenager was arrested for defacing Lennon's grave.

Another issue regarding the lynching of Lacy that the police overlooked or ignored to investigate, apart from the defacing of the grave, was that Lennon was found hanging from a 7ft 6" height when he was only 5ft 9". It would have been impossible for him to have hanged himself considering the height. Another intrigue was the report that a 52 year-old-woman had reportedly taken down the 207lb teen "while she was on the phone with an emergency dispatcher." How was that likely? Why did the 52 year-old-woman take down the body and where did she get the strength to do so? Was the 52-year-old woman involved in the lynching? The police did not bother to ask these questions because the victim was black, which parallels the discourse about the insignificance of blacks' lives in America.

Another intrigue that the police overlooked and or ignored was the fact that the noose or belt that Lacy had been hanged with did not belong to the teen. The mother of the deceased teen said she was sure the belt did not belong to her son since she was still buying his clothes up to the time he was lynched. The Bladen County Coroner and Medical Examiner, Hubert Kinlaw, stated that the belts "might have been dog leashes." Another overlooked evidence of a hate crime was that Lacy had been hanged with somebody else's shoes, a size 10.5, on his foots. There had been no laces in the size 10.5 tennis shoes. The teen had left home for a walk wearing a size 12 Air Jordan. The shoes found on the teen had been two sizes too little. Someone had obviously stolen his brand new pair of the popular pair of Air Jordan. Someone who was obviously involved in the hanging of Lacy!

Another unanswered question was how the teen got to the dirt road late at night to a swing set in the middle of the trailer park where he was hanged from a tree. Two things may have occurred, says the deceased's brother. Either he was strangled and brought to the scene of the lynching or he was carried to the dirt road and lynched there.

Why was it necessary to declare the death a suicide when there were obvious signs of racial crime? According to CNN, "Dr. Radisch noted that her determination of (manner of death) in this case as suicide was based on the information she was provided by law enforcement and the local medical examiner." The determination of suicide was not based on any medical analysis but on the uninformed prejudgment of a few small town cops!

For trigger happy police officers, it is legal to accidentally shoot a black man under the pretext of self-defense and being in the line of duty. According to USA Today, based on FBI report, in 2013, over 461 black males were killed by the police in unjustifiable homicides. The FBI indicated that "homicide database during a seven-year period ending in 2012 found an average of 96 incidents each year in which a white officer killed a black person." Accidental discharge of weapon and actually shooting a black man in the line of duty has become synonymous with self defense.

With no legal repercussions and redress for victimized blacks, white police officers see their homicidal actions as immunity from the law. With total impunity and lack of fear of the wrath of the law, several white police officers seldom worry about the consequences of killing unarmed blacks in the U.S. Appalling for a country like the U.S. that champions fundamental human rights in developing and underdeveloped countries. It is not surprising that the policy of the U.S. government to defend the defenseless in Burma or the Republic of the Union of Myanmar, Kosovo, Ukraine, Afghanistan and Iraq and many parts of the world is often seen as a laughingstock.

For poor blacks and the not-so-poor blacks, it is not uncommon for justice to fail them. Recently, a black Harvard professor was hardly differentiated from a poor black man when he was confronted by a white police officer who thought he was a burglar, as he tries to enter his home in a white neighborhood. The first black U.S. Attorney General and the current and outgoing

Attorney General of the U.S., under the Obama Administration, Eric Holder, Jr. had reportedly been unjustly profiled. The 65th Secretary of State, Colin Powell, under Bush 41, was also reportedly profiled in New York. The reason police brutality has become ubiquitous among blacks is that blacks everywhere in the U.S. have come to accept police brutality as a norm, a black activist recently said. Elsewhere in the world in Africa and the Caribbean Islands, blacks have silently accepted police brutality and use of deadly force, according to Amnesty International.

Though the chances of a white police officer admitting to his trigger-happy readiness to shoot a black man is tantamount to a homicidal drunk driver admitting to being drunk, which is always slim; a white police officer would often hide his homicidal instincts toward a black man, under the pretext of being in the line of duty. The police secret code of *omerta* - code of silence and the non-interference in the illegal actions of other officers, and not telling on fellow officers often protects officers from ratting on each other. An officer involved in "an accidental" discharge of his weapon will often be overlooked because of the code of silence, even when the action was premeditated and intentional.

Trayvon Martin was shot by Zimmerman because Martin looked black with a hoodie and possibly a potential burglar, even though Martin was not breaking any law at the time. His crime was being black and wearing a hooded sweatshirt in the dark of night. Zimmerman's chosen action to tail Martin, with a deadly weapon, was premeditated. Justice would fail Martin as it has, and continues to fail many blacks in similar situations as prosecutors often deliberately choose white jurors, knowing that white jurors will favor the actions of fellow whites. The mostly white jurors failed to see that it was illegal for a white Hispanic to shoot an unarmed black man. Why will prosecutors pick 90% white jurors in a predominantly black community? "Your guess is as good as mine," says a black activist in Florida.

Like Ebola had stigmatized Africans in the U.S. blacks face being relegated, to being irrelevant and insignificant in the scheme of things, by most whites and in some cases, by nonwhites. It is not uncommon for a black man to be carefully monitored and watched as he shops in a convenience store owned by an Asian immigrant, in a black neighborhood! Why open a store in a black neighborhood and expect black business if you think that some black customers will walk in and steal your merchandise? The slavery, and marginal effect, has grown some ripple effects to where immigrants whose deplorable conditions back home are even worse in their countries will want to act like white, and discriminate against blacks.

How did a poor immigrant from India, China, Vietnam and elsewhere in Asia, who manages to swim his way or get smuggled into the U.S. suddenly becomes an overlord who now acts as if he is more superior to a black man, in the black man's own backyard? A prominent black activist wondered. The Asian immigrant saw the deplorable condition of poor blacks and cashed in on it; opened a store in his neighborhood; often illegally swaps food stamps for cigarettes and beers, and in some cases, cashes the food stamps for 50% less than the value, for the unsuspecting poor black who is eager for hard cash. Even with that, the poor black is perceived as a crooked drug dealer who can be shot in front of the convenience store for suspicion of drug dealing, or better still, for minding his own business in front of the store.

Are blacks unworthy of fair treatments that other racial groups receive in the United States? Nina Pham was treated like a heroine and even given a presidential reception at the White House when she had survived the Ebola disease. Amber Vinson, a fellow nurse, was barely acknowledged, save for the subdued press conference, in the media. Why do blacks continue to be marginalized in obvious situations? Is there something in the DNA of blacks that relegate them to the socioeconomic backseat? One observer asked. Is the past perpetually coming home to roost in every sundry occasion, a past forgotten but not buried? The past servitude and subjugation of blacks appear to still haunt and stigmatize them, even when the obvious has been achieved. It is as if the image of servitude is ingrained in the minds of the perpetrators and those who admired the curse and scourge of history! When will the stigma give way to a well earned respect for the black man?

African Americans continually face police brutality and profiling on a daily basis. Like the deadly Ebola virus that took the lives of two Africans in the U.S., the profiling and killing of defenseless black people, because of the color of their skin, continue to take center stage. The lives of blacks, based on the manner police officers kill them regularly appear to be less worthy, and meaningless, than people of other color in similar situations.

Trayvon Benjamin Martin, an unarmed 17 year old black teenager who was shot and killed by George Zimmerman, a neighborhood watch guard volunteer, was chased down as he walked back to his father's fiancée townhouse at the Retreat at Twin Lakes in Sanford, Florida. Martin had reportedly "gone with his father on a visit to the father's fiancée at her townhouse at the Retreat at Twin Lakes in Sanford." On his return from the convenience store where he had purchased a candy and juice, Martin was accosted and shot by George Zimmerman, a neighborhood volunteer, on February 26, 2012.

Though Zimmerman was indicted and eventually faced justice in court, a jury of mostly white jurors found him not guilty and freed him. On February 24, 2015, three years after Martin's death, the Justice Department concluded "that there is not enough evidence to bring civil rights charges in the case," involving the slaying of Martin by Zimmerman. Eric Holder, the Attorney General, called the case "a devastating tragedy," during the press conference, according to CBS-News.

Like most white jurors before them that did not care much for black victims, Zimmerman was found not guilty. Some of the female jurors were reportedly flirting with Zimmerman during the trial. Critics believe prosecutors deliberately chose white jurors knowing they would not convict Zimmerman. And like several white jurors before them, in previous cases involving a white man killing a black man, Zimmerman was not only acquitted but also made a celebrity. While Zimmerman was on trial, so many white Americans donated lots of money towards his legal defense fund as a show of support. It was felt that killing a black man was reducing one less unwanted miscreant in the society!

The justice system that was designed to protect all and sundry failed Martin for several reasons. The first reason was that Martin was black and unimportant in the grand scheme of things! After all, he was just a 17 year old black high school student who was probably on the verge of dropping out of school! If that wasn't the case why was he out strolling by himself in the dark of night, on February 26, 2012, in Sanford, Florida, a community that was not totally packed with African Americans? It didn't matter that the shooter was a mixed-race Hispanic man who happens to be a neighborhood watch coordinator; who had volunteered for the job, in a gated community where Martin was visiting with his father at the time of the shooting. All Zimmerman saw was the fact that a young black man was out in the dark, wearing a hooded sweatshirt, and probably out to commit a crime. Zimmerman didn't look beyond the teenager's skin color. Zimmerman's attitude towards

Trayvon Martin can equally be compared to the way Duncan and Dr. Martin Salia were treated when they had contracted Ebola. Thomas Eric Duncan had been prejudged to be unimportant to the grand scheme of things, and was untreated and allowed to rot away in a ventilator while sedated until his organs started to fail. A few months before, a white American, Dr. Kent Brantly was successfully treated of Ebola, and was hailed as a hero for surviving the disease. Why couldn't he have survived, when he was given every opportunity, and treatment to survive!

Upon surviving, he was treated like a hero by the media and even honored as Time Magazine's "Person of the Year." According to the magazine, the other Ebola fighters were also honored because they "risked and persisted, sacrificed and saved." Why didn't Brantly volunteer to donate his blood to save Duncan like he had done for Nina Pham a month later when the nurse had been infected? Your guess is as good as mine! And why didn't one of the Ebola survivors donate blood plasma and antibody to Dr. Martin Salia who was a Sierra Leonean living in America? Again, your guess is as good as mine! The same Dr. Kent Brantly was being honored for sacrificing and saving lives!

Trayvon Martin's life had been as unimportant as Duncan's when the mostly white jurors had refused to convict Zimmerman of chasing and shooting Martin, an unarmed teenager, during an altercation between the two. The altercation had been instigated by George Zimmerman who had gone after the teenager who was just exercising his rights as an American citizen, visiting an American neighborhood. As expected and not surprising, the police had taken Zimmerman into custody and had reportedly "treated his head injuries," before questioning him about the shooting, for five hours. Rather than immediately arrest him, and let the jury decide his innocence, the police had let Zimmerman go back to his life, a free man. Zimmerman had just killed a human being, taken a life, and the police allowed the man to go back home after questioning him. Questioning him? When he had just killed a man! Though Zimmerman was later arrested after a huge public outcry and was later found not guilty, the police had treated the case with total triviality.

The police had claimed there was no evidence to hold Zimmerman on, when he had just killed a man! What further evidence did the police need to hold a person when a man lay dead in the street, and the perpetrator claiming self defense? Shouldn't the police have arrested him and let the court decide his innocence? The police had decided that Zimmerman was innocent, long before he was indicted and found not guilty by the jury. It wouldn't be implausible to say that the police prepared his case for an eventual acquittal!

Another false and unsupported claim the police made in Martin's case was that under Florida's Stand Your Ground statute, the police could not arrest anyone since it was a case of self defense. Even if that was true, which it wasn't, shouldn't the case of Stand Your Ground statute be allowed to be interpreted by the court rather than by the police? The statute was enacted to protect individuals who may resort to defending themselves when faced with imminent danger that involves life and death. But there was no evidence of Zimmerman facing any imminent danger since no weapon was recovered from Martin at the scene of the crime. Why did the police use a one-sided case of self defense to determine that Zimmerman had acted in self defense? Even before a judge or jury could decide, the police chief had stated that Zimmerman had the right to use lethal force for self defense, which explains why Zimmerman was allowed to go home that night, after he had unjustly taken the life of another human being.

If a black man had used the same line of argument after killing a white man, would he have been sent home after being questioned for five hours? My guess is that the black man would have been locked up, refused bail, and indicted until his fate was decided by a jury, and not allowed to go home, regardless of the Stand Your Ground statute.

Another disturbing factor in the case of Trayvon Martin and George Zimmerman was that the latter was not charged by a grand jury. Rather, Zimmerman had been charged with murder by a special prosecutor appointed by Governor Rick Scott. If the case had gone to a regular grand jury, what had happened in Ferguson Missouri when officer Darren Wilson was not indicted by the grand jury would have happened, and Zimmerman would not have been charged with murder! Grand juries across the nation have created a parallel and a pattern of not indicting white officers and white people when the case involves the shooting of a black person.

And prosecutors across the nation have developed the habit of appointing white grand jurors in cases involving black victims and white perpetrators, in murder cases.

The Trayvon Martin case proves that the life of a black person is not only unimportant but utterly marginalized, especially when compared to the life of a white person or of other colors, close to the white color. George Zimmerman was not a white man; but he was treated like a white man; and even called a white man; and hailed for killing a black man. Conservative talk radio hosts across the nation like Mark Levin, Michael Berry, Sean Hannity, Rush Limbaugh, and many others, praised Zimmerman for his actions and even contributed to his legal defense fund. Some talk radio hosts even reportedly invited Zimmerman to their shows. Zimmerman's rose to fame had been for killing a black man! Before that, he was an unemployed neighborhood watch volunteer coordinator who had taken the law into his own hands to kill an unarmed black man.

Zimmerman's ability to kill a black man and get away with it made him a hero to so many racist think tanks who appointed themselves as America's last conservative frontiers. And there were those on the extreme right that felt Zimmerman did the right thing by helping to prevent a crime from happening. There was no doubt that those sentiments were reminiscent of the National Socialism – Nazism! The same far-right groups were the ones that donated to Zimmerman's legal defense funds to help him fight the charges of murder against him. They were also the same racist groups that had paraded the streets of Sanford, Florida and elsewhere in the country, to counter black protests that followed the unjust slaying of Trayvon Martin.

What made the hypocrisy and racism of Zimmerman's case so palpable was the twofaced manner of some of the same undercover racist elements who had praised him; and who had also pretended to be friends with the black community. Some of the so-called friends of the black community were part of the dissenting voices that had denounced the unarmed black teen for being out in the street at night and wearing a hooded sweatshirt when it wasn't cold. The same twofaced elements were the ones that said Martin was a drug dealer.

They were also the ones that claimed the teen had brutally beaten Zimmerman. How on earth could a frail looking teenager like Trayvon Martin have been strong enough to overpower someone as heavyset and as strong as Zimmerman? Recall that Zimmerman was armed and Martin was not. A man with no gun being intimidating to a man with a gun? Hard to believe; but the jury believed it! Martin weighed 158lb and was over a hundred pound lighter than Zimmerman. Yet the arresting police said Zimmerman had bruises consistent with a brutal beating!

To Zimmerman, the presence of a black teenager minding his own business, walking in the neighborhood toward his father's fiancée residence, was enough to qualify the victim as being "up to no good."Zimmerman had told the police that Martin attacked him and that he had shot the teen in self defense, when it was actually Zimmerman who had rudely accosted and confronted the teen to ask him why he was in the neighborhood. Even after shooting Martin to death, Sanford Police Chief, Bill Lee, (who later resigned), reportedly said "until we establish probable cause to dispute his claim of self-defense, we don't have the grounds to arrest him," meaning Zimmerman. When did the police start to use probable cause to determine whether a person should be arrested for killing another human being? The court and the grand jury determine probable cause, never the police!

If the Stand Your Ground *clause* in the Florida law is to be believed, that a citizen "has no duty to retreat and has the right to stand his or her ground and meet force with force, including deadly force if he or she reasonably believes it is necessary to do so to prevent death or bodily harm to himself or herself or another or to prevent the commission of a forcible felony," then Martin should have been the one to exercise his rights to stand his ground since he was violently accosted and confronted by an armed Zimmerman! Zimmerman went to Martin and confronted him with a gun in hand.

How does the clause apply in defense of Zimmerman when he was clearly the aggressor? Martin was simply going about his business and was not committing any crime when he was accosted by another citizen (not a peace officer or a law enforcement agent), who did not have the legal authority to do so. Was Zimmerman making a citizen's arrest because Martin was breaking the law? No! He was using his self-appointed authority to violently confront Martin who was exercising his constitutional right of freedom of movement. Martin's exercise of his constitutional right to move freely did not harm or break any law. He had gone to the store to buy things he needed. He did not rob the store or threaten the clerk, to warrant an aggressive confrontation from Zimmerman, who was volunteering to protect a neighborhood that didn't need his protection from Martin. Did the police officer, Timothy Smith, who was the first on the scene, lie to protect Zimmerman when he said Zimmerman's "back appeared to be wet and was covered in grass, as if he had been laying on his back on the ground," and "bleeding from the nose and back of his head," to exonerate the killer? It would have been unarguably so, as it would have been logically impossible for a man as heavy as Zimmerman to be wrestled to the ground by someone as light weighted as Trayvon Martin. Zimmerman's father, Robert, who was not even at the crime scene when it happened, told Fox News, a conservative news media, that Martin had punched his son, breaking his nose and knocking him to the ground.

The father, Robert, also reportedly said "it is my understanding that Trayvon Martin got on top of him and just started beating him, in the face, in his nose, hitting his head on the concrete." How is that possible that an unarmed teen would wrestle an armed man almost twice his size, to the ground and be beating him mercilessly?

Martin was not a criminal and was never even arrested, and had no juvenile record. Though it was reported that he was investigated in October of the previous year, in 2011, after a school police officer had found women's jewelry in his backpack, the "jewelry did not match any that had been reported stolen."

On the other hand, Zimmerman had been arrested "in July 2005 on charges of felony resisting arrest with violence and battery on a police officer," even though the charges were later reduced to a single misdemeanor and was eventually dropped. It wouldn't have been inconceivable to think that the case was dropped because Zimmerman was considered a white male. Had Zimmerman been a black male the case wouldn't have been dropped under any circumstance, that is if he wasn't even shot on the scene

To further prove the kind of man Zimmerman was, a month after he was acquitted for killing Martin his ex-fiancée filed a temporary order of protection against him. Zimmerman counter-filed against her and not surprising, the court had granted both orders. As part of the order, "Zimmerman was prohibited from having a firearm or ammunition." Again not surprising, the order was "lifted in August 2006." Lifting that order empowered Zimmerman to use his firearm again, and this time, fatally, killing Trayvon Martin. And again, Zimmerman would beat the system that he had gotten good at beating because of his status as a white man.

To prove that Zimmerman's father, Robert, and Officer Timothy Smith, did not tell the truth, a video that was ironically released by the same police department that Officer Timothy Smith represents, showed no "obvious injuries to his head," CBS News had reported. The funeral director, Richard Kurtz, who had prepared Martin's body for burial had said "we could see no physical signs like there had been a scuffle." And to further buttress Martin's innocence and his unjust killing, there were no bruises on Martin's knuckles at the time his body was prepared for burial. If there had been a struggle, and punches were involved, as Robert Zimmerman, and Officer Timothy Smith had claimed, it would have been impossible for the bruises not to have been on Martin's body.

As if the conspiracies were not enough, Zimmerman's brother, Robert Zimmerman Jr. – obviously named after his father, Robert Zimmerman, reportedly told CNN's Piers Morgan that "he believes medical records will show his brother's nose was broken." No medical record was reportedly released to confirm the claim made by Zimmerman's brother that the killer's nose had been broken due to the confrontation he had had with Martin.

George Zimmerman had displayed his dislike for blacks when he had reportedly told a 911 operator, while following Martin (even when he was told not to) that he was tired of these "fucking coons." With all the evidence made available to the jury, how did George Zimmerman walk without a conviction? Not only did Zimmerman breach Martin's civil rights which is a federal crime, and an offense, but also killed him, and for all of that, the jury could not find any reasonable ground to convict him! And on February 24, 2015, the Justice Department said it could find no evidence to charge Zimmerman on Martin's death!

Did the police cover up for Zimmerman because they thought he was white? The original police report, made available to the public, revealed that Zimmerman was identified as a white male. The fact that Zimmerman was protected because he was white was not surprising. In Florida, CBS News reported that police often label Hispanics that don't have black skin color as whites, regardless of their ethnic features that represent them as Hispanics. According to the Associated Press, Zimmerman's mother, Gladys, is an immigrant from Peru. The family is said to officially identify themselves as Hispanics, which in Florida is considered white. Zimmerman's father, Robert, listed himself as a white male in his voter registration card, which incidentally made George Zimmerman to think of himself as a white male; which would qualify him to refer to blacks as coons! There is no doubt that the police were on the side of Zimmerman from the beginning of the deadly encounter, to the time Zimmerman was acquitted. He was not arrested when it was obvious he had just killed a man. The police had taken his side of the story because he was, in Florida, considered white, and needed to be protected for killing a black man whose life was unimportant, to start with.

The fate that befell Martin is similar in scope to the fate that befell Duncan and Dr. Martin Salia. Martin was seen as a "fucking coon," that shouldn't, and wasn't, allowed to live and exercise his God-given and constitutional rights. Duncan was seen as an unwanted immigrant who deliberately and intentionally brought the Ebola disease to the U.S. It didn't matter that Duncan was inadvertently infected (if he was), while helping a pregnant woman that was suffering from convulsion, not Ebola. Duncan had been immediately isolated and put on a ventilator while sedated, and refused the Ebola treatment that had saved Dr. Kent Brantly and other Americans who had been infected and cured, months before. Duncan's organs had withered away while sedated and on a ventilator.

Dr. Martin Salia had paid his own way to be treated in the U.S. after he had contracted the Ebola disease while working as a general surgeon in Sierra Leone. A Nebraska Medical Center that had saved the lives of other Ebola infected Americans could not save an African surgeon with Ebola! The excuse was that his Ebola was already too advanced when he arrived, even when he had tested negative a week before his death!

Michael Brown's case was another case of utter disregard, and marginalization of blacks' lives in the United States. The shooting death of Michael Brown, an 18 year-old teenager, on August 9, 2014, in Ferguson, Missouri, a suburb of St. Louis was another case of police brutality and utter disregard for the lives of blacks in the United States. The death of Michael Brown marked a turning point in the lives of black males in America. Officer Wilson, 28, saw Michael Brown as an unwanted nuisance and felt the best way to handle the situation was to make sure the teenager was sent back to his maker. The officer did not hide his disgust for Brown when he took out his gun and shot the teenager dead, multiple times. It was the first time the Officer reportedly used his gun, and his mission was to target a black man, and this time, a teenager just entering adulthood. Like most teenagers his age who often cherish being mischievous as part of growing up, Brown had stolen a merchandise from a store and had been confronted by the owner of the store, earlier in the day, before he was shot dead. He had not been armed like most teenagers his age who commit such crimes. He had stolen a grocery that he had no business stealing. He had been unruly, yes, but not enough for him to be murdered by an Officer, for an unrelated offence, hours later, in a different scene and setting. The officer had obviously seen the likes of Brown as a threat to the white minority in Ferguson. Blacks represent 68% of the population in Ferguson. Was Brown committing a crime when he was shot by Officer Wilson? According to the Cable News Network, CNN, Brown and his friend, Dorian Johnson, had been walking down the street like most teenagers their age, when Officer Wilson drove up in his patrol car.

Seeing them, Officer Wilson reportedly told the teenagers to use the sidewalk and not walk on the street, which is a normal and justifiable instruction. The events that unfolded were not normal. An instruction from Officer Wilson to Brown and his friend to use the sidewalk instead of the road reportedly culminated in an altercation that resulted in Brown allegedly struggling with Officer Wilson in the officer's police car.

How a routine instruction became a fight for the officer's gun in the officer's police cruiser is unexplainable since there was no video of the event when it had unfolded. According to the officer's account, Brown had tried reaching for his gun and the gun had unloaded at the same time, hitting Brown. It didn't make sense that the officer's gun would suddenly discharge as the two were struggling. How did the situation ensue in a struggle in the first place? Was Brown being disobedient and didn't want to move away from the road and use the sidewalk?

What was reported was that Brown and his friend Johnson, had run for their lives, fearing imminent danger from the officer's aggressive behavior. The two friends reportedly fled in two different directions, each hoping to evade the officer. The officer, in an obvious murder rage, chose to pursue Brown, the bigger of the two friends. According to Officer Wilson, he had to fire more shots as Brown was running, for fear of the teenager turning on him. How is it logical that the teenager that was running would suddenly turn around and be a danger to an officer with a loaded gun? But the officer had said he was afraid that Brown would kill him first if he didn't shoot to kill the teenager. In a more deadly altercation, as the officer's bullets hit Brown and the teenager slowed down, the officer would shoot him several more times to make sure he was dead. During the deadly altercation that was obviously instigated by Officer Wilson, 12 shots were fired at the teenager by the officer, with all the shots hitting the teen. The teen, fearing that the end was near, had raised his hands in surrender to let the officer know that he was no longer a danger to him. But the officer reportedly kept shooting until the teen twitched in death.

Bystanders and spectators watched in horror as another unarmed teenager was being killed before their very eyes. It was an awe-inspiring moment for the bystanders and spectators. Not too long ago, on February 26, 2012, in Sanford, Florida, another teenager had been killed in the same fashion by a "white" self-appointed neighborhood volunteer. Here now, before their very eyes, an officer had just killed an unarmed black teenager who was minding his own business, walking in the street!

The unjust killing of Brown was enough to spark civil unrests by a community that has seen many of its teenagers killed by trigger-happy white police officers. They felt changes needed to be made in the way black males were being profiled and killed. The resultant protests attracted attention from all and sundry, from all walks of life, and from all over the world. It was unheard of that a country as civilized as the U.S. would permit such a racist-motivated killing in its own shores.

The U.S., for all its preaching of democracy and equality for all could not tolerate the existence of blacks in his own shores. It was not only twofaced and double standard but almost hypocritical. For the rest of the world it was a case of *do what I say and not what I do*. The world has seen the U.S. struggle with civil rights and the segregation of blacks, and eventual Civil Rights Act of 1964, that outlawed discrimination based on race, color, religion, sex or national origin. The Act was supposed to end unequal coexistence. But in the 21st U.S., it appears the Civil Rights Act was not protecting the rights of blacks to walk freely in the streets of the land of their births, without getting killed by law enforcement agents, and by those who pretend to be law enforcement agents, like George Zimmerman.

Here was Brown, an 18-year-old teen, probably enjoying his first perception of young adulthood and being shot down by a volley of a racist officer's bullets. What were Brown's and Martin's offences for getting shot to death other than they were young black males walking in the streets of the land of their births, in America?

Though the shooting death of Brown by Officer Wilson reinvigorated the debate about race, and the unfriendly and tense relationship between the police and African Americans; and the police use of excessive, deadly force when it comes to African Americans, little if any, has ever been accomplished by such debates.

In an era of the supposedly black power, when an African American is elected president of the United States, not once but twice, in a landslide victory, it is almost inconceivable that some would still prefer to see the black man in chains, a protested said. If that is not the case how else does one explain the shooting of a black man strolling in the street in Sanford, Florida, by someone claiming to represent the law – a neighborhood watch volunteer? Or in the case of Ferguson, Missouri, of Brown getting killed as he strolls in the street with his friend? Is it now a crime for a black male to walk in the street? Has walking in the street now become a homicidal offense in America, for a black male? Two teenagers, Martin 17, and Brown 18, were killed for walking in the streets, not robbing anyone!

As if the killing of Brown wasn't enough, the police would, with impunity, pounce on the already aggrieved protesters, in Ferguson, Missouri, with force and militarized responses, with insensitivity. The governor, Jay Nixon, according to CNN, declared a state of emergency, calling in the National Guard, Highway Patrol, and increasing the size of police, all in an effort to squash the peaceful protests. The state of emergency, according to critics, was another attempt to suppress a peaceful protest. During the protests, there were reported deaths of yet more African Americans, with several more brutalized and arrested. The situation in Ferguson was reminiscent of the Tiananmen Square protest of 1989 that resulted in the massacre of protesting Chinese students, in Beijing, China, by police and the military, in the June Fourth Incident; and of the Egyptian protest in Tahrir Square, during the Egyptian revolution of 2011, during the Arab Spring that resulted in the deaths of many Egyptians, and the eventual toppling of the Egyptian dictator, President Hosni Mubarak.

But this was not happening in Egypt, or in Tunisia or in Tiananmen Square in Beijing, China, it was happening in the United States – the land of the free and the home of the brave! Blacks, one by one, and in different cities, were being shot to death by police officers for little or no offenses. In the U.S., whether it is in Dallas, Austin, Houston, Cleveland, Bridgeport, New York, and major cities across the U.S., it was a wrong time to be black!

Since the death of Michael Brown, on August 9, 2014, over 50 more black teens have been shot to death by white police officers. Between the shooting death of Michael Brown on August 9, 2014 and February 14, 2015, over 50 black males have been shot to death by white police officers in cities across the U.S. In Cleveland, Ohio, on November 22, 2014, Tamir Rice, a 12 year-old- boy was shot to death by a rookie police officer after the 12 year old reportedly brandished what turned out to be a BB gun while playing in a park. On September 21, 2014, an unarmed Cameron Tillman, a 14 year-old African American, was shot to death by a deputy sheriff, in Terrebonne, Louisiana.

In October, VonDerrit Myers Jr. was shot 17 times by an off duty white police officer in the Shaw neighborhood of St. Louis, in the same vicinity that Michael Brown was shot to death. And also in October, Laquan McDonald, a 17 year-old, was shot to death by a police officer in Chicago. Another disturbing death involved the shooting death of an 18-year-old girl, Carey Smith-Viramontes, in Long Beach, California, who was shot to death by a police officer on the scene. The girl was an African American.

In Kansas City, an 18-year-old Jeffrey Holden was killed by a police officer in October. And in another Ohio shooting, Qusean Whitten, was killed by a police officer, also in October. And also in October, a 19 year-old boy, Miguel Benton, an African American, was shot to death by police in Georgia. On September 26, 2014, Dillon McGee, an 18 year-old, was shot to death by a police officer, in Jackson, Tennessee. Also in Georgia, Levi Weaver, an 18 year-old, was shot to death by a police officer.

And in September, 2014, a 19-year-old Karen Cifuentes was shot to death in Oklahoma City by a police officer. In August, Sergio Ramos, an 18 year-old, was shot to death by police, multiple times, in Dallas. Roshad McIntosh, 19, was shot to death by police in Chicago. Diana Showman, a 19 year-old mentally ill woman, was shot to death by police.

In Houston, Texas, Jordan Baker was shot to death by a Houston police officer, Juventino Castro, on January 16, 2015. In Bridgeport, New Jersey, a black male, Jerame Reid, 36, was shot to death by a Bridgeport police officer for running a stop sign on December 30, 2014.

All these cases reflect extreme police brutality in the United States. The police appear to have taken it upon itself that the lives of stray animals are more precious than the lives of black males. One protester in Washington DC said "the police will sooner shoot a black male than a stray animal!" If only that protester had realized how true his comments were! In July 2014, a Texas man was sentenced to prison for two years, for animal cruelty! The loss of, and death of a stray dog, sometimes invite more condemnation than the same fate for a black man! The black man, according to a recent article, has become an object of ridicule when it comes to punishing those that made it their mission to kill or maim him.

In Ferguson, Missouri, the body of Michael Brown was abandoned after Officer Darren Wilson, a white police officer, had shot and killed him. No one had bothered to pick up the body for four hours! A dead stray dog would have received a better honor than Brown received! According to the New York Times, the body of Brown had remained where he had been shot on Canfield Drive, for four hours in that summer sun, uncollected!

"Neighbors were horrified by the gruesome scene: Mr. Brown, 18, face-down in the middle of the street, blood streaming from his head. They ushered their children into rooms that faced away from Canfield Drive. They called friends and local news stations to tell them what had happened. They posted on Twitter and Facebook and recorded shaky cell-phone videos that would soon make their way to the national news."

The dishonoring of Brown's lifeless body on Canfield Drive was palpably racist and an utter disregard for a human life. When Brown had been shot dead by the police, no attempt was made to call an ambulance by Officer Darren Wilson. Brown was left to bleed to death, when he did, and had remained in the same spot, on Canfield Drive, for four hours. Patricia Bynes, a committee woman in Ferguson, observed that "It was very disrespectful to the community and the people who live there. It also sent the message from law enforcement that 'we can do this to you any day, any time, in broad daylight, and there's nothing you can do about it."

Trayvon Martin, the 17 year old teen, who was shot to death by a neighborhood watch volunteer, George Zimmerman, presented a case of utter marginalization of the values and significance of African Americans. Zimmerman shot and killed Martin with a 9mm, after the teen was confronted by him for walking the street in the gated subdivision of Sanford. Martin was shot, not because he was a criminal but because he wore a hooded sweatshirt and was walking alone, in the dark, in the gated neighborhood. Zimmerman felt it was his responsibility to prevent "coons," like Martin from his neighborhood and, proceeded to kill the teen. There was no doubt that he had every intention of killing the "coon," and reducing their numbers in his neighborhood. He obviously felt a profound dislike for blacks like Martin, and nurtured the belief that "coons" like Martin, often break into homes and commit crimes.

The death of Martin marked a turning point in the unjust deaths of black males in the hands of racist and trigger-happy white police officers in the U.S. Martin's death brought out the reality of the unimportance of the lives of blacks in the U.S. when a Hispanic male is categorized as a white male and allowed to get away with the murder of a black teen. The refusal of the Sanford Police to arrest Zimmerman, claiming that the killer had acted in self defense, was a rush to judgment that was racially motivated, said a black activist. "If it had been a white person that had been shot, the situation would have been totally different," another black activist had protested. The black shooter, regardless of the race would have been in custody the moment the police arrived at the scene, another black activist said.

The ensuing protests, following the shooting death of Martin, proved that blacks felt they have had enough from racist police forces across the nation. "Shooting and killing black males with impunity has become the norm among trigger-happy white police officers in the U.S.," another activist said, after he was arrested for peacefully protesting the death of Martin in the hand of Zimmerman.

Did the background of Martin prepare him for an untimely death? Born February 5, 1995, Martin was a 17 year-old black teen from Miami Gardens, Florida, when he was fatally shot by George Zimmerman, a neighborhood watch volunteer in Sanford, Florida, where Martin had gone with his father to visit the latter's fiancée, at her townhouse at The Retreat at Twin Lakes in Sanford. Though he was a byproduct of a broken family, Martin clearly had a bond and a cordial relationship with his father that was good enough for him to go with his father to visit his fiancée, and future stepmother, in Sanford Florida. On the evening of February 26, 2012, Martin, like most people, wanted to enjoy a leisurely walk to the neighborhood convenience store to buy a juice and a candy bar, not knowing the trip will be his last, cut short by an overzealous cop impostor. Martin had made his purchases, didn't steal them, and was returning to the townhouse his father's fiancée was staying, to meet his father. As he walked through the neighborhood that had allegedly been burglarized and robbed in the past, being black, he was easily taken for a would-be burglar or robber, by Zimmerman, who saw him as a miscreant and a coon, who was up to no good. The fact that Martin wore a hooded sweatshirt further fueled Zimmerman's already prejudiced mind towards what he called coons or blacks with hooded sweatshirts.

Zimmerman's untrained and misguided, and prejudiced feeling, that coons are the thieves robbing and burglarizing his neighborhood, prompted him to follow Martin, who was lawfully minding his own business. The self-appointed cop and neighborhood watch captain acted on his prejudice toward coons and immediately called the police upon spotting Martin who was walking back, in the street, to his father's fiancée's townhouse. Rather than let the police handle the situation, Zimmerman proceeded to follow Martin, acting against the instruction of the police dispatcher not to do so. Zimmerman followed martin on foot, tailing him. Zimmerman's motive was to make sure the coon did not steal anything from the neighborhood. But that wasn't enough for the already prejudiced Zimmerman. He wanted to kill the coon.

After he had tailed Martin for a short distance, Zimmerman obviously made his presence known to Martin, and accosted the teen in the process as to what he was doing in the neighborhood. Martin, seeing that Zimmerman was not a law enforcement agent, probably replied and said it was not anybody's business what he was doing walking in the street toward his destination – his father's fiancée's townhouse. Zimmerman was obviously angered by the rude response of Martin's, and feeling disobeyed, decided to take the law into his own hand by confronting Martin, who was probably scared to death that he was being confronted by an armed man.

Seeing that Martin did not give him the response he wanted, he probably tried to delay the teen until the police arrived since he had already called the police before the pursuit. But Martin was obviously feeling threatened and wanted to keep moving to his destination. Zimmerman probably grabbed him; and Martin, as any reasonable person would do, spurned and rejected, with disdain, Zimmerman's unlawful attempt to detain him. Zimmerman resorted to the use of force, imposing his huge bulk to impose his will on Martin. The ensuing struggle as Zimmerman tries to detain Martin for the police to arrive led to an altercation in which Martin was shot (deliberately?) in the chest.

Did Zimmerman shoot Martin in the chest as Martin turned to see who was following him? Did Zimmerman order Martin to stop and when Martin turned to see who was ordering him to stop got shot in the chest by Zimmerman, whose motive was to stop Martin by any means possible? Going by Zimmerman's past mishandling of, and careless use of, guns, it wouldn't be wrong to assume that Zimmerman's intention was to kill Martin whom he thought was a potential burglar or robber.

The police did arrive, obviously from Zimmerman's earlier call, and found that Zimmerman had already killed the teen. The police made what would only be a racist move. They took Zimmerman to the station, questioned him, took pictures of his so-called injuries, and sent him back home, a free man. It was bad enough that Zimmerman had acted against a police dispatcher's instruction not to follow Martin, and it was bad enough that Zimmerman made several racist innuendoes about the teen to the dispatcher. The police would also treat him like a victim when he (Zimmerman) had just killed a man who was going about his business, in the street. The police, would, at that moment, help Zimmerman prepare a case of self-defense by making it look like he had sustained injuries in the scuffle and altercation that supposedly and allegedly developed during his accosting of Martin.

The police excuse for not arresting Zimmerman was that Florida's stand your ground statute prevents law enforcement agents from arresting or charging anyone in that situation, was fraught with, and laden with, legal errors. By refusing to arrest Zimmerman on the spot, the police made it its business to be the interpreter of the law rather than the court. Legally, it is the business of the police to enforce the law, not to interpret it. If Zimmerman was acting within his rights under the stand your ground statute, shouldn't it have been the responsibility of the court to interpret the statute?

If the police claimed to have seen injuries in the body of Zimmerman, where did those injuries come from? Were they self-inflicted to make it look like Martin had overpowered Zimmerman, in order to justify the use of his gun as a form of self-defense? Highly likely since the funeral place that prepared Martin's body did not find any injuries or evidence of a struggle. And the video camera that had captured Zimmerman in the police station when he was questioned, immediately after the murder of Martin, did not reveal any injury on Zimmerman, which means the injuries were borne out of a conspiracy to create a case of self-defense.

To further prove that Martin was a much better person than Zimmerman, a closer look at both Martin's and Zimmerman's background is imperative. According to the Associated Press, in July 2005, Zimmerman was arrested for resisting arrest with violence, and for scuffling with a police officer. The charges were dropped after it was agreed that Zimmerman should enter an alcohol abuse program. A month later, in the same year, in 2005, Zimmerman's former fiancée filed for a restraining order against him for domestic violence. Zimmerman also countered with a restraining order against the fiancée. Both restraining orders were granted, and no criminal charges were filed. Before killing Martin, Zimmerman was already known to the police for alcohol related violence and domestic abuse.

Since charges were never brought against him in 2005, and since he had developed a knack for evading the law, he felt he enjoyed a rare impunity from the law and decided to take it upon himself to kill. In February 2012, Zimmerman shot and killed Martin, and as always, he was able to beat the system, and was acquitted of all charges. Still unremorseful, in July 2013, the same month he was acquitted for killing Martin, Zimmerman was stopped in Foley, Texas, for speeding; probably for drunk driving as has often been the case with him. Once again, Zimmerman was allowed to proceed on his journey, with a warning, even though he was a danger to other drivers, drunk. In September 2013, two months after he beat the rap for killing Martin, Zimmerman was again stopped for excessive speeding in Lake Mary, Florida, for driving 60mph in a 45mph zone. As often the case, Zimmerman was only given a ticket even though it was obvious he was drunk.

The same month, in September 2013, Zimmerman's wife, Shellie, called 911 to report that Zimmerman had physically assaulted her and her father, and had threatened them with a gun. Shellie declined to press charges and, not unexpected, the charges were dropped by the police! In the same month of September 2013, a Florida highway patrol trooper stopped Zimmerman for driving a car that was tinted beyond legal limit. The plates and windows in the car were heavily tinted beyond legal limit. Once again, he was able to beat the system, with no ticket or citation. In November 2013, a few months after charges were dropped for hitting, and threatening his wife, and father-in-law, Zimmerman was arrested for yet another offense, this time for domestic violence and disturbance, at a home in Apopka in the Seminole County.

Zimmerman had had several run-ins with the law and Martin hadn't, not even a juvenile record. Martin's death was protested by hundreds of students at his high school, following his death. The protesting students had held a walkout in support of Martin. The shooting of the teen was so unjust and infamous that it generated 2.2 million signatures that called for a full investigation and prosecution of Zimmerman. It wouldn't be the first time Zimmerman would be investigated.

The utter disregard for the lives of blacks by non-blacks has often been a cause for concern to blacks, especially when that utter disregard is coming from other disadvantaged minority groups. The word 'disregard' is appropriate here because regard is synonymous with respect, and the absence of it is disregard. Disregard from whites is something blacks have come to put up with it while disregard from nonwhites is something blacks do not think they have to put up with it.

Years of suppression and oppression have prepared blacks to expect any form of disregard from whites, but not from nonwhites and other races. George Zimmerman falls into the category of nonwhite that pretends to be white. Though Zimmerman is seen as a white person in Florida, he is clearly a member of the Hispanic ethnicity. The same can be said about those that resemble the white skin but are not really white but who cling to the white race for significance. Among police forces across the United States, several of these nonwhite officers are sometimes more prejudicial and brutal than white police officers. The same group of nonwhite officers is often the group, that usually target blacks in the streets, and in stores. An example is the black man who was shot and killed for holding a pellet gun inside a walmart store in Ohio, in 2014.

The black man, John Crawford III, had been holding a pellet gun when he was shot, after failing to respond to an officer's instruction to drop the weapon. The gun was on the shelf when the black man had taken it to examine it. It had all happened on August 5, 2014, in Beavercreek, Ohio, inside Walmart. Someone had called 911 to report that Crawford III was holding an assault rifle style model, inside the store, which was actually a pellet gun that was on Walmart's shelves. The caller was a white person who was frightened by the sight of a black man holding a pellet gun that was being sold by Walmart, inside the store. The black man had just been examining the pellet gun, no more, no less.

If the 22 year-old black man, John Crawford III, had known that taking a pellet gun from a shelf to look at would end his life, the poor black man would have desisted from looking at the merchandise that he was probably thinking of buying. Crawford III had simply done what most customers usually do when they pick a merchandise to take to the cash register for payment. But someone had raised a false alarm that Crawford III was holding an assault rifle inside the store. The police had responded in full force. The police, seeing a black man with what they thought was a real gun, had ordered him to drop the weapon. Crawford III had been slow to respond or had been frightened out of his wits which cost him his life.

Crawford III had just picked up the pellet gun in the sporting goods section of the store with the intent to buy it, but that decision to buy that pellet gun became a fatal mistake that got him shot as he was on the phone talking. The question became whether the police shot him as he was on the phone holding the pellet gun or was actually ordered to drop the weapon and was shot when he failed to respond. According to the surveillance video, Crawford III was holding the pellet gun, and was talking on the phone when the first bullet hit him, apparently shot by the police. Did the police shoot Crawford III first and then ask him to drop the weapon when he was already shot and probably half dead to make a case of nonresponsive to an officer's command? The surveillance video clearly spoke for the deceased black man who was holding the pellet gun, not pointing it, and talking on the phone, when he was shot.

The police apparently responded to a 911 call, and upon seeing the black man with the pellet gun and on the phone, quickly shot him and then realized it was not a real gun, and proceeded to make it look like the black man had refused a command to drop the pellet gun. Was Crawford III a threat to anyone other than just attempting to purchase a pellet gun from a Walmart store? The surveillance video clearly indicated that Crawford did not present a danger to anyone but was simply shopping with the pellet gun in hand, and a cell phone to his ears, talking. The surveillance video showed Crawford holding the pellet gun which was designed to look like an AR-15; but was actually a Crossman MK-177, a pellet gun. But the police did not know it at the time, when they reportedly shot Crawford III. The police thought Crawford III was holding "a black assault rifle."

If Crawford III had been a different race, would he have been shot and killed? Probably not! But according to NBC News, the gun had resembled a real gun, an assault rifle. But Crawford III was not threatening anyone nor was he using it menacingly in the store. He was simply holding it. Did he intend to commit a crime with it? Probably not since it was only a harmless pellet gun! Did the customer that called 911 feel threatened? Probably, since the gun was designed to look like a real AR-15.

One fact is obvious and that is that a black man lay dead, his intentions misconstrued. Who is liable for Crawford III's death, walmart or the police? NBC News reported that the owner's manual for the pellet gun warned that the air rifle should not be brandished or displayed in a public place, as police and people may think it is a real gun. But walmart was selling the pellet gun, and had displayed it on the shelf. Did walmart breach the instructions in the manual that the gun should not be displayed in the public? After all, Crawford III was just holding it, in an attempt to make a purchase, not to display it or to frighten anyone!

The death of John Crawford III is similar to the death of a 12 year-old boy who was shot to death by the police in Cleveland, Ohio, for holding a fake pistol. It had all started when a man called 911 and told the police dispatcher that a guy who appeared to be a juvenile was pointing a pistol at people and scaring them. The caller was not sure if the guy was a grownup or a juvenile and had told the dispatcher so. The caller also mentioned to the dispatcher that the gun was probably fake and not real. As customary with 911 dispatchers, they sent two police officers. The two police officers arrived at the scene and reportedly ordered the boy to raise his hands. According to the New York Times, the boy refused "and reached for a gun in his waistband." Seeing that the boy was reaching for "a gun in his waistband an officer fired two shots, striking the boy once," the police reportedly said.

Why didn't the police use a taser to immobilize the boy instead of shooting him? The person that called 911 said he wasn't sure if the gun was real or not, and that the person might be a juvenile. The police did not bother to investigate the scene before shooting the boy. They had reportedly ordered the boy to raise his hands, and there was no telling if the boy obeyed or not, since there was no video to rebut the claim made by police. The only witnesses were the two police officers who had shot him. Would the situation have been different if the boy had been white instead of black?

The boy, Tamir E. Rice, had lived near the park and often goes there with his friends and family to play. The park was the only playground the boy knew. Saturday November 22, 2014, was not the first time Rice had played in that park but it was his last. It is impossible for the person that called 911 not to have known that the gun the boy was holding was a fake pistol. Kids play with fake pistols all the time. Fake pistols adorn store shelves everywhere. Fake guns are not illegal as anyone can own one. But on that fateful day, it became illegal in the hands of Tamir Rice, who was reportedly taken as a miscreant that was waving and allegedly pointing the gun at people in the park.

Rather than question and treat him like a child, the police had treated him like a criminal that he was not. He was only a child, playing like a child with a toy! Only in America will a child be killed for being a child!

In other parts of the world, in developing countries, children the same age as Rice are often enlisted in the military to fight with real guns. But that only happens in underdeveloped and primitive warfronts in Africa and in the Middle East, never in a civilized and ultra modern society like a 21st century America, where children are supposed to enjoy the privileges of being children.

Tamir E. Rice had been shot in a recreation center where he often played. Someone had called 911 to report that "a guy was pointing and waving a gun at people." Within minutes, two officers had arrived, and within seconds the boy was reportedly shot in the torso "when he reached for a weapon that turned out to be a fake pistol," New York Times Reported. The boy later died at the Metro-Health Medical Center in Cleveland. Another obtuse report was that one of the officers was taken to the hospital for an injury he had sustained in his ankle during the shooting! Why was the report about the injury to his ankle necessary? Was the report a cover-up to imply that the boy had confronted the officers in a scuffle and that one of the officers had sustained an injury during the altercation? In Trayvon Martin's case, George Zimmerman said he sustained head and nose injuries from the scuffle he had with Martin. That would later form the basis of his legal defense, that he had defended himself under the stand your ground statute, in Florida. Officer Wilson, in shooting Michael Brown, had said he had been in a scuffle with Brown and that he had shot the teen because he had feared for his life.

Why would an officer knowingly kill a 12 year-old without probable cause? "Like the Ebola epidemic that took the life of Duncan and the life of Dr. Martin Salia, it is all about the color of the skin rather than about probable cause," one black activist said. Rice did not commit any crime. His only crime was that he had held a toy gun in his waistband. And the police had killed him thinking he was reaching for the gun to shot them. The police could have used other means to determine that the boy was not posing a threat. Instead they had preferred the only method they are familiar with, to kill the boy!

It is obvious that the boy did not present any danger to the people at the park and to the police, at the time of the shooting. Will the grand jury indict the two officers for killing the 12 year-old boy? Statistically, grand juries seldom, if ever, indict police officers involved in fatal shootings. And in the case of stand your ground statue; the statute is always interpreted to suit the whims of the interpreters. It is okay for a grand jury to indict a homeowner who shoots a burglar that enters his unclosed garage to steal, but it is not okay for a grand jury to indict an officer who kills an innocent person?

The homeowner has often been targeted by teens in the area; and they had burglarized and stolen from him before. The homeowner had gotten tired of being robbed, and decided to defend himself. Two teenagers had testified "that they had stolen items from the garage of a Montana man charged with killing a high school student in that very place weeks later, and one of the teens said that may have been one factor that led to the German exchange student's death." Is something not wrong with a system that denies a homeowner the right to defend his family and property and yet gives the police the license to kill innocent citizens?

There are factors determining the indictment and trial of the Montana man charged with killing a burglar in his garage. The first is the ethnic background of the shooter and of the dead burglar. The second is that the shooter is of the Asian ethnicity while the dead burglar is of the Caucasian ethnicity. "If the reverse had been the case, the grand jury, would not have indicted," one Asian immigrant was reported saying. And in the same token, if the burglar had been a black person, the case would have been long concluded as a stand your ground case. When critically examined, it would seem as if police brutality and unjustifiable killing of black males is part of a larger conspiracy to eliminate blacks from the U.S. If an innocent man can be shot and killed for selling loose cigarettes in the street, in Staten Island, where then is justice for the common man? How is America different from a brutal autocracy in Africa and in the Middle East? Has America gradually become a police state, where police determine and interpret the law according to their whims and caprices?

Garner, 43, a father of six, and an unarmed black male died in July 2014, after a white police officer, Daniel Pantaleo, put him in a chokehold by wrapping his arm around his neck with a tremendous amount of pressure to cut off Garner's breathing and oxygen supply; thereby making it impossible for him to breath. By the manner Officer Pantaleo manhandled Garner, there was no way his death would not have been ruled a homicide. But as expected, the grand jury, as in every case involving an officer killing an innocent black man, refused to indict the officer!

Why will a grand jury be so blatantly racist as not to indict an officer that cold-bloodedly murdered an innocent citizen by chokehold? The grand jury by default and design are regular citizens like Garner, but unlike Garner, most of the members of the grand jury were predominantly white; while the rest were mainly comprised of brown/yellow racial groups who were likely to side with fellow white jurors.

The prejudiced grand jury was composed of 14 white jurors and nine nonwhites. "The grand jury was not racially balanced as it should have been in a controversial case such as this," a black protester said. Why would a prosecutor knowingly select a grand jury that was racially one-sided, knowing how predictable the outcome would be? The explanation to that is that the grand jury was deliberately selected to create an outcome that was predictable.

CNN reported that during the fatal encounter Garner had raised both hands and told the police not to touch him, fearing the worst. But the police would not listen to that simple instruction that he shouldn't be touched. Garner was not committing any crime at the time of the fatal chokehold. He had been simply hawking loose cigarettes that were legal to hawk. The only issue was that there were no tax stamps on the cigarettes! When the officer had taken it upon himself to manhandle and chokehold Garner, the latter had repeatedly said "I can't breathe." Ignoring the dying request of Garner to allow him to breathe, the officer proceeded to snuff out his life. Did the officer feel challenged when Garner told him not to touch him? From the look of things, that would be the case! Barely seconds after Garner told the officer not to touch him, and apparently seeing the way and manner the officer was talking to him menacingly, Garner knew trouble was afoot. Officer Pantaleo would put Garner in a fatal chokehold that would snuff out his life. How a grand jury that saw the video recorded killing of the innocent black man would say there was no "reasonable cause," to indict the officer is both shocking and appalling in a 21st century America. But the grand jury did. Just like the other cases involving police shootings. They refused to indict the officer, even in the face of such an overwhelming evidence of culpability.

"The grand jury was not being objective, and has never been known to be," one famous black activist said. They were influenced by the color of the shooter and the victim. To them, it will be an injustice to send a white man to jail for killing a black man! After all the black was just a property owned and often auctioned in slave stops, a few decades ago. Why sacrifice the precious life of a white man for a liberated property? Though freed and unchained, the black man is, and always will be a slave, to a lot of white people!

Slavery mentality has always been the catalyst prompting the decisions pertaining to white officers killing blacks in America. That same slavery-mentality-decision was displayed in Ferguson, Missouri when Officer Darren Wilson was not indicted for killing an unarmed 18-year-old black male. That same decision was displayed when a jury refused to convict George Zimmerman when the neighborhood watch volunteer cold-bloodedly murdered Trayvon Martin, 17, in Sanford, Florida.

The New York police had a history of racial profiling and killing of black males in unjustifiable homicides. According to CNN, African Americans are often stopped for frisking, under the old New York police policy of stop and frisk. You would think New York City was a city carved out of the old South African apartheid regime where black South Africans were often stopped and searched by the police for no reason other than they were blacks. But it is

New York City, in 21st century America where blacks are still being treated as if they are in an apartheid country. Apartheid was adopted by the white minority government of South Africa to suppress black South Africans from having political and economic rights as white people in South Africa. During the South African apartheid regime, blacks were often forced to live separately from white people. Though segregation ended in 1954, following a Supreme Court decisions on Brown v. Board of Education, it is still prevalent everywhere in 21st United States.

Like apartheid in South Africa, the policy of segregation was to keep people of different races and religions, separated from each other. Segregation was also the denial of socioeconomic equality. Blacks could not use the same restrooms, bus, and restaurants as white people, and if they did, they were only permitted to sit in the backseats while white people would sit in the front seats. It was taboo and illegal for a black person to sit in a bus while a white person stands. The same was true of restrooms. There were separate restrooms for blacks as there were for whites, under segregation.

In apartheid South Africa, blacks were required to carry passes. The pass laws were designed to segregate blacks. Passes were like a passport system that was created by the South African apartheid government to segregate blacks from white South Africans. The pass laws existed in South Africa from 1800-1994, when Nelson Mandela became the first black president of South Africa in 1994, having served 27 years in prison as a political prisoner.

In the United States, segregation still exists to a large extent; and that can be seen in the manner the police indiscriminately kill blacks in every city, town and state, in the country. Just like in apartheid South Africa where police were used to suppress, terrorize, oppress and segregate blacks, the police in the United States have also become the instruments of black oppression, homicide and brutality.

In Sanford, Florida, the police refused to arrest George Zimmerman because of the stand your ground statute. Just like in apartheid South Africa, where the police mainly carried out most of the policies of the government, in the United States, police officers often give their own interpretation of the law, as happened in Sanford, Florida, when the police interpreted the stand your ground statute to mean that a killer cannot be arrested if it is assumed to be a case of self defense. If the law is to be interpreted it should be the responsibility of the court, not the police!

In Staten Island, New York, on July 17, 2014, a black man is killed for selling loose cigarettes. Here again, the police transitioned itself from being the enforcer of the law to being the executioner of innocent citizens. The New York case was not an isolated case. According to the FBI, over 461 unjustifiable deaths resulting from police shooting of blacks occurred in 2013 alone. Since the death of Trayvon Martin on February 26, 2012, over 1,000 black males have died in the hands of white police officers; and 99.9% of the cases had been unjustifiable homicides!

Why do blacks continue to die in the hands of the police? A lot of reasons contribute to the increased percentage of deaths among African Americans, in the hands of the police. The first of the numerous reasons is that there is usually no fear of any form of repercussion for killing a black person. Police officers and even those who are not police officers (like George Zimmerman) know that a police officer will seldom be arrested or investigated for killing a black man. A case in point is when Officer Darren Wilson was not arrested for killing Michael Brown in Ferguson, Missouri. George Zimmerman who was not even a police officer was not arrested when he had unjustifiably shot and killed an unarmed teenager, Trayvon Martin. The killing of Brown was so outrageous that a lot of black people who usually do not get involved in injustice towards blacks stormed the streets to protest the injustice and inhuman forfeiture of a life so young!

For a lot of the 68% of the blacks in Ferguson, Missouri, the refusal of the grand jury to indict Officer Wilson was a slap in the face, yet again, of black people. How else does one explain why a black man minding his own business and walking in the street with his friend is confronted and shot for refusing to move to the sidewalk? If that was really the truth since Brown was not around to tell his side of the story. Did the officer use a racial slur to tell the teen to move to the sidewalk and the teen felt insulted? One thing is clear; Officer Wilson said the two friends ran off to two different directions. Officer Wilson chose to follow Brown whom he then shot several times, killing him. Why did the officer choose to follow Brown and not the other teen? Did the officer have a preconceived prejudice towards Brown for his size and attitude? It can be highly improbable for an unarmed teen to be rude to a heavily armed Officer Wilson, knowing that he could be shot by the officer.

There was no doubt that Brown was aware of the race relations among the various racial residents in the city of Ferguson. There was no way the teen would not have known the risk of challenging an officer with a gun. In Ferguson, blacks are often profiled, and unnecessarily arrested for minor traffic offenses that a white person will hardly get stopped for, a black resident in Ferguson said.

The ongoing racial profiling in Ferguson would not have been new to Brown who was old enough to know that blacks and white police officers do not often get along, especially in Ferguson. He would have especially known that when it comes to blacks that the police were trigger happy. At the age of 18, Brown was already profiled by the police for several minor infractions. Brown would have known that blacks do not get their props for being good citizens. He would have known that blacks were readily criminalized for insignificant infractions and were never given a break in the town of Ferguson. He would have known that racial injustice exists in the town.

Little wonders he ran at the sight of the police! Even though he ran, he was still chased, shot and killed! How did a fleeing man pose a threat to Officer Wilson who was armed? Officer Wilson reportedly said he was afraid that Brown would kill him if he didn't kill the teen. For an Officer that weighs over 200lbs and is 6'4" and armed, how can an unarmed teen be a threat to such a big officer? The dead do not talk, if they could, a different version of what really happened would have emerged. Alas! Even if the teen had lived to tell his own side of the story, it would not have mattered since the police was always right in the eyes of grand juries in America!

Chapter 14

Police Brutality/Killings of Black Men

There is hardly a day that passes without a reported incident of police brutality against unarmed black men in the U.S. Police killing of black men have become so ubiquitous and prevalent in the U.S. that the media sometimes overlook the occurrence as a norm. In some cases, reporters do not even bother to report it as newsworthy and as an abnormal incident any longer. "It is pretty much like killing a dog or any animal. Sometimes a dog killer has a greater chance of facing justice than a police officer that kills a black man," a black activist in Houston said.

If past and current occurrences of police killings and incrimination of black men in the U.S. is carefully looked at, one will easily see that the rate of police killings of black men has increased more than ever before, in the history of race relations between blacks and police in the U.S. A recent poll indicated that over 70% of black men in the U.S. feel their lives are in danger because of the police in their communities, cities and town.

In New York City, the police have sworn to take the fight to the 109th mayor, Bill de Blasio, of that city for sympathizing with families of victims of police killings, by publicly humiliating the mayor; by turning their backs on him and putting up placards that say "God bless the NYPD. Dump de Blasio." The mayor's transgression or sin was, according to the New York Police Union's president, Patrick Lynch, that the mayor has "blood on his hands," for showing sympathy when a black man, Eric Garner, was unjustifiably murdered in a chokehold by a New York Police officer, Daniel Pantaleo, on July 17, 2014.

Garner was selling "loosies" or single cigarettes from a cigarette pack that did not have tax stamps. Tax evasion does not carry a death sentence for offenders!

What made Garner's death more inhuman was the behaviour of the officers who caused his death. According to media reports, Garner repeatedly told the officers surrounding him that "I can't breathe," before taking his last breath. Even when the officers realized he was unconscious no one tried to resuscitate him with a CPR. They left him there, dying, while they waited for an ambulance to arrive. Garner reportedly lay on the sidewalk for over seven minutes; and by the time ambulance arrived, he was half dead or on the throes of death. The EMTs and the officers reportedly did not do anything to try to resuscitate the dying man. Garner was killed for selling loose cigarettes! A crime not even worth a citation!

Since the shooting death of Michael Brown by Officer Darren Wilson, on August 9, 2014, more blacks have been shot to death by police across America. "There is not a day that passes in which a black man is not shot to death by a white police officer. Why shouldn't they? I would kill too if I know I won't be charged," a black activist said. "The police have a job to do and if it involves taking down someone to do it, so be it," a Los Angeles Police Officer said. "There has to be a better way. Police can't just be killing black men with impunity. Very soon black men may have to take up arms against the police. They can only push us so far," a black activist in Berkeley, Missouri, said. "Black men can't be breaking the law and not expect some repercussions," a white activist said in St. Louis, Missouri.

In the current debate about police brutality, some white Americans often take sides with white police officers involved in the shooting of black males. In the same token, black Americans or African Americans often take sides with the victims, no matter what triggered the shooting. In Houston, Texas, a black man was shot and killed by a Houston Police officer for arguing with him. According to the media, the unarmed black man was stopped for not wearing a seatbelt, and for having an expired license plate sticker. When the police approached the man, the officer ordered him to come out of the car with his hands raised above his head. The suspect immediately obeyed the officer. And as the officer approached the suspect, the suspect was said to have allegedly reached for something in his waistband, which made the officer to fire his gun in self defence. The unarmed black male was shot three times, and died on the spot.

A month after the incident, the grand jury refused to indict the officer, saying the police officer acted in accordance with department procedures. "The officer was left with no choice but to shoot the suspect. If the suspect had obeyed the officer and not tried to reach for a weapon, he will be alive," another police officer, in the same department as the errant officer, said. "The duty of the police is to protect lives, not take them, as they have been doing lately. They now use black males as target practice because they know there will be no consequences for killing them," a black female activist in Staten Island, New York, said.

Adrian Davieson

In a controversial case involving the shooting of a 26 year old Jordan Baker, by a Houston Police Officer, who was working off duty, as a security guard, in a strip mall, the grand jury refused to indict the officer saying the officer acted in self defence. But did the officer act in self defence? The officer was not even working as a police officer at the time of the shooting. He was working as a security guard, not working to protect, but working to prevent a crime, in his off duty job. According to CBS News, Baker reportedly struggled with the officer, and then ran away. While running, Baker reached for his waistband and "charged toward Officer Castro." Officer Castro then reached for his gun and shot Baker, killing him in the process. Officer Castro's story did not add up as Baker was found to be unarmed at the time of the shooting. If Baker was not armed, what did he charge Officer Castro with that resulted in the former being shot and killed?

Jordan Baker was a student, not a street hoodlum as the Houston police tried to portray him. "He was a good man", an activist said. The Houston police tried to criminalize him because of his race; that he was in the strip mall to rob someone and to break into a store in the strip mall where there have been several break-ins. But Baker was not in the strip mall to break into any store; nor did he try to shoot Officer Castro. Officer Castro was not acting in his capacity as a police officer, as he was working as a security guard at the time of the shooting. Though a police officer, he was, at the time of the shooting, a security guard. The shift in his taxpayers' funded profession from a police officer to a security guard made him liable for his actions, of careless homicide.

The fact that Officer Castro "lied about the incident should have been enough for the grand jury to indict him," a local activist said. Another reason the grand jury should have indicted him was for shooting Baker under the presumption that the 26 year old college student was a criminal rather than a citizen minding his own business. The grand jury's refusal to charge Officer Castro with murder is justice denied, for Baker, and for all the black males that will be killed by police in unjustifiable homicides, in the future.

"It is not fun to kill another human being. But if I am faced with a situation that requires me to discharge my weapon, I will not think twice about discharging it. As for me, any form of threat imaginable or unimaginable is enough for me to discharge my weapon. I have killed three times before, and each time I was not indicted, because those bastards deserved to die. It didn't matter whether they were committing crimes at the time. What matters is that one less criminal was off the street because of my police work," a Sugar Land deputy sheriff, said. It is fundamentally wrong for an unarmed man to be killed because he is assumed to be a criminal! But because grand juries and prosecutors continue to make it impossible for police officers to be indicted, unjustifiable homicides continue to be more prevalent.

To create a just and equitable society, prosecutors and judges across the U.S. need to be more objective in the discharge of their duties, and in legal proceedings. Taking the sides of the police against a tax paying citizen is counterproductive and unconstitutional. Prosecutors only embolden police officers to kill when erring officers are not brought to justice. The killing of several unarmed black men by white police officers proves that police officers are above the law and able to kill on and off duty whenever they feel the urge to kill. Government officials cannot continue to allow, or ignore, this type of trend if the U.S. is to be spared the agony of terrorism and jihadist uprising that is spreading across Europe and Africa. Home grown terrorism is on the rise in the West, and to avoid this trend in the U.S., where it is currently gaining momentum, efforts must be made to avoid bitterness by the citizenry, especially among the youths, and the downtrodden and marginalized members in the minority communities.

By criminalizing and killing innocent black males, the police are sending a message that the lives of black people are not relevant in the scheme of things. That sort of message is what Islamist recruiters look for when they recruit jihadists and suicide bombers. They preach their sermons of doomsday conspiracy message to the vulnerable youths who feel marginalized and forsaken by their governments and societies. Those vulnerable members of society are usually unemployed, misguided, discriminated against, and often profiled and brutalized males in the minority communities such as blacks and Hispanics.

The implication of such police impunity and policy to brutalize and criminalize black males is that those who are not yet victimized by them become more prone and susceptible to terrorist and Islamist recruitments. In *France* for example, black males and minority children of immigrant parents, who are unemployed and marginalized, have become vulnerable to terrorist and jihadist recruiters, who use their unemployment status, as a tool to goad them into terrorism.

The U.S. can avoid a replica of what happened at Charlie Hebdo when three gunmen entered the offices of the satirical newspaper and killed 12 editors and cartoonists on January 7, 2015. When it was all over, 17 French citizens had been killed in the terrorist attack. Al-Qaeda in the Arabian Peninsula had immediately claimed responsibility for the attack. Al-Qaeda and ISIS were quick to claim credit for the Paris massacre because the violence manifested the kind of publicity they crave. Even though there were sceptics that doubted that al-Qaeda funded the attack, there was no doubt that the three gunmen had been influenced by Islamic extremism and jihad. After all, one of the gunmen had said he was funded by Al-Qaeda right before his death.

The subsequent hostage taking at a Jewish supermarket that resulted in the death of additional French citizens, and the fleeing of a 26 year old jihadist woman, to Istanbul and thereafter to Syria, to ISIS stronghold in Syria, confirmed that the terrorists were influenced by both al-Qaeda and ISIS.

And there is the case of the unmasked Jihadi John, Mohammed Emwazi, who had felt harassed and threatened by M15, as his reason for joining ISIS, and becoming the most deadly terrorist since the holy war started by the jihadist crusader, Prophet Muhammad, in earlier centuries. School authorities where Jihadi John had once been a student said Jihadi John was a good student. How did a quiet, well behaved student become the most deadly terrorist in modern times? The way authorities handle gullible and impressionable citizens who already feel marginalized needs to be re-examined, to prevent more Jihadi Johns from turning against their countries, in the West. The jihadists that killed editors and satirists at Charlie Hebdo were also French citizens who at one time or the other had been harassed, threatened and watched by security agents, before they took the ultimate plunge of joining terrorist organizations.

According to the New York Times, the French massacre had first occurred when three gunmen wearing ski-masks stormed Charlie Hebdo, a satirical newspaper based in Paris, France and started shooting. The grievance of the extremists had been that Charlie Hebdo had insulted Prophet Muhammad by portraying the revered prophet in a disrespectful manner. The al-Qaeda in Yemen or al-Qaeda in the Arabian Peninsula had quickly claimed credit for the killings which had included 12 editors and cartoonist, and five others, including Jews and a police woman. Charlie Hebdo had suffered the most casualties with 12 of its members of staff losing their lives. It would have been impossible for Al-Qaeda or ISIS to brainwash the militants who had carried out the slayings at Charlie Hebdo if the perpetrators had been gainfully employed and were useful citizens of France. Terrorism is said to be so bad in Paris that some places, reportedly, are a no-go for the police. The question is how authorities allowed such places to exist in the first place, and why known terrorists on international watch-lists were allowed to walk around, free? And if the terrorists were known to authorities why were they not under surveillance?

As the vanguard of press freedom, Charlie Hebdo was a target. The magazine had been firebombed in the past; and worst of all the editors had been threatened in the past. France should have been more vigilant and watchful of such known extremists who live in the midst of decent and god-fearing citizens. Allowing deadly terrorists, who enjoy harming others, and who cherish martyrdom in the name of Allah, to freely move around is the "ultimate laxity on the part of authorities in charge of preventing terrorism," a French woman waving placard that read "Jesuis Charlie," said. Some part of Paris neighbourhoods are, reportedly known, for terrorist activities and the preaching of religious extremism.

The Boston marathon bombing on April 15, 2013, in which two pressure cooker bombs were used by two Chechen brothers to bomb the Boston marathon participants, is an example of what disgruntled, misguided and gullible youths can do. Though the casualties had been less severe with three fatalities and over 264 people injured in the Boston Marathon, than the Charlie Hebdo slayings, the fact that terrorists, albeit home grown, were able to infiltrate such a popular event, was an eye-opener to authorities.

While it is not certain what led the Boston marathon bombers to carry out such a deadly terrorist act other than that they were self radicalized and motivated by extremist beliefs, the fact that it happened at all on U.S. soil was a major concern; especially after the al-Qaeda funded terrorist attack of September 11, 2001. The Chechen brothers, Dzhokhar and Tamerlan Tsarnaev, were immigrants from the old Soviet Union of Chechen who had converted to Islam. Converting to Islam and being brainwashed by the radical preaching of radical imams convinced them that the only way to be true followers of Prophet Muhammad was to kill and carry out a jihad. The Tsarnaev brothers were like the French-Algerian brothers who had been among the shooters of the editors and cartoonists at Charlie Hebdo in Paris, on January 7, 2015.

For years, the U.S. has had to deal with the upsurge in home grown terrorism, especially among the children of immigrants who converted to Islam or whose parents are Muslims. For these newly converted Muslims in the U.S. and in Europe, the wars in Iraq and Afghanistan, and the current U.S.-led bombings of ISIS strongholds in Iraq and Syria, is to them, an assault on Islam. These new Islamist converts see Muslims as victims of Western hegemony and oppression.

The radical imams in the Middle East, U.S. and in Europe, spewing preaching of hatreds know that there are those marginalized, uninformed, impressionable, and gullible youths who will easily buy into their deceits about jihad. The Tsarnaev brothers, according to CNN and other media, learned to build explosive devices from an online instructions posted by Al-Qaeda in Yemen. The two Chechen brothers had also planned to travel to New York City, to bomb Times Square. The brothers had been ready for the ultimate martyrdom because they believed it was the way to salvation, and to achieve significance. They had reportedly learned from al-Qaeda that killing in the name of Allah was the acceptable proof that one was truly a jihadist fighting to protect the virtues of Allah and Prophet Muhammad.

How did the Tsarnaev brothers turn against the country they once loved? According to an FBI investigation that followed the bombing, the brothers were unhappy that they were not able to fully fit in, into the American society. With loss of significance at having failed to fully belong in the American society, they had sought and found solace in Islam. The brothers, according to the New York Times, were influenced by Al-Qaeda, though they were not affiliated with the group. There were also media reports that the brothers said they were tired of being marginalized in the U.S. They had felt that the only hope they had was to identify with religious extremists and jihadists in Chechen, Iraq and Afghanistan, in order to achieve significance in life.

Unlike the French brothers, Cherif Kouachi and Said Kouachi, who were French citizens and who had carried out the killings of the editors and cartoonists at Charlie Hebdo in Paris, the Tsarnaev brothers were not born in the U.S. Tamerlan Tsarnaev was born in 1986, in North Caucasus within European Russia, in the Kalmyk, in the Russian Republics of the North Caucasus. The brother, Dzhokhar was born in 1993 in Kyrgyzstan or Dagestan. The somewhat dysfunctional nature of the family may have made them naive, gullible and susceptible to the hateful preaching of radical imams in Yemen, according to the media. But there is no denying the influence that radical Islam had in changing them from decent members of society into jihadists that were ready to sacrifice their lives as martyrs.

While it is hard to really understand the motive of the Tsarnaev brothers, it is not hard to understand what motivated a 28 year old black man, Ismaaiyi Brinsley, to shoot two New York Police Officers: Officer Rafael Ramos and Officer Wenjian Liu, to death as they sat in their patrol car in downtown Brooklyn. Brinsley had felt marginalized, having seen enough killings of young black men by white police officers across the U.S. He had seen how police officers get away with murder. He was already marginalized by the system. He had a record, a long one that would forever make it impossible for him to live a decent life. As far as he was concerned, he was already ruined, ruined by the same police that was killing his fellow black males, across the U.S. He saw how Michael Brown was killed and how the officer, Officer Darren Wilson, got away with murder.

He saw how Trayvon Martin was murdered in cold blood and how justice failed the dead teen as it had failed and ruined him. He didn't see any future that was worth hoping and living for. He felt he was already dead, dead to the system where he doesn't count, or ever counted. It was impossible for him to vote, get an apartment, and to get a job. It was even impossible to get an apartment to lay his head. He felt he was finished.

Since justice had failed his peers who had been unjustifiably killed, he felt something had to be done. He saw himself as a martyr of some sort, who could go out leaving a trail of hope for those who had been fallen by the bullets of the police. He felt if jihadists could sacrifice themselves for their beliefs that he could do the same for a worthy cause. After all, his is a more tangible and just cause that a lot of people could agree and identify with, he had mused. He could teach the police what pain meant. He knew he could make the police feel the pains that black families who have lost loved ones have felt over the years. He knew there will be people that would secretly praise his martyrdom.

He knew there will be those that will despise his actions. He also knew that there will be no headstone for him. He was not worried about a headstone. The important thing was that he was going out as one whose place was secured in history. Even if his life wasn't significant he knew he will be a hero to some, and a villain to others, in death. He would finally achieve fame, even if a notorious one. He would be known by all and sundry. He will no longer be ignored, as his name will become a household name. For him, it was the end and the beginning of a new era. An era that would only be defined by him! It was the end of marginalization for him. Even in death he knew he would be a hero!

He also knew that many will be persecuted, prosecuted and criminalized for agreeing with his deeds. He was tired of hearing the grieving voices of the families of black victims. He knew they were powerless against a system that was created to make them powerless. He was tired of hearing that grand juries will not indict murderous police officers who continue to take the lives of young black males, with impunity. He was tired of being profiled. He had nothing left. The only thing that mattered to him was his girlfriend, whom he had shot. He hopes she recovers fully. He had loved her but that was over now. She will never love him again, even if she ever recovers.

There was a time he had thought of suicide. Many a time he had thought of so many painless ways to take his own life but didn't have the guts to do it. It had occurred to him that his death should mean something, some sort of sacrifice for those unjustly killed by the police. It had pleased him to no end that he could, and would, make history. A final farewell would be befitting, he had thought. Armed with renewed courage and hope, he had travelled from his accursed neighbourhood, to his old turf, where he figured it will be newsy to carry out his deadly plans and acts.

He had watched with sadness how Eric Garner was killed in a chokehold by Officer Daniel Pantaleo, while other police officers had looked on, with arms akimbo. He had also seen how the officer refused to help the dying Garner as he cried "I can't breathe," to the contemptuous and snobbish officers who ignored his cries for help. He had seen how Officer Daniel Pantaleo was allowed to walk scot free, uncharged by the grand jury. He had wept silently for the hapless black man and how his life was rendered meaningless by the society he thought he belonged.

Elsewhere in the country that cherishes freedom and human rights, he had witnessed the slaying of Jordan Baker by a Houston Police Officer and how that officer had not been charged by a grand jury. It was not too long ago that an unarmed Trayvon Martin was shot dead by George Zimmerman in Sanford, Florida, on February 26, 2012. He had also wept silently when the mostly white jury had found Zimmerman not guilty and dismissed all charges. Three years later, in February 2015, in his grave, he had turned, when the Department of Justice had said it did not have enough evidence to bring charges against Zimmerman!

He had also seen how Michael Brown was shot to death by a white police officer who claimed he had no choice but to kill the teen because "it was his life or the teen's life." He had seen how the grand jury of mostly white jurors had refused to charge Officer Darren Wilson. He had always known that he lived in a racist world but he never knew it was racist enough to place little premium on the life of a black person.

Posthumous, and from his grave, he had seen how over 20,000 police officers from around the country had attended the deaths of the two police officers he had killed. He had witnessed, as he stood there in the hereafter, watching from the afterlife, how the two dead police officers were praised and celebrated by all and sundry.

He had been bemused and sad that so many would come to celebrate the deaths of two officers while innocent black men are being killed by police officers everyday uncelebrated, without media-covered burials and memorials.

He could see now in the afterlife, how his life had unfolded. He knew now he was never given a chance to be what he could have been. He had been condemned to end the way he had ended, long before he was born. His parents had suffered the indignity of being profiled; and were openly discriminated against, long before he was born. But his birth and childhood had been marked by fewer celebrations and joys than others, of a different race. He had grown too quickly, before he knew how he could manage his inherited disadvantage. He was born with a disadvantage of being black in a racist environment. An environment that pretended to be compassionate and liberated at heart! He could see now that it was all a sham. He had known, growing up, in the fast lane of Atlanta and Baltimore, that life held little promises for a better future.

He knew he had little chances of success. After all a black man was just killed trying to make a living selling loose cigarettes in Staten Island! What else could he have done differently? He asked himself. Maybe he should have been born in the future, in a post-Obama presidency, when it would have been common knowledge that blacks were just as good, if not better than other races.

As he watches the funeral procession of the slain two police officers in the afterlife he felt a sigh of relief and a sense of accomplishment. Maybe his life wasn't wasted after all! If the 47th

Vice President of the country, Joe Biden, and the 109th mayor of New York, Bill de Blasio, could find time to attend the funeral of the slain officers, maybe his death was not a waste. He knew his name will be ingrained in the sands of time, somewhere along with the slain officers. Wherever the officers' names are mentioned, his name will be mentioned somewhere too, he mused.

In the afterlife, he watched as his corpse was carried with ignominy. He also watched as some quietly praised and celebrated him. He couldn't blame those who silently wept for him. He knew it was a bad time for freedom of speech, in a country that promotes and cherishes freedom for the modern man. In the afterlife he had seen how a black man was arrested for saying that white police officers should have been killed instead of the two slain officers who were not even white. He had also seen how black men had been criminalized for their comments in support of his actions.

He had also seen in the afterlife the many black men and women who had been arrested for supposedly saying they want to kill police officers. He knew what police officers were capable of doing. He had experienced it himself when he was among the living. He could see now how they managed to marginalize and criminalize the black man. It was all coming clearly to him now. Yonder, in afterlife, everything becomes so clear. He could see the past, the present and the future.

As he walks around unseen, around Atlanta, Baltimore and New York, in his afterlife in his restlessness, he wondered about the future of the black man. Even after the protests in cities across the country, black men continue to die, day by day, across the U.S. in the hands of white police officers. Maybe in his next life he would come through Africa, a better and progressive Africa where the black man is not looked down upon. An Africa where there is no terrorism and where the black man is not double-checked at international airports because of the color of his skin. Maybe that Africa will never come to fruition. Not with increased terrorism and barbarism in the 21st century Africa! Maybe if Western conspiracy will cease, Africa will be truly free and be allowed to prosper, maybe! He said as he watches and walks around the country, restless. He knew he would wander the nook and cranny of the land. He would finally have a chance to visit the places he never visited in life! Perhaps afterlife wasn't so bad! He thought, grimly.

Like France, where terrorism is more prevalent an d home to home grown Islamic jihadists, the U.S. is already breeding its own home grown terrorists of Somali and other foreign descents. Most of the home grown terrorists blame the U.S. for whatever reasons they chose to join Islamic jihad. Some of the home grown extremists have either copied jihadist extremism or have been influenced by it. There are also those home grown terrorists who are fascinated by Islamic extremism and fundamentalism. They love the idea of being outlaws and of being in the news as wanted fugitives and jihadists. For them, there is significance in jihad! These troubled members of the youthful generation seek significance; and feel being associated with fundamentalists and jihadists is the route to significance.

Some of them are susceptible to the preaching of radical imams who preach about a blissful hereafter; where there is greater paradise in the afterlife, when one kills in the name of Allah and Prophet Muhammad. These faith-strapped and gullible teens believe that the only way to gain favour in the eye of Allah is to kill in his name. That belief has made several teens to become susceptible to recruiters from Al-Shabaab, Boko Haram, Al-Qaeda, ISIS and many terrorist organizations across the world

The killing of the editors and cartoonists in the offices of Charlie Hebdo, because the satirical newspaper purportedly desecrated and disrespected Prophet Muhammad, is a prime example of the extent gullible believers will go, to defend the name of the revered prophet. Al-Qaeda in the Arabian Peninsula blamed the satirical newspaper for disrespecting Prophet Muhammad. Even the pontiff, Pope Francis, said "you can't make a toy out of the religions of others," and not expect consequences. Was the pontiff endorsing the killing of the editors and cartoonists, at Charlie Hebdo as a justifiable act of terrorism?

Critics believe the pope indirectly agreed with, and endorsed, the actions of the jihadists that killed the 12 editors and cartoonists at the offices of Charlie Hebdo newspaper, when he made those comments. Other critics further asserted that the pope agreed with the actions of the terrorists instead of condemning it as an act of terrorism.

World leaders, except the pope, had condemned the act as a barbaric act that has no place in a civilized society where freedom of speech and of the press is paramount. Since Islamic extremism gained prominence in the 21st century with the emergence of Boko

Haram, Al-Shabaab, Al-Qaeda, ISIS, Pope Francis became the most prominent and recognizable world leader to endorse the acts of terrorism when he said ""You cannot insult the faith of others. You cannot make fun of the faith of others. There is a limit. Every religion has its dignity." The pontiff felt every act of indignity toward the faiths of others has its consequences.

The pontiff goes on to add that "There are so many people who speak badly about religions or other religions; who make fun of them, who make a game out of the religions of others. They are provocateurs," for disrespecting the faiths of others. The pope blamed Charlie Hebdo for the acts of terrorism that was visited upon the satirical newspaper, because the satirical newspaper provoked the consequences that led to the deaths of its 12 editors and cartoonists. For an influential pope who is the leader of millions of catholic faithful and pilgrims to make such a comment, made jihadists across the world feel justified in their ongoing jihad against infidels.

According to USA today, the Pope went on to say that "Considering the impact of the media, their leaders are invited to offer information that is respectful of religions, their followers and their practices, thus favoring a culture of encounter." The pope is a highly influential religious leader with teeming millions of religious catholic adherents hanging on his every utterance. Some critics think the pope has a personal grudge against the satirical newspaper that has for years made fun of several religions, including Catholics. If that is the case, should the pope have chosen the moment of national mourning in Paris to endorse the acts of terrorism committed against Charlie Hebdo by the al-Qaeda influenced jihadists? Religious experts believe the pontiff's comment was not an endorsement of Islamic extremism or jihad; that the pope has earlier condemned the terrorist acts committed against the satirical newspaper of Charlie Hebdo.

While acknowledging that "freedom of speech was a fundamental human right," Pope Francis, according to the Guardian, added that "every religion has its dignity." When asked about his opinion on the attack that killed 12 editors and cartoonists at the offices of Charlie Hebdo, that was targeted for printing cartoons depicting Prophet Muhammad, the pontiff declared that "One cannot provoke, one cannot insult other people's faith, one cannot make fun of faith." Is the depiction of Prophet Muhammad in a cartoon enough to kill 12 people? The Pope appears to say yes and no at the same time. On one hand he condemned the terrorist attack, and on the other, he condemns the actions of the satirical newspaper that led to the attack. A lot of observers would see the pontiff wanting to appease both sides in the argument. Critics believe the pope endorsed the actions of the terrorists that brought 44 world leaders together in Paris, to condemn the attack on the satirical newspaper. The world leaders condemned the attack as an attack on the freedom of speech and the freedom of the press.

In a direct endorsement of the terrorist attack of the offices of Charlie Hebdo on January 7, 2015, the pontiff turned to Alberto Gasparri, who organizes his trips and who was standing on his side, during a recent trip, and said: "If my good friend Dr Gasparri says a curse word against my mother, he can expect a punch. It's normal. It's normal. You cannot provoke. You cannot insult the faith of others. You cannot make fun of the faith of others."

A lot of people think the pope meant that it is normal to kill or fight back when insulted as was the case when three armed men stormed the offices of Charlie Hebdo and killed 12 editors and cartoonists. Did the pope realize his comments were an endorsement of an eye for an eye philosophy?

Can the Pontiff's words also apply to the cop killer, Ismaaiyi Brinsley, who took the lives of two New York police officers on December 20, 2014, because of police brutality towards black men in the U.S.? The reason given by Brinsley for killing officers Rafael Ramos and Wenjian Liu was because of police brutality and killings of blacks across the U.S. Brinsley named the police shooting deaths of Eric Garner and Michael Brown as the reason for his actions. While the action of Brinsley was a condemnable act by all and sundry, can the pope, with the same belief of "If my good friend Dr Gasparri says a curse word against my mother, he can expect a punch," endorse Brinsley's actions? Many would quickly say no, and would not see a correlation between the cop killing and the slaying of the 12 editors and cartoonists at the offices of Charlie Hebdo. But they were both acts of terrorism, and blatant assassination of innocent people who were engaged in the performance of their various duties at the time of their deaths. Did they deserve to die? Brinsley thought so. And the three jihadists that killed the 12 editors and cartoonists also thought so!

Could these acts of barbarism have been stopped? Certainly! Does the pontiff think so? Probably not, going by the weight and implication of his comments! Preaching intolerance as the pontiff did, following the Paris attack, is unprecedented and sets an unprecedented example for future terrorists and jihadists!

But terrorism can be eradicated in the U.S., France, Nigeria, and in the Middle East, if disadvantaged and marginalized youths, and minority groups across the world are made inclusive and productive members of the society, and not rendered insignificant. They can probably become decent and useful members of society if they are given the same chance and opportunity that privileged citizens of the world enjoy.

Could Brinsley have become a productive member of American society? Probably yes. But since he was never given a chance by society and by the system that created and nurtured him, it will be hard to tell. Could those jihadists that killed 12 satirists and editors at Charlie Hebdo have been decent members of global societies instead of jihadists who cherish protecting and avenging the undefined cause and reverence of a long-gone prophet? Hard to tell since they never attained the mindset to be free of religious extremism.

Chapter 15

How Ebola Marginalized the African

In the United States, and elsewhere in the civilized and Western world, the black man was already marginalized because of the color of his skin. The arrival of Ebola gave further credence to the marginalization of the black African. For Africans arriving from sub-Saharan Africa, they became stigmatized for being Africans. Immigrants from Sierra Leone, Liberia, and Guinea, where the Ebola virus continues to resist international efforts to minimize it, face ongoing discrimination and stigmatization at airports; when they depart and arrive in their destinations the world over. In some cases flight attendants reportedly serve Africans on international flights dressed in protective clothing as if all Africans have Ebola!

Months before, it was Liberia that was stigmatized, but now it is Sierra Leone. It is as if these sub-Saharan African nations haven't suffered enough stigmatization. The economies of the affected countries have suffered as their borders have been shutdown, and schools closed. Tourists are now afraid to go to Africa, even to those countries not affected by Ebola. A recent poll indicated that the tourism industry in Africa has been negatively impacted by as much as 80% shortfall in tourism in Africa.

As far as most already prejudiced Westerners are concerned, the African continent is contaminated with Ebola. The Ebola virus has only mainly affected six countries in sub-Saharan Africa, with three cleared of the virus. There is no Ebola infection in East Africa, South Africa and North Africa. East Africa's safari now faces tourism disaster as tourists have reportedly abandoned traveling to Africa, according to recent reports.

It is not surprising that tourists and investors would abandon Africa. In Sierra Leone where Ebola is today wreaking havoc, a doctor recently died of the disease, making him the 11th doctor to die of the virus in that country. According to BBC, Ebola has infected over 30,000 people in West Africa, killing over 11,000, with most of the dead (3,900) in Liberia.

The doctor that recently died of the Ebola virus in Sierra Leone died, on Thursday December 19, 2014, hours before the arrival of the experimental drug, Zmapp, that could have saved his life, according to Reuters. The doctor, Victor Willoughby, was reportedly diagnosed with Ebola after he had treated a man with

organ infections. The patient, who was a banker, was later
discovered to have Ebola, but it was too late for Dr. Willoughby
who had unknowingly treated him of organ-related infection. The
senior banker died of Ebola, and Dr. Willoughby who treated him
of organ infection, also died days later from Ebola that the banker
had unknowingly infected him with.

The question is why is the Zmapp drug just arriving in Sierra
Leone when the experimental drug has been around for months,
and has been used to save the lives of Westerners, mostly
Americans, who had been infected with Ebola? Why do Africans
continue to die of the virus while Westerners, again mostly
Americans and Europeans, continue to be cured, and saved from
the disease? The discussion again goes back to the marginalization of
Africans. If not, why do Africans continue to die of the disease
when the experimental drugs, Zmapp, and ZMab have been
available since the early part of the year?

According to Reuters, "ZMab, was transported in frozen form
on a Brussels Airlines flight that arrived overnight. Before it could
thaw, Willoughby's condition deteriorated." Why was the drug not
already in sub-Saharan African countries, especially in countries
most affected by the Ebola virus? If Westerners are serious about
helping to combat the Ebola virus, why does it have to be flown
from Europe every time it is needed?

A similar situation had occurred when another Sierra Leonean
doctor, Dr. Martin Salia, was transported to the Nebraska Medical
Center for treatment, and had died because his infections had
reached an advanced stage! Now, another Sierra Leonean doctor,
Dr. Willoughby, could not be saved because his condition had
deteriorated. Why do Africans infected with the disease always get
the same final diagnosis of the "Ebola reaching an advanced stage,"
when Westerners infected within the same number of days do not
get the same diagnosis and eventual deaths?

This brings the analysis back to the African being the subject of
marginalization wherever he or she is. Dr. Martin Salia had believed
so much in the country he chose as his home, the United States, that
when he was infected in Sierra Leone, where he had been using his
medical skill to save lives, he paid his way to receive treatment in
Nebraska. He had paid for medical transportation to the United
States for treatment. Unbeknownst to him that his decision was a
death knell that would quickly herald his death! He had felt, and
wrongly so, that he would be saved once he made it back to the

United States, which he had called home. Upon arriving a week later, he was received without the hoopla that the likes of Dr. Kent Brantly and Nancy Writebol had received. His condition was categorized as too advanced to be treated. He died within days of arriving at the Nebraska Medical Center, a place he had expected solace and cure, but had instead received misery and death!

Dr. Martin Salia was also not given the experimental drug, Zmapp, even though he was on American soil; and the drug had been used to save Dr. Kent Brantly and five other Americans who had been infected with the Ebola virus. The excuse was always that the disease had reached an advanced stage for the patient to be cured. In the case of Dr. Martin Salia, he was declared Ebola-free on November 6, 2014 and would die of the disease days later because the disease had reached "an advanced stage."

For Dr. Willoughby who became the 11th doctor to die of the Ebola virus in Sierra Leone, a perception of marginalization pervades the availability of the Zmapp drug to Africans, especially the African doctors who risk their lives daily to treat those infected with the virus. African doctors are not just treating Africans infected with Ebola but also making sure that the disease is contained so that it does not spread to Western countries where it could become a global epidemic crisis like the black death of the 14th century.

Unlike the Black Death that killed over 200 million people in Europe and Asia, Ebola has only killed over 11,000 people in West Africa, and counting. The brave men and women healthcare workers in sub-Saharan Africa should receive equal treatment and cure when they fall ill of the Ebola virus. These brave African doctors and healthcare workers chose to be in the heart of the Ebola crisis because of their love of humanity and continent and most of all because of their commitments to save lives. And if it hadn't been for these healthcare workers, the Ebola virus would have spread more than it has, and probably would have been gradually approaching the magnitude that Black Death had attained before it was finally contained in the 19th century, having reoccurred several times between the 13th and 19th centuries.

Black Death had been caused by the Yersinia pestis bacteria which had infected and killed people in northern and southern Europe during the pandemic of the 14th century. Like Ebola which started in Zaire in 1976, the Black Death had started in the arid plains of central Asia where it had reportedly spread along the Silk Road to Crimea in Ukraine, in 1343, where it was carried by oriental rat fleas that were living in black rats. The merchant ships of the 13th and 14th centuries were often populated by black rats. And the black rats had traveled with the merchant ships, spreading the oriental rat fleas along, to as far as the Mediterranean and Europe, where the plague wreaked havoc and killed over 60% Europeans, reducing the population of Europe from 450 million to 375 million in the 14the century.

The Ebola virus has not reached the proportion of the Black Death but if Western countries continue to marginalize African doctors who are infected in the field, other African doctors who have seen the pattern of deaths among African doctors will refuse to help in the fight against Ebola; and the virus could spread just as the oriental rat fleas that plagued Europe in the 13th century. The Black Death had only started in the arid plains of central Asia, and when the dust had settled, millions of Europeans in faraway land had died of the plague.

The Ebola virus has continued to reoccur since its advent in 1976, just like the Black Death had reoccurred between the 13th and 19th centuries. It had taken 150 years for Europe to recover from the scourge. The Ebola virus can easily be another Black Death if Western countries continue to marginalize and treat only their own kind. In fairness, Europe has successfully treated Africans infected with the disease but not so in America where two Africans infected with the disease had died, and where over five American doctors infected with the disease had recovered, and had been cured!

The death of Dr. Willoughby makes the reluctance of Western countries, especially the United States, to cure the disease a conspiracy. Europe has been very helpful in making sure that infected Africans are given the necessary medical attention, including experimental drugs, and all the proper processes of recovery, including rehydration of body fluids. Europe obviously learned its lesson from the ravages and plagues of the Black Death. It is not easy to forget a disease that took 150 years to recover from, that reduced the population of Europe from 450 million to 375 million people, within a short time, in the 13th century. Europeans know the consequence of allowing an epidemic like Ebola to spread.

The black rats that carried the fleas with Yersinia pestis bacteria that caused the plagues of the 14th century traveled from Asia to Europe just like Ebola had traveled with Thomas Eric Duncan to the United States, on September 19, 2014, until Duncan died of the disease at the Texas Presbyterian Hospital in Dallas on October 8,

2014. In Sierra Leone alone, 12 doctors had been infected with 11 dead. Over 142 healthcare workers had been infected, and according to the World Health Organization, 109 of the 142 infected healthcare workers had died of the disease. While the rates of infections had subsided in Liberia, Sierra Leone's infections have surged. The World Health Organization indicated that over 30,000 people have been infected in sub-Saharan Africa and that over half of those infections have occurred in Sierra Leone, which is a huge proportion compared to other infected countries like Liberia, and Guinea.

The death rate continues to rise in West Africa. The World Health Organization reported that the number of recorded deaths in sub-Saharan Africa has now reached over 11,000, as of March 10, 2015. Though there are reports that the rate of infection has slowed in Sierra Leone and Liberia, the number of those who are continually infected continue to be alarming.

The Center for Disease Control (CDC) continues to increase its stockpile of protective gear for several clinics and hospitals, especially U.S. hospitals that are involved in the treatment of Ebola in West Africa. According to Reuters, the CDC ordered $2.7 million worth of protective equipment that had been supplied to hospitals in Sierra Leone to prevent and combat the Ebola virus. The equipment "is being configured into 50 kits for rapid deployment to hospitals," the CDC said.

If the CDC is worried about preventing Ebola, how come the Zmapp drug is not being made available to healthcare workers in the three affected countries? So far it has proven that the Zmapp drug can cure Ebola, as it has done in several cases where it has been used. Dr. Kent Brantly, Nancy Writebol and many others had survived due to the Zmapp drug. If it is that effective, why not supply affected African countries such as Liberia, Sierra Leone and Guinea with the drug?

Sending troops to build clinics and medical centers is commendable; why not provide the right medication to cure those infected? If the U.S. is going to provide any meaningful help it should not be about sending 3,000 troops. It should be about sending what is really needed – drugs. The troops are not doctors or nurses but just soldiers! There is no war to fight in the affected countries other than the war against Ebola. And to fight the Ebola war, what Liberia, Sierra Leone and Guinea need is not soldiers but medicine which appears to be in short supply.

Though protective gears and equipment are equally important in the fight against Ebola, there has not been a serious effort on the part of Western countries to fight the disease. There have been lip services about fighting the disease but nothing concerted. The financially strapped World Health Organization is doing its best but member nations are not doing enough to prevent what will likely become a pandemic that could be as dangerous as the Black Death plague of the 13th century.

Reuters indicated that some of the protective equipment that the United States ordered had been stuck in backlogs due to growing domestic demands in the U.S. For Western countries like the U.S., it was about priority! The orders for domestic supply must be met first, before fulfilling the orders for the affected African countries. After all, it was just Africa, a continent that was used to death, poverty and misery! What was another 100 deaths per day from Ebola when tribal wars, terrorism, armed robberies and kidnappings claim as many lives, on a daily basis?

While manufacturers were enjoying unprecedented demands for protective gears and equipment, and making huge profits as a result, the same cannot be said of the pharmaceutical companies that are reluctant to manufacture the Zmapp drugs for financially strapped sub-Saharan African countries. For the manufacturers of protective gears and equipment, there was no need to worry about payments since most of the orders were placed by aid agencies trying to curb the outbreak of Ebola in sub-Saharan Africa. As long as Ebola continues to ravage lives and the people of West Africa, the demands for protective gears and equipment will continue to flood in, from aid agencies and Western countries.

As for the manufacturers of fluid-resistant gowns, gloves, hoods, shoe coverings, and face mask, they would prefer Ebola to continue to spread as it means big businesses and huge profits to them. In times of war, while misery, deprivation and deaths pervade the air, others often profit tremendously, as has been the case with Ebola. Billions of dollars will be made from the epidemic by the manufacturers of protective gears and equipment. The manufacturer of Zmapp and other experimental drugs would also enjoy the boom if they think sub-Saharan African governments can afford to pay for the drugs. As for Western countries, there has been very limited willingness on their parts to supply the drugs to the affected countries, on humanitarian grounds.

It will be fair to quickly point out that several European countries are just now recovering from the recent global financial meltdown. European countries like France, Italy, Germany, England, Greece, Ireland, to name a few, are still struggling with their own financial problems, as their public and capital expenditures continues to challenge their receivables and their GDP, GNP.

As for the United States, which Forbes reportedly said had beaten every Ebola infection that occurred on its soil, the disease is conquerable. Not so for Africans who have died of the disease on U.S. soil. Every American patient taken to an Elite U.S. medical facility had survived. The Zmapp drug was used for Americans infected with Ebola. Africans infected with Ebola in the U.S. had died because the drug was *never used* for them! According to Forbes "you don't need to be scared that the deadly disease carries an automatic death sentence – especially in the United States," but it still does for Africans in the U.S., as Thomas Eric Duncan died in Dallas, months after the Zmapp drug was used to save Dr. Kent Brantly and Nancy Writebol – both white Americans.

Ebola was also an automatic death sentence for Dr. Martin Salia, a resident in the U.S. who was working in Sierra Leone where he had contracted the disease. Dr. Salia had paid his way back to the U.S. to get treatment at the Nebraska Medical Center, and died. The so-called "elite U.S. facility," could not, and did not save him.

Forbes wrote that the rate of Ebola survival in the U.S. was 80%! When the Africans who didn't survive the Ebola because they were refused the Zmapp drug, or did not have access to the drug, is considered, it will be right to say there is an 80% survival rate. After all, every American that contracted the disease survived while the same cannot be said of the Africans that didn't survive the disease in the U.S. It can also be possible that the "Zmapp drug does not work for Africans," one Sierra Leonean U.S. resident said! In sub-Saharan Africa, in Sierra Leone, 12 doctors have been infected and 11 have died from the disease. The only doctor that survived was saved because he was transported to Europe for treatment. If that doctor had "come to the U.S. he would not have survived as his Ebola would have reached an advanced stage," one Liberian in Houston said. It is obvious that "when it comes to using the Zmapp drug for Africans it never works," a Nigerian restaurant owner said. It is not surprising that many Africans feel they have been marginalized and "taken for granted because of the color of their skin," says a Ghanaian.

NBC News cameraman: Ashoka Mukpo, who had contracted the Ebola disease in Africa (not an African but an American), was treated at the Nebraska Medical Center for Ebola and survived. Dr. Martin Salia was treated at the same hospital and did not survive! Mukpo had contracted Ebola while working for NBC News in Liberia, which means NBC paid his medical bills. While the survival rate in the U.S. is 83%, it is 30% to 40% in the affected countries of Sierra Leone, Liberia and Guinea.

Dr. Kent Brantly, Nancy Writebol, Nina Pham, Amber Vinson, Ashoka Mukpo, Rick Sacra, and a World Health Organization doctor who was infected with the Ebola virus, and who did not want to be named, and a few others, survived the Ebola virus and they were all Americans. Dr. Martin Salia, and Thomas Eric Duncan were Africans and did not survive the disease in the United States. The difference was that the Americans that survived had received the Zmapp drug and blood donation from those that survived the disease. The Africans did not get the same treatment.

The Ebola disease did not only marginalize the African but also reduce his ability to mingle among the citizens of the world. Several European countries had temporarily banned Africans from entering their countries. In some cases, precautions were taken in admitting tourists and visitors from Africa because of the Ebola virus. Prior to the Ebola epidemic, all the African immigrant had to worry about was getting a visa to travel to any country he or she wishes to travel. With Ebola, that choice had been taken away as every African was seen as an Ebola carrier. "First it had been aids and HIV coming out of Africa, now it is Ebola," a Malawian student in central London wrote on his facebook page. For the African, the stigma follows him everywhere.

Most Africans do not feel the West should be blamed for the marginalization and humiliation they continue to face everywhere they go. African governments have not done enough to improve their various countries to make them attractive enough with employment opportunities to stop the brain drain and immigration of Africans to Western countries. Africans risk their lives daily to cross the Mediterranean seas to European countries like Italy, France and Spain, because of the proximity of those two countries to the African continent. For instance, Spain's mainland is bordered to the south and east by the Mediterranean Sea. Spain has both the Atlantic and Mediterranean coastlines, which makes it attractive for human smugglers.

Thisday Newspaper, a Nigerian daily reported that "Several Africans believed to be fleeing harsh economic conditions in their home countries have often resorted to crossing into parts of Europe, using unofficial channels. Many of them have died in what is described as 'the immigration crisis.'" The proximity of Morocco to Spain often makes it possible for human smugglers to smuggle Africans across the dangerous Mediterranean waters to Europe, at exorbitant rates. Recently, in January 2014, over 233 Africans were rescued from a rickety and dangerous boat, by an Italian Navy.

Every year, thousands of Africans die crossing the deserts to escape the harsh economic and social conditions in their countries. Most of the Africans are mostly from East and West Africa where terrorism is rampant. In Nigeria for example, Boko Haram has created a caliphate in the northeast of the country. Those who refuse to pledge allegiance to the caliphate are often beheaded and shot, and in cases sentenced to death through the Sharia Court. Over 14,000 Nigerians have died from the jihadist extremism of Boko Haram since July 2009.

Nigerians living in the northeast of Nigeria where Boko Haram has its stronghold often flee to safe haven in Europe. And since several of these Nigerians have lost their parents and siblings to the murderous and suicide-bombing Boko Haram, they no longer have any confidence in the Nigerian government to protect them. Their choice of destination is usually Europe; and since immigration visa is usually not easy to get they often turn to human smugglers who charge exorbitant fees for such services.

For the Nigerians escaping terrorism, armed robberies, insurgencies in the Niger Delta, kidnapping, unemployment, and other social ills, they have very little choices left to them. They are often caught in a limbo. Risking their lives to cross the deserts and the dangerous Mediterranean Seas presents a better future than being a sitting duck in Nigeria where they remain susceptible to getting killed by Boko Haram, Nigerian soldiers, police, kidnappers, and armed robbers.

For Malians, the story is the same. Terrorism, unemployment, hunger, political strife make the country a bleak and gloomy prospect to achieve any future ambition and economic mobility and substance.

For Somalis, Sudanese, Kenyans and other Africans living in the countries at war with al-Shabaab, the Somali based terrorist and jihadist extremists, risking their lives to cross the desert and the Mediterranean Seas is better than being a sitting duck for the bloodcurdling terrorist extremists.

The African is continually left with limited choices as his government has robbed him of his choices. Corruption, Embezzlement, political rivalry and greed has robbed Africa of its greatness. For European countries, African leaders have no credibility as selfless and committed leaders who have the best interest of their countries at heart. As far as the West is concerned, African leaders care more about being presidents for life than in actual governance.

African leaders often hide their stolen money in European banks. And because of the nature of their thievery and crookedness, there is very little respect for these crooked African leaders. And for the countries that allow these corrupt and thieving African leaders to stash stolen monies, it is of little concern to them if these African leaders choose to plunder their coffers to buy properties in Europe and America. After all, the monies are from bank loans and donor countries that will never be repaid.

In the meantime, the downtrodden African is left to bear the brunt of the staggering debt, and stark thievery of his unconscionable leader who often steal monies meant for salaries, infrastructural projects, building factories, road repairs, and developing electrical grids.

After taking the risks of traveling across the Sahara desert and the Mediterranean Seas; and the African makes it safely to his destination, the last thing on the mind of the African is to bite the hand that feeds him – to question the condition he is subjected to in his foreign land. After all, he is better off in the foreign land than in his country where death is meaningless and where human life has less value. At least in his adopted land, he has potentials. Opportunities abound for him to grow and be all he can be. Back home he has a greater likelihood of getting killed than of making it, economically.

For the African, what is a token of discrimination to the naked and often, unquestionable police brutality back home? At least in his adopted country a police officer often get to face some justice even if he doesn't get indicted, and for killing unarmed black male teens.

Back home, the African had often seen police officers round up innocent people for execution to make it look like they are doing their job to reduce crime and fight terrorism. He had also seen police officers run away from armed robbers when confronted. He has heard the voices of the citizens of the northeast of Nigeria crying and begging for the police and soldiers to come to their aid as Boko Haram invade their homes to behead them. He has heard people in the northeast say that soldiers often flee with fleeing residents as Boko Haram approach them. For him, being a fortunate foreigner in a foreign land is better than constantly facing death in his country.

After all, his country has never offered him anything other than misery, danger, poverty and hunger. What is a small price of marginalization when his country was the first to marginalize and leave him to die in the hands of terrorists in the northeast of Nigeria?

Thomas Eric Duncan may have been untreated for Ebola or he may not have had Ebola at all, but his country did not offer him better choices. He would have probably died anyway if he had remained in Liberia. After all it was his government that was the first to condemn him in his deathbed when he had contracted Ebola, or when they thought he had it. It was at the same time citizens of the civilized world were being called heroes for contracting Ebola when he was being called a villain by the president and government officials of his own country. Though he arrived in the United States not knowing he had the symptoms, he probably would have stayed back if he had known. Nobody knew he had it, not even the test he took at the airport in Monrovia and upon arrival in the United States revealed any symptoms.

What is known is that the relatives who had lived with Duncan when he supposedly had the Ebola did not contract the disease, not even the fiancée he slept in the same bed with. In the affected countries in West Africa and everywhere Ebola has claimed lives anyone with close contact had contracted the disease. It was weird and strange that someone who had very close contact with his relatives before and after the symptoms showed in his system did not transmit the disease to his relatives.

Though there can never be a greater marginalization than the ones suffered by blacks in the United States; for Africans there is a greater disregard for human lives than anywhere, save Asia, in the world. The African in African does not have emergency response or what some called first responders in an emergency. When someone is sick or there is an accident, a relative or a friend will have to quickly rally around for transportation to get the person to the hospital. Sometimes the patient dies before transportation can be found, to get the patient to the hospital. In some cases when help or transportation is readily available and when a patient is transported to the hospital, the hospital will reject the patient if the injury or sickness is too severe. Sometimes a patient dies by the time a hospital is found to accept him. In some cases a patient will be rejected if there is no bed or there are no doctors to attend to the patient. Only in Africa!

So the African is used to being treated inhumanly, even in his own country where first responders do not exist or where authorities seldom care about the lives of their own citizens. For the African, police shooting of young black males or black males in general, in the United States is nothing compared to what he is used to back home. It does not appear strange to the African that only black males are getting shot and killed daily by white police officers in the United States. He has seen, back home, how police would gather innocent people - their fellow citizens, and shoot them en masse! And the police, as often the case in the United States, would act with impunity "as if they are above the law," one Nigerian mechanic said. And in some cases "they are!" a Nigerian student at the University of Houston added. "In Nigeria police do not think they are above the law, they just know they are!" A Nigerian architect based in Houston said.

The shooting of a 12 year old playing in a park in Cleveland with a toy gun is nothing new to the African as he has seen worse back home, in his country. In his African country, the police do not need to be provoked to kill, just like their counterparts in the civilized United States. A mere whim or suspicion can lead to death in the hands of the police, as happened in St. Louis, Missouri where another black teen was shot to death for supposedly pointing a gun at a police officer. It didn't matter that eyewitnesses said the teen was only holding a sandwich. After all, it is whatever the police say that matters. The police had to justify its homicidal actions against blacks. If they said the black teen in St. Louis had a gun, then that is what happened! Eyewitnesses do not matter, when the police have spoken. It was just a few short months ago that another unarmed teen was shot to death by a white police officer, with impunity from the law.

With renewed impunity and empowerment by grand juries that never seemed to find the killings of black males, by police, a crime, police across the United States have become more daring and trigger-happy than ever before. The year 2014 had seen more black males shot to death by police in unjustifiable homicides in the United States than ever before, polls have shown. The increased police killing of black males is, according to a black activist, "because grand juries often do not indict police officers when they kill black males. It is always different when one of their own dies. The shooting death of two police officers drew a huge public outcry and condemnation as if the lives of the two police officers were more precious than the lives of the innocent black males police continue to kill on a daily basis across the country," another black activist in St. Louis said.

"Just look at what happened! What did an 18 year old boy, Vonderrit Myers, do to justify his being shot to death by the police? Nothings! They said he was pointing a gun at a police officer when he was actually holding a sandwich! How does a gun resembles a sandwich?" A protester, protesting the death of the teen said. According to the cousin of the teen, Teyonna Myers, "He was unarmed. He had a sandwich in his hand, and they thought it was a gun. It's like Michael Brown all over again." It is unlikely the grand jury will indict the officer, judging by the abysmal record of past grand juries. It is also unlikely that the grand jury will even take the evidence provided by the eyewitnesses into account. In the past incidents involving police shootings of black males, grand juries have never sought, nor considered eyewitnesses' account to reach a predictable verdict.

It wouldn't take a soothsayer to know that the police in the shooting of Myers will not be indicted.

The shooting of the black teen in St. Louis, Missouri, is a typical example of what has become the fate of black males in the United States. According to The Atlantic News, Police Chief Sam Dotson told the Associated Press that "the officer was spotted by three men while patrolling his designated security guard area in his car, and after one of the men ran away, the officer made a U-turn." When did spotting a police officer and running away start to constitute a crime? Didn't it occur to the police officer that the three young black males probably ran away from him because they were worried that they may get shot for just being blacks? Chief Dotson did not say the three black males were caught committing a crime. They simply ran away when they saw a police officer, not charged the officer! Where is the justification for chasing the black teens in the first place? It wasn't that the teens started shooting at the officer when they spotted the officer. They simply ran away because they feared for their lives.

How can anyone blame the three black teens for running away when in, Ferguson, Michael Brown was just shot to death a few short months before? Chief Dotson reportedly said Myers was reaching for his waistband as he ran that "the officer believed he was carrying a weapon." In 21st century America, a mere whim or suspicion that a black teen is armed is enough justification to kill him, even when the gun is not visible and the teen is not pointing it. It happened in Cleveland, Ohio where a 12 year old child was killed for also supposedly reaching his waistband for a toy gun! The statement of Chief Dotson about Myers reaching for his waistband to justify the teen's death is as bogus as the Cleveland Police saying a 12 year old child was reaching for his waistband when he was shot!

Another baffling part of the St. Louis slaying of a black teen was the number of shots the white police officer had fired. The officer reportedly shot Myers, 17 times! Assistant Police Chief, Alfred Atkins said the officer "ended up in a struggle with the teen after the teen jumped out of the bushes during the chase." If there was a struggle as the police officer claimed, how did the teen reportedly shoot at the police officer three times before the officer shot the teen 17 times? The inconsistency in the story told by the Chief and his assistant, points to a disconcerting fabrication of what really happened. There was the version of the assistant police chief, Alfred Adkins, that the "teen jumped out of the bushes during the chase;" and there was the version of the police chief that the officer believed the teen was carrying a weapon and decided to chase the teen and later, tailed him, before shooting him, 17 times.

The officer reportedly got out of his car to chase the three teens, on foot. Why was that necessary when the teens had not committed any crime? According to the Police Chief, the officer chased after the teens because the teens ran away when they spotted the officer. How is that a crime in an America where black teens are killed daily for not breaking the law? Chief Sam Dotson said the "chase escalated as the officer got out of his vehicle and pursued one man on foot." How could the teen have jumped out of the bushes if the officer was chasing him on foot? It doesn't add up, does it? The officer must have seen the teen to chase him or he was suddenly surprised by the teen jumping out of the bushes to confront him. Which version is true? If the officer was surprised by the teen's sudden jump, and shooting, the officer would have been hurt or killed in the process. But the officer was not hurt because the teen did not shoot at the officer! To shoot someone 17 times amounts to unreasonable and excessive use of force by the police. There had to have been a willingness on the part of the police officer to make sure the teen was dead to have shot him 17 times.

If the officer was off duty at the time of the shooting, why was it the business of the officer to chase after three teens who were just minding their own business? "It was an execution, and nothing to do with police work or an unavoidable incident in the line of duty," a Missouri activist said. "Why not kill another 'coon,' since they will not face the law for doing so. They might even get a promotion for killing innocent black males. Maybe there is a secret police mission to reduce the number of black males in the streets of America by killing them," another protester in Missouri said.

On December 23, 2014, in Berkeley, Missouri, another 18 year old black male was shot to death by a white police officer for reportedly pulling a 9mm handgun on the officer. Berkeley is a few miles from Ferguson where another teen, Michael Brown, was shot to death by a white police officer, Officer Darren Wilson, on August 9, 2014. According to the Associated Press, the officer had been reportedly questioning the 18 year old black teen when the teen allegedly pulled a 9mm. St. Louis County Police Chief, Jon Belmar, said the "police officer stumbled backward but fired three shots, one of which struck the victim." The victim, Antonio Martin, was 18 and black. "Perhaps white police officers are in complicity to get rid of all 18 year olds in Missouri because the killing of Antonio Martin brings the total number of 18 year olds killed by police to, about six, within the last six months," a 21 year old black protester said in Berkeley, while protesting the teen's death.

The Police Officer, according to the St. Louis County Police Chief Belmar, had been questioning the teen about a theft at a convenience store when the teen reportedly pulled a 9mm. If the questioning was ongoing when the teen reportedly pulled a gun, if that is accurate, then something happened because the teen was already being questioned! It wasn't as if the teen pulled a gun before the officer could question him. He reportedly pulled the gun when the officer was questioning him. If it is true, and it seems doubtful, could it be that the officer's behavior was becoming threatening to the teen, who had seen so many of his peers unjustifiably shot to death in the area by police, and pulled his own gun?

The 34 year old police officer who is reportedly a six year veteran of the Berkeley Police Department, no doubt knows that killing the teen will be a justifiable homicide since the teen reportedly had a gun, if he had a gun. He knew there was no need to use a less deadly method to apprehend the teen. Death was a preferred method to an officer who knew that there will be no consequence for his action. After all, it was not too long ago that another police officer, in the same vicinity, was unindicted by a grand jury, for killing a black man. There was also the case of Eric Garner's chokehold death in which the officer was not indicted. Why let the allegedly thieving teen live to steal another day when the problem could be solved by just killing him!

"He will carry the weight of this for the rest of his life, certainly for the rest of his career," Chief Belmar said of the officer. There was no mention of the loss that the grieving victim's mother had suffered. A life had been taken and will never return, yet the police chief was talking about the guilt that the officer will carry "the rest of his life." Why was the police officer not wearing his body camera and why was the dashboard camera on the police car not activated when the shooting occurred? Did the police officer intentionally kill the teen, having deliberately deactivated his body and dashboard cameras before the shooting? Why will a police officer who is provided with a body and dashboard camera in his car, forget to activate the cameras for the very same reason the cameras were provided?

The blurry surveillance video obtained from the parking lot surveillance camera outside the store where the teen was shot was reportedly edited "to back up the police claim of self defense," a protester said. The officer must have been informed that a theft was taking place at the convenience store. And yet the officer did not activate his body camera or his dashboard camera? The cameras were provided to protect the public and the officer in volatile situations such as the convenience store shooting. And the police officer conveniently forgot to activate the cameras!

The two minute clip of the edited video "shows two young men leaving the store as a patrol car pulls up. The officer got out of his patrol car and spoke with the teens. About a minute-and-a-half later, the video appears to show one of the men raising his arm, though what he is holding is difficult to see because they were several feet from the camera," Police Chief Belmar said. How do we know what really happened if the video had been vetted and edited to remove proof and evidence of the police intentionally slaying the black teen?

The Associated Press reported that "It was the third fatal shooting of a black suspect by a white police officer in the St. Louis area since Brown was killed. Kajaime Powell, 25, was killed Aug. 9 after approaching St. Louis officers with a knife. Vonderrit Myers Jr., 18, was fatally shot Oct. 8 after allegedly shooting at a St. Louis officer."Black males across the United States continue to be shot to death by police, for unfathomable crimes. And the police officers involved continue to get away with the crimes," an activist said. Just like the stigmatized African, has it come to where black males are targeted because they are blacks? A black protester in New York's Staten Island said "blacks are continually targeted by the police across the United States because of the color of their skins and they often do not need justifications to kill black males."

The African has been marginalized in more ways than one. To the African, living in the United States has been easy and difficult; but it was much better than the life he had lived back home. He sees the blacks in America as his kinfolks and brethrens even though the feeling is not always mutual. He watches with awe and bafflement how the blacks in America are treated. He follows events as they unfold about police brutality and killings of blacks in America. He remembers how it was back home in his native country, how police would often kill with impunity. He tries to compare his native country with his new foreign home, and shudders. Back home he knew things were bad, very bad, but sometimes he sees America as even worse.

Not too long ago, he saw a video of a black man being searched by a police officer and then being handcuffed, and soon after, being shot to death by the same police officer. He was confused. He couldn't understand how a country he had dreamed of, and respected, as the beacon of civilization, could suddenly become so barbaric. He knew there were still some remnants of racism, left from time past, but he never knew it was as bad as it has become, of late. The deaths of Trayvon Martin, Michael Brown and Eric Garner shook him to no end. He grieved in silence for the defenseless and unarmed black males that were shot to death for no reason at all. He was also shocked by the attitude of the grand juries in Ferguson and New York that did not indict the killers of the black males. Somehow he sees no difference between the police in his native country, in Africa, and the police in the so-called civilized country called the United States. He listens to talk show radio hosts and is often appalled by the racist commentaries of Rush Limbaugh, Sean Hannity, Michael Berry and Mark Levin, and shudders that such racist sentiments still exist in a country he loves. Whatever happened to the country that cherishes and exports freedom to countries bereft of it?

In New York City he reads about the comments of the police union members commending the chokehold death of Eric Garner as self defense. He also reads about the union members criticizing the 109th mayor of New York, Bill de Blasio, for being too sympathetic towards the grieving family of Eric Garner who died in a police chokehold. He wonders how these racist elements are still in the payroll funded by taxpayers. He realizes that perhaps the police union members were reechoing the sentiments of the undercover racists who often display their smiling faces in public to hide their racist tendencies.

The African also remembers South Africa and how the blacks in that country were mistreated and subjugated for many years. He tries to compare today's America with apartheid South Africa, and fails to see a similarity. Yet the feeling that there is a similarity remains in his subconscious. In apartheid South Africa, blacks were brutalized and often killed with careless abandon. In the 21st century America, blacks are also being killed with the same careless abandon while the police enjoy total immunity from the law.

Just like in apartheid South Africa where police acted with total impunity from the law he can't but help notice that most of the police killers, killing blacks, have mostly been white officers. Perhaps there is a similarity, he muses.

There was Duncan and Dr. Martin Salia; and how they were marginalized because of their color and country of origin. How else could one explain the way Thomas Eric Duncan was put on a ventilator and sedated while his vital organs rotted away? Duncan was refused the Zmapp drug that could have saved his life. Or did Duncan really have Ebola? The African sometimes wonders if Duncan had Ebola in the first place, since the relatives Duncan had lived with while he supposedly had the disease never contracted the disease. If he did have it, why was he denied the same experimental drug that was given to Dr. Kent Brantly and Nancy Writebol months before? Or why was Dr. Martin Salia not given the same experimental drug and treatment that had saved many Americans before him who had contracted the Ebola disease? It wasn't like Dr. Salia couldn't afford the medication. After all he paid his way to get admitted at the Nebraska Medical Center.

The African never stops to wonder why he didn't stay back home in the first place. He had sacrificed everything he had acquired in life to come to the land of the golden fleeces, the land of milk and honey, where opportunities abound. But beneath the surface of the boundless opportunities lie deep rooted hatred for the African, he has found out. He has seen it in the eyes of the white man who sometimes refuses to shake his hand because of Ebola even when there was no Ebola where he lives in America. He has always taken the indignity with pride. After all, he was a foreigner in the land!

Ebola has robbed the African of the last vestige of dignity that he once possessed. At work, working with white colleagues, he sees the difference in the treatment he receives. He feels marginalized in his every endeavor but he has learned to accept what he couldn't change. Perhaps he should have gone home, he often muses. Sometimes he feels if he had gone back home that he could have made some changes that could have made his country more attractive to the thousands of Africans that risk their lives to go to foreign lands to receive indignities in Europe and America.

Sometimes the words of William Shakespeare resonates in his head, that *the fault is not in our stars but in ourselves*; he would often reflect on those wisdom to gather courage to return back home. Perhaps home wasn't too bad after all. He also knew it was too late to return. He knew his essence has eroded with time. Time was no longer on his side. His greatest fear was raising children that may become susceptible to police brutality someday. He feels for his children.

He realizes soon enough that America was not a safe place for a young black man. He watches his children grow up, and feels a pang of guilt that he has chosen to raise his children in an environment so hateful and despiteful of black males. He knew he must make a change to rescue his children from a future that was fraught with danger from the police. He was no longer worried about drive-by shooting or black crime against black. He was more concerned that his children may not be safe when they walk the streets, buy gas at the gas station, eat at a restaurant, or go to the movies; and anywhere in the streets of America! He fears there will always be a George Zimmerman or a racist cop lurking somewhere in the dark, ready to pounce and kill. Maybe education will set his children free and apart from the black males being killed daily by white police officers. If he gives his children the right education perhaps they could become meaningful contributors that will earn the respect of all and sundry. Not so fast, he cautions himself. After all it wasn't long ago that a black Harvard Professor, Henry Louis Gates, was arrested for trying to get into his own home! He had seen it in the news. Professor Gates was a prominent scholar of African American studies at the Ivy League Harvard University.

The crime Professor Gates had allegedly committed was trying to get into his own home! A woman had alerted the police that a black man was trying to break into a home. Professor Gates was only trying to get into his own home through the front door! Even though Professor Gates had told the officer that he lived in the home, and that he was a faculty member at Harvard University, the officer still arrested him. Gates would later reechoes the sentiments of the downtrodden black man when he said "this is what happens to black men in America." Even Gates knew that education does not set a black man apart from the other black men. As far as the white police officer was concerned Gates was just another black man, not different from the many black males he had seen. The fact that Gates was a prominent scholar who was renowned for his work at Harvard University did not set him apart. The police officer only saw the color of his skin to rush to judgment that he was trying to break into a home, even though that home belonged to the Harvard Professor!

Chapter 16

The Impact of Ebola and Police Brutality

The Ebola virus arrived when the black man was already grappling with police brutality and racism in America. He had barely survived the civil rights movement that got his leader, Dr. Martin Luther King, assassinated for fighting for equality. It has been a difficult struggle to maintain any modicum of significance, and to exist in a country his ancestors were sold into slavery, to till the soil, many years ago.

He has never been presented with a choice of another country though he had heard of his ancestral root in Africa. But he has been told that Africa was ravaged by the scourge of unemployment, poverty, terrorism, disease and now Ebola! Who would want to identify with a continent so full of misery, strife, war, terrorism, armed robberies, kidnappings, and violent insurgencies? The Africa he has heard of was home to the most dangerous infections and diseases like the polio disease, aids/HIV, malaria, yellow fever, and now Ebola!

Why couldn't Africa be like other continents like the Asian continent where China, India, Vietnam, Indonesia, Singapore, Japan and other progressive countries continue to dominate the headlines with their economic growth and prosperity? He has often been ashamed to identify with anything African. Who would blame him? After all, Africa has not done enough for itself to attract its own people who are risking their lives to escape to Europe through the dangerous deserts and Mediterranean Seas. If Africa couldn't be made attractive to Africans living in Africa why should it be attractive to him, in America?

He has seen the Africans who live in America and hasn't been impressed with what he has seen. Most of the ones he knows, the Nigerians, have developed an infamous reputation of defrauding unsuspecting and gullible people that often believe their bogus stories of huge amounts of unclaimed cash waiting to be transferred to banks in America, to bank account holders. He has heard of the Nigerian 419 fraudsters and their confidence tricks and stratagem; how they defraud people by gaining their confidence and trust. He has seen in the media how people who are guided by greed, dishonesty, naivete, credulity, often fall victim of the 419 scam. He has often been embarrassed by the scam, even though he was not a

Nigeria or even an African. The mere coincidence of being black has also been embarrassing, that a land he secretly calls his motherland is so scandalized with infamous scams.

Though he has often been embarrassed by the 419 fraudsters and advance-fee scam, perpetrated by Nigerians, he has always felt the victims got what they deserved. If they were not dishonest themselves why would they fall victim to a ploy to transfer illegally obtained large sums of money they were told belonged to someone who had died in a plane crash or shipwreck, to their bank accounts? Though the media often condemns Nigerians for their confidence tricks and scams, he has always secretly admired them even though he has also, always been embarrassed by the media coverage of their nefarious activities.

He has also heard of the bountiful mineral resources and oil in Africa, especially in Nigeria. He has seen and heard of wealthy Nigerians who come to America to buy expensive cars and furniture to take back home as if Nigerians back home were incapable of making simple things like furniture! Nigerians and Angolans often brag about the wealth that abound back home in their countries; and yet they still come to America. If only he could go to Nigeria and Angola to see for himself!
To the black man in America, Nigeria is a country so well spoken about by the many Nigerians living in America that he maintains a secret urge to visit. He never ceases to wonder why several Nigerians continue to arrive on American shores and soils everyday looking for greener pastures.

If the Pastures of Nigeria are so green why are Nigerians sacrificing so much to come to America? Why do they come to America to do odd jobs with so much education they claim to have when their country is flowing with oil and gold?

And then there is terrorism in the northeast of Nigeria and he often reads of how Boko Haram invades villages and cities in the northern part of Nigeria and how the Nigerian military is unable to combat the jihadists. He reads about the corruption of Nigerian government officials and how they often loot government treasuries to enrich themselves. He watches Nollywood, the Nigerian version of Hollywood and sees the extravagantly built beautiful homes and expensive cars on display amid squalor, poor roads and inadequate or nonexistent electricity. He has often wondered why the Nigerian government does not try to use the huge revenue it gets from oil to develop the roads and amenities in the country. Perhaps it wouldn't be a bad place to visit if the place was worth visiting. But he fears that he might fall victim of kidnapping, armed robbery and worst of all, the Ebola virus!

And then in all the confusions, he feels trapped with nowhere to go. The Jews could go back to Israel when things don't work out wherever they are. The Irish could go back to Ireland. He has read of how the Nazis, under Adolf Hitler, drove German Jews out of Germany and how the Austrian-born German politician killed and gassed many Jews in an attempt to get rid of the Jews in Germany. Suppose a white supremacist, and racist, like Adolf Hitler, becomes President of the United States as Hitler became the leader of the Nazi Party and Chancellor of Germany, and starts to kill and gas blacks like Hitler did to Jews, in Germany? Where would he go? He often asks himself. After all, the Jews had a place to run to, but where will the blacks run to? Africa is unsettled and still backward, despite all the rumored oil wealth.

And then amid all the worries that occupy his thoughts, he thinks about Ebola and how it has infected over 30,000 lives in sub-Saharan Africa. Why can't famine, diseases, misery, and ill-luck leave Africa alone? Why does Africa continue to be the home of the worst type of bad things? Why is everything bad, black? He often wonders. But despite his mind's odysseys, he is yet to find a comforting answer to his many questions.

Just when he thought he had some questions about Africa answered, he is faced with a new one. Just when he thought he knew how Africa inherited its problems, Ebola entered the equation. The Ebola epidemic completely changed his perception of Africa. Yesterday, Liberia was constantly in the news; about how Ebola was wiping out the citizenry; and how dead people littered the streets, to no end. He had read in the papers that schools were closed indefinitely and the borders closed. And then, just as it had started, it had suddenly subsided with the Liberian government lifting the state of emergency, and opening its borders and schools. Though the Liberian president said the country would be Ebola-free by December 2014, there were still some remnants of new infections in the country, months later.

Ebola still continues to ravage the lives of Liberians in 2015, albeit in a small scale. The President, Ms Ellen Johnson Sirleaf, said there had been fewer reports of new infections. Liberia will have to be free of Ebola for a period of 42 days without new infections for it to be Ebola free, according to the United Nations. But she had reopened the borders and had even allowed the senate election that had been earlier postponed to take place.

According to the New York Times, Liberia will go ahead with the senate election that had been delayed by the scare of Ebola. With the ban on political gatherings lifted and the senate election allowed to proceed, Liberia had sent a message to the world that there was no longer any need for tourists and investors to avoid the country; that it was now safe to visit and invest. Liberia has been hard hit with near economic collapse when the border had been closed and curfew had been imposed to contain the Ebola disease.

The Ebola disease and scare almost crippled the Liberian economy with workers, especially healthcare workers, abandoning their posts for lack of wages and salaries. It was reported that a lot of healthcare workers and government employees had not been paid their salaries and wages for several months. Some, according to the media, had abandoned their jobs for fear of Ebola. Healthcare workers who were scared of exposure to Ebola had left their jobs. "Lots of indigenous healthcare workers have died from exposure to Ebola patients," one government official was reported saying. And to add to the already bad situation, there were no protective gears and clothing when the Ebola disease had first hit Liberia, and many healthcare workers, including nurses and the few available doctors, had died from the disease.

The World Health Organization would later confirm that the rate of infection had subsided in Liberia. "New Ebola infections in virus-ravaged Liberia appear to be declining for the first time in months," the World Health Organization said, after it became clear that Ebola had slowed down; due to the efforts of the government to contain the disease and the international help the government of Liberia had received. Western countries had provided protective gears, medical facilities, including the influx of foreign healthcare workers.

According to the Washington Post, reports of slower infections had initially been met with skepticism by officials who felt the decline in new infections was due to poor data collection. It was hard to believe that a country that was reportedly having over 10,000 new infections every week would suddenly have such a reduced rate of infections. It was just a month ago that the country was overwhelmed with the Ebola crisis, when President Ellen Johnson Sirleaf made a clarion call to the president of the United States, Barack Obama, for help to stop the spread.

And the United States president, President Barack Obama, had responded by sending over 3,000 troops and medical equipment to the country. Several medical clinics and equipment were provided by the Obama administration to the Liberian government to help it fight the disease. Other countries such as Britain, France, Germany, Cuba, amongst others, had donated money and equipment to help fight the disease. Though several skeptics, including health officials, were surprised that the rate of infection had declined in Liberia, not many were surprised because of the international presence in the country helping to fight and contain the disease.

Officials with the World Health Organization had cautioned that though the rate of infection has slowed, the danger was still very palpable and tangible. There was the reported case of genetic mutation. Scientists, according to the media, warned that potential Ebola treatments could be hindered by mutations in the virus. The genetic changes may make it seemed as if the rate of new infections has slowed when it was actually undergoing genetic mutation in the virus. The genetic mutation in the Ebola disease could change the way the disease is contracted as it could become airborne, scientists warned. Scientists also warned that Ebola may become symptomless in its new genetic mutation.

The World Health Organization also cautioned that Ebola was unpredictable, that though it has declined, it could surge at anytime in West Africa, especially in the affected countries. "But Liberians are happy and eager to return to their normal lives that had been disrupted and ruined by Ebola," one Liberian government official was reported saying. Bruce Aylward, assistant director-general in charge of the Ebola response with the World Health Organization thinks people should not take Ebola for granted that it could easily surge. According to Aylward "it's like saying your pet tiger is under control," when it remains palpably dangerous. The Ebola disease, according to Aylward remains "very dangerous."

In an earlier prediction, Aylward had said if concerted and serious efforts were not made to combat and contain the Ebola epidemic that 5,000 to 10,000 new Ebola infections would start to occur, starting in December 2014, in the affected countries of Liberia, Sierra Leone and Guinea. International health officials and epidemiologists had earlier made the same gloomy prediction a month before "there would be catastrophically high numbers of Ebola cases without a robust response."

In confirming the decline in new infections of Ebola in Liberia, Aylward attributed the reduced rate of new infections to the increase in the rate of safe burials, success in finding people who may have been exposed to Ebola patients, and aggressive government campaign to make people aware of the danger of Ebola. The World Health Organization continues to emphasize the importance of safe burials. Unsafe burials had, reportedly, been one of the reasons for the high rate of infections in Liberia, when the Ebola outbreak had first occurred and was at its height. The World Health Organization cautioned that if the practice of safe burials was not consistently practiced that new outbreaks could flare up in places where the disease had been successfully contained and prevented.

Since the latest outbreak in sub-Saharan Africa, the World Health Organization has estimated that over 30,000 infections have occurred in the three affected countries of Liberia, Sierra Leone and Guinea. In five days alone, officials with the World Health Organization said over 3,000 new cases had occurred in the three countries. Out of the 30,000 cases of new Ebola infections, over 11,000 deaths have occurred in the three countries. Healthcare workers have also been hard-hit with over 600 infected, and with over 300 reported deaths in the three affected sub-Saharan African countries. Officials continue to remain cautious, because of the shifty nature of Ebola; that it often subsides in some places while flaring up in other places. For example it has shifted from Liberia where it had temporarily faded and moved to Sierra Leone where it has recently flared up.

The Obama administration had kept its promise to build treatment units, and had sent over 3,000 troops to complete the construction of 17 new Ebola treatment centers in Liberia. Though the U.S. focus had been primarily focused on Liberia, in part due to the clarion call made by the Liberian President Ellen Johnson Sirleaf, and also because Liberia had been the country hardest-hit by the disease before it recently shifted to Sierra Leone where it is currently raging, the U.S. is also helping other countries in the region to help curb the disease.

In the western border of Liberia lies Sierra Leone where Ebola has shifted its raging epidemic of increased infections; and where more infections than previously reported, continue to occur daily. The Guardian reported that "A fresh outbreak of Ebola in a part of Sierra Leone where the virus was thought to have been contained has raised fears of a new, uncontrolled infection chain that could send the death toll soaring." With Ebola having infected over 6,338 and claimed 2,510 lives in Sierra Leone, the fear is that Ebola infection is now on the increase in Sierra Leone, even though reports abound that it has slowed down.

The new fear facing the world is how the Ebola virus continues to mutate and shift to where it had once subsided. The remote district of Koinadugu which had not been affected when Ebola first occurred has now become the source of new infections in Sierra Leone. The Guardian reported that over 50 corpses were collected by the Red Cross for medical burial. All the corpses were reportedly due to Ebola related deaths. Two months before, health officials with the World Health Organization had thought the rate of new infections had slowed down in Sierra Leone. It was a major surprise that the disease made a comeback in Sierra Leone after it had subsided in Liberia.

Was the Ebola infection really contained in Sierra Leone or the report of a reduced infection was due to lack of reliable data about the rate of Infection in that country? According to the World Health Organization, Ebola had been "kept at bay," in many areas in Sierra Leone for a while until the recent new infections and subsequent deaths from the disease. In places like Koinadugu the people in that district have been reportedly self-quarantining themselves to contain the spread of the disease.

Scientists and health experts indicated that complacency and unsafe burials may have been responsible for the new infections in areas like Freetown, Nenie and Kabala. The Red Cross, according to the Guardian, continues to collect dead bodies from villages to villages for medical burials in the districts most affected such as the Nenie fiefdom.

The biggest problem facing health officials in Sierra Leone, according to the Guardian, is the inability of health officials to track down those who have been in contact with those who have contracted the disease in remote places where many new infections have occurred and where many are being monitored for the 21 day incubation period.

African villages and towns are often difficult to monitor because of inadequate amenities such as electricity and good passable roads. The Koinadugu district is close to the country's border with Guinea where Ebola outbreak had first occurred, and the district reportedly has an estimated population of over 260,000, that is susceptible to new infections. If the new infections are not contained, health officials feared that the remote villages and towns within the district of Koinadugu could further spread the disease outside the district and possibly back to Guinea where the disease had subsided and contained to a large extent.

Other areas in Sierra Leone that health officials with the World Health Organization worry new infections could spread much faster are the districts of Bombali and Port Loko, because of the lack of treatment centres and medical facilities to treat infected patients in the areas. Most of the Western countries that have shown interest in helping to contain and prevent the disease have shifted their interests elsewhere to troubled spots in the world since the infections in Liberia subsided, one health official said.

While the interests had been on Liberia with hitherto most infections, the virus has quietly reared elsewhere, with new infections in Sierra Leone. In districts like Bombali and Pork Loko, there are hardly healthcare workers to treat Ebola patients. And worst of all, there are fewer nurses and doctors. And the few nurses and doctors, according to local health officials, do not have protective gears and clothing to even protect them in their line of work.

The Guardian reported that the new surge in infections in the districts of Koinadugu, Bombali and Pork Loko had been caused by an infected man who had travelled to the eastern province of Sierra Leone for a funeral, where he had been exposed to an unsafe burial. Unsafe burials, according to the World Health Organization, is responsible for the upsurge of new infections in several parts of Sierra Leone; just as it had been the case in Liberia before the process of cremation was introduced in that country.

With over four cases of new infections and deaths on a daily basis, Sierra Leone appears on the verge of bringing Ebola back to world headlines, one health official observed. "Life has been very difficult for healthcare workers, with 11 of our doctors dead from Ebola it has not been easy," one health official said. The Sierra Leonean government, like the Liberian government, is waiting for the international community for help when the government could initiate safety measures to contain the spread of the disease just like the Guinean government had done. As always with African governments, there is a tendency to be dependent on outside help for simple measures, one Sierra Leonean nurse stated.

Another problem facing African countries, especially sub-Saharan African countries, is unnecessary red-tape and bureaucracy. There are countries for example that would like to help but because of government lukewarm attitude towards decision making, and in approving measures necessary to combat the disease, it has been difficult, one Cuban team leader said.

The Cuban medical team had reportedly been trying to start a new medical clinic to treat Ebola patients but government policies have essentially made it impossible, in Sierra Leone. The Cubans eventually built a medical facility in the area but many lives could have been saved had there not been a delay in approving the project.

Chapter 17

The 21st Century Ebola vs 14th Century Black Death

Ebola, like modern infectious diseases and terrorism, continues to defeat efforts to contain and eradicate it in sub-Saharan Africa. Frustrated and financially strapped sub-Saharan African countries that see Ebola as a roadblock to their economic survival have declared themselves to be Ebola free, even when there is every indication that Ebola is still raging in their countries. In Liberia for example, though the government asserted that the rate of new infections has slowed, there are reports of new infections every day. The government of that country, according to health officials, prematurely declared that the rate of new infections has slowed down when it has only shifted from one region of the country to the other.

As of March 1, 2015, there had been no new infections in over a week in Liberia, according to the World Health Organization. But Liberia will need to be free of new infections for 42 days to be free of Ebola.

In Sierra Leone, where the government has made feeble efforts to contain the disease for example, new infections continue to make headlines every day. A recent World Health Organization's report indicated that new Ebola infections are on the rise and not on the wane as earlier reported in various media outlets. International monitoring organizations have warned that the number of new infections may be underreported by as much as 50%, which means that the Ebola virus may be claiming more lives than previously admitted to, by the governments of the three affected countries of Liberia, Sierra Leone and Guinea.

Since the beginning of December 2014, according to doctors without borders, the rate of new infection continues to rise because of lack of concerted international efforts to support containment and prevention of the Ebola disease in West Africa. There is every indication that the rate of new infections will surpass the summer 2014's infection, unless drugs are made available to the affected countries in West Africa.

Experts also predicted that by the time a new clinic is finally opened in Port Loko that the disease would have spread to several communities in that district because of the delay in establishing medical facilities and getting needed healthcare workers in that part of Sierra Leone. Though Ebola drugs are currently at the experimental stage, they still need to be made available to West Africa where Ebola has infected over 30,000 people and where over 11,000 people have died of the disease.

In its recent assessment of the state of the disease in Sierra Leone, Doctors without Borders/Medecins Sans Frontieres (MSF) stated that the country needs over 4,000 beds than the 500 beds it currently has to admit those newly infected. And since there is very little international and western presence in Sierra Leone, compared with Liberia, more people continue to die from the disease, one indigenous healthcare worker said. Though countries like Nigeria, Cuba and several other poor countries have sent a handful of healthcare workers to help fight the disease, there is not enough medical equipment and facilities to make their efforts effective, a health official said.

The United States has mostly concentrated its efforts in Liberia where the rate of new infections has slowed down; but Sierra Leone continues to face crisis, for lack of international support. There are fewer beds, and most of all, there are fewer doctors and nurses in the country. The country needs more nurses and doctors to combat the disease. Since 11 doctors have already died in the country, other doctors will be hesitant to join the efforts to fight the disease; unless drugs are made available to cure the doctors and nurses when they do get infected.

The problem facing Sierra Leone, according to the World Health Organization, is the increased mortality rate of doctors and nurses in that country. Since the recent outbreak in Sierra Leone, over 12 indigenous doctors have been infected with 11 dead. To start with, there is already a drastic shortage of doctors; and the increased risks the few available doctors face makes it discouraging for the others to risk their lives to treat Ebola patients in that country.

According to ABC News, "Ebola has taken a particular toll on health workers, killing more than 350, depleting the ranks of doctors and nurses in countries that already had too few to begin with. Because Ebola is spread by body fluids, it is only transmitted through close contact. It is often called the 'caregivers' disease' because those infected are typically family members caring for the sick or health workers treating them." The rate of infections cannot be stopped by West African countries alone, without the help of rich Western countries.

If the West has been serious with its commitment to prevent and contain Ebola in sub-Saharan Africa, experimental drugs and adequate protective gears and clothing would have been made available to the health ministries of the effected countries. If drugs and equipment are made available to West Africa, doctors currently helping to fight the disease will be embolden to put in more efforts. But when they see more and more of their colleagues dying of the Ebola disease and there is no help forthcoming from rich and advanced Western countries, there will be reduced inclination for the doctors to risk their lives.

And when the brave African doctors start to die in large numbers because of their exposure to the disease and lack of Ebola drugs, then there will be increased new infections and deaths, one local epidemiologist said.

"When the disease travelled to the United States through Thomas Eric Duncan and got people infected there was interest on the part of the West," one Sierra Leonean healthcare worker said. If the West does not continue to try to fund more experimental drugs in West Africa, there will be more deaths and there "will be more Thomas Eric Duncan travelling to the West to spread the disease," a Liberian carpenter said.

Though wealthy donors have reportedly been donating money towards providing medical equipment and protective gears, there is the need for more cash donations from wealthy individuals and countries. In several districts in Sierra Leone, there is the need for more beds for patients; and protective gears and clothing for healthcare workers. Providing protective gears and clothing will help prevent more deaths among healthcare workers. And if the West would make the Zmapp drug readily available to treat the brave doctors and nurses currently in the field, fewer of them will be dying than currently occurs.

The death of the 11th doctor, Dr. Victor Willoughby, in Sierra Leone, was due to lack of Ebola drug to treat him when he had first contracted the disease. If the drug had been readily available the doctor's life would have been saved from the disease. By the time the drug arrived from the West, it was already too late. Dr. Brima Kargbo, Sierra Leone's chief medical officer, who had seen more of his colleagues succumb to death through Ebola, said the death of Dr. Willoughby "was a major loss to Sierra Leone."

It is not only a major loss to Sierra Leone it is a loss to West Africa, Africa, and to the world. Without the courage of brave doctors like Dr. Willoughby the disease would have probably claimed more lives in West Africa.

The death of a senior doctor like Dr. Willoughby was a blow to junior colleagues whom he was a mentor to. Dr. Willoughby was reportedly an inspiration to the physicians and medical personnel in Sierra Leone; and his death was a big shock and blow to those who depended on him for moral support, among the medical professionals in that country. There will no doubt be fear among the medical professionals left behind that they are next to die. If their senior colleague could so easily succumb to death through Ebola, what hope do they have?

One of the reasons given for the experimental drug not being available to West Africa was because the drug was waiting for FDA's approval. "Though it doesn't make sense for infected medical professionals to have to wait for drugs from overseas to get treated, it is just that the drugs are not ready for the market," a health official with the World Health Organization said. "Regardless of the experimental stage of the drugs, they should still be made available to infected doctors in West Africa," a Sierra Leonean nurse said. Adequate medical equipment and protective gear should be made available to protect those who are risking their lives in the field; since the drugs are not ready.

The West doesn't have to send their own citizens to West Africa to treat Ebola patients. They can financially support the brave African doctors and nurses in the field by providing needed drug to treat them when they get infected with the disease. If they can use the experimental drugs for infected American doctors in America, they can also use the drugs for infected West African doctors in West Africa. The world has 1800 billionaires, and is producing more everyday; some of those wealthy individuals can donate a fraction of that money to provide drugs and medical equipment to the poor and infected countries in West Africa. Rather than be donating money to meaningless causes, and research on cure for less dangerous diseases, wealthy individuals around the world can put their money where it is most useful, to fight infectious diseases like Ebola.

If serious efforts are not made to combat the disease, there will be more deaths to follow the ones that have already occurred in West Africa. And as has been proven with Thomas Eric Duncan, Ebola does not care where it strikes. It can strike anywhere in the world, regardless of the wealth and power of the country. It was proven with Duncan that Ebola can travel anywhere, when the Liberian unknowingly brought the disease to Dallas. It can happen again. The worst part of Ebola is that it does not often show right away. Sometimes it can take days if not longer to show, as happened with Thomas Eric Duncan.

Duncan had left Liberia on September 19, 2014, and was screened for the disease at the airport, before departure; and did not have the symptoms. He was also screened at the airport in the United States and did not display any symptom of the virus, until he was firmly settled in his destination, on September 26, 2014, when he started to display the symptoms. Other travellers could take the disease to the comforts of those rich Western countries if they do not make concerted efforts to contain and prevent the disease in West Africa.

It was not long ago when people who had travelled to, and returned, from Dallas were being put on a mandatory 21 day incubation period because they had travelled to that city! It can happen again. Just like a school teacher was put on a 21 day incubation period for travelling back home to her native Tanzania for vacation, even though that country did not have Ebola, so it can happen to the countries in the West if the disease is not eradicated with serious efforts.

History has proven that the world cannot take another disaster as happened with the Black Death when millions of Europeans were wiped out by the plague that was caused by a severe epidemic of bubonic plague that causes an inflammatory swelling of a lymph gland in the groin, in the 14th century. The Black Death was not preventable at the time of its outbreak due to little or nonexistent scientific knowledge about epidemics, and plagues. Unlike Ebola that was easily identified when the outbreak first occurred in 1976, the Black Death was not easily identified and would claim the lives of an estimated 2 million Europeans in less than two years between 1348 and 1350.

Since there was no way to contain the disease it had spread like wildfire, infecting and killing its victims within days of infections. Just like Ebola, it was a dangerous plague that was easily spread through contacts; but unlike Ebola, it was airborne, its contamination was widespread throughout the European continent.

The Black Death had originated from Asia just like Ebola had originated from sub-Saharan Africa. The arrival of the Black Death had initially been perceived with confusion and fear. Patients of the disease had easily succumbed to it because of lack of understanding of the disease. And since lack of medical knowledge pervaded every nook and cranny of Europe, lives were lost to the plague.

There were no medical equipment and protective gear to prevent the spread of the Black Death so the plague reached an epidemic proportion. England and the rest of Europe were helpless; and the plague was first thought to have been caused by fleas carried by rats that travelled in merchant ships. Recent scientific and archaeological evidence proved that it would have been impossible for fleas, carried by rats, to have caused so many deaths. The medieval belief that people bitten by rats carrying fleas in the 14th century were infected with the disease was discarded using modern medical and scientific analysis.

According to English scientists and archaeologists, the disease had to be airborne to spread as fast as it did in the 14th century. Human remains that were examined and analyzed by forensic scientists and archaeologists indicated that fleas could not have been responsible for the plague that spread as fast as the Black Death. It had to be an airborne disease, the study suggested. Another finding was that people who were malnourished were especially susceptible to the disease because it was said to prey on low immune system.

Unlike the Ebola that causes abdominal pains, hemorrhagic bleeding, dehydration, and transmitted through body fluids, blood, and kisses, the Black Death was airborne and transmitted through sneezes and coughs. Like the Ebola, death from the Black Death was often quick as it often claimed its victims within days. The disease would often spread into lungs where death was quickest. The mystery of the disease causing the Black Death baffled Europeans for many centuries up till the 19th century when it faded.

Like the Ebola virus that has reoccurred several times since its first outbreak in 1976, the Black Death reoccurred several times between the 14th and 19th centuries, claiming millions of lives as it spreads through sneezes and coughs. The symptoms of the Black Death were often signs of lumps in the armpits and groin. The disease would often progress to other parts of the body as black spots on limbs such as arms, thighs and legs. Death was usually within days.

Though the Black Death disease was airborne and was spread through coughing and sneezing, patients did not display fever or any symptoms related to flu or cold that is usually associated with Ebola. The belief that the rats that carried the fleas that caused the Black Death came from merchant ships that arrived from Asia to Europe was disproven but not altogether ruled out, according to the analysis done on the remains of victims. It was just that it did not add up that fleas were capable of causing so many deaths among Europeans in the 14th century. One undisputed fact was that millions of Europeans died from the disease, thereby significantly reducing the population of Europe during that era.

Like Ebola that is easily spread through contacts and body fluids, the Black Death killed many Europeans in the 14th century because of the proximity of homes, towns and cities during those centuries. One of the reasons, according to forensic scientists, was that contagious diseases were unheard of prior to the outbreak of the Black Death. Lack of experience with contagious diseases exposed several victims who unknowingly transmitted the disease to others, resulting in many deaths.

According to archaeological and forensic findings, the Black Death could have been avoided if people did not live so close to each other in cities and towns. If those who had contracted the disease had been quarantined like those who are contracting Ebola today, many lives would have been saved, scientists opined. Another preventive method that could have saved lives would have been simple measures of covering the mouth and nose when coughing and sneezing. But because of inexperience with contagious diseases it was not reportedly known to those 14th century Europeans that quarantining the sick and following simple guidelines of covering the mouth and nose would have saved their lives.

Like Ebola, ignorance played a significant role in the spread of the Black Death in the 14th century. Historians opined that blind religious beliefs rather than facts led so many to die from the disease. Those who became victims of the disease causing Black Death thought the disease was due to a curse that came about as a result of their sinful ways. They thought that inflicting self-administered punishments would solve their problems. Lots of Europeans resorted to flagellation when all else had failed; and because they did not know what else to do, according to historians.

Most of the people infected with the disease causing Black Death had thought that repentance through flagellation would spare them from the death caused by Black Death. For millions of Europeans who were yet to be infected it was felt that the only way to escape death was to show unconditional love to God. And to prove their readiness to turn a new leaf, they resorted to flagellation, but alas, the problem was just a simple measure of self-quarantine and avoidance of those who had fallen sick, or contracted the disease.

Historians believe medieval leaders of the 14th century did not have experience about preventing the disease and isolating the sick from those uninfected. Unlike the leaders of medieval Europe, African leaders who were faced with the outbreak of Ebola in 1976 quickly knew to separate those infected from those uninfected. Many areas in sub-Saharan Africa were quarantined to prevent the disease from spreading to other parts in sub-Saharan Africa, in 1976. And during the 2014 outbreak, Liberia, Sierra Leone and Guinea closed their borders, imposed curfews and quarantined those who had contracted the disease in order to contain the infection. But this sense of simple leadership measure was not known to the leaders of medieval Europe at the time.

The Black Death, like Ebola, left its economic upheavals as fields were left unploughed and crops uncultivated as sharecroppers became victims of the disease. The Black Death also led to the shortage of sharecroppers in Medieval Europe, and with that, untold hunger. The Black Death also brought untold hunger in Europe which may have also caused many deaths because the grounds were left untilled and uncultivated. Though reliable data was not available to separate the number of those who died from hunger from those who had died from the disease, it was felt that those who died in that era died because of the Black Death. Historians believe a lot of Europeans died from hunger as well as from the disease, in the 14th century.

If leaders of the 21st century do not make concerted efforts to eradicate Ebola, it could easily become another Black Death. According to the United Nations, world leaders need to make serious efforts to contribute drugs and medical equipment to sub-Saharan Africa in order to contain the disease. Failure to do so, the World Health Organization cautioned, could lead to the disease moving from West Africa to the West, just like the Black Death moved from Asia to Europe in the 14th century, and subsequently claimed several millions of lives. Though desperate laws and decrees were made to contain the Black Death, they were mostly limited to peasants and farmers who had to take permission from their leaders to leave their villages and towns. This method of containing the disease did not have any significant effect on the disease as it had spread even more rapidly throughout Europe in the 14th century. Some of the provisions of the feudal system were unenforceable due to the shortage of labour as most of the peasants and farmers were restricted from leaving their villages.

To combat the shortages of labour, the lords or leaders of the era had to introduce the Statute of Labourers, of 1351 to combat labour shortage and to reduce hunger by making it impossible for labourers to look for better paying labour among farmers willing to pay more.

The Statue of Labourers was enacted to curb the movement of labourers to look for better pay and also to make labourers available to farmers who needed their services in their farms. The Statute of Labourers of 1351 became necessary when it was felt that the feudal law prevented labourers from leaving their villages without permission. It also gave the labourers the freedom to find better pays for their labour. Both the feudal law and the Statue of Labourers were enacted to prevent food shortages rather than to contain the spread of the disease causing Black Death.

Like now with Ebola in the 21st century, the Black Death was not seriously tackled as it should have been, experts opined. Had the European leaders of the 14th century quarantined those infected from those uninfected and separated the areas infected from the areas uninfected, the disease causing Black Death would have been contained. But that did not happen. The emphasis was placed on trying to prevent hunger, and to cultivate more crops than to contain and prevent the disease.

The source of the Ebola disease is still linked to fruit-bats that feed on ripe fruits, pollen, and nectar that is said to usually use visual navigation rather than echolocation. According to CDC the Ebola virus is usually spread through direct contact with blood and body fluids of an infected person. Unlike the disease that caused the Black Death, Ebola is not airborne and is not spread through the air, water, food and mosquitoes. Forensic scientists and archaeologists that examined the remains of the victims of Black Death opined that the disease was spread through sneezing and coughing, and that it was an airborne disease that resulted in the bubonic plague that first occurred in Asia and later spread to Europe in the 14th century. The Ebola disease bears some parallel symptoms to the disease that caused the Black Death. Both epidemics had resulted from developing and poor countries. Ebola had started in sub-Saharan Africa and has infected some in the West who had survived the disease. Ebola continues to infect Westerners who travel to the infected parts of West Africa in Liberia, Sierra Leone and Guinea, to treat infected Africans in the region.

The latest Westerner to be infected as of late December 2014 was a Scottish nurse who had been helping to treat infected patients in Sierra Leone.

The Scottish nurse, Pauline Cafferkey, had contracted Ebola in Sierra Leone, where she was treating patients with Ebola. She had arrived in the U.K. without any symptoms of the disease; but that would later change when she started experiencing the symptoms. According to the Morning Star News, nurse Cafferkey became the first person to be diagnosed with Ebola in the U.K. after she had returned with Ebola from West Africa. Morning Star News wrote that the nurse had not displayed any symptoms of Ebola when she had arrived in the U.K. but had fallen ill days later and had tested positive for the Ebola virus when she had been tested. The nurse "had returned to Glasgow on Sunday via Casablanca and London from working with Ebola patients in Sierra Leone."

The unwillingness of Western countries to provide needed medical equipment and drugs to prevent the disease in West Africa continues to make the West susceptible to the disease. Nurse Cafferkey is the latest Westerner to contract the disease. Another British healthcare worker is still being monitored for the disease, also in the U.K. The bubonic plague that caused the Black Death had also been carried by infected people into Europe in the 14th century. And the lack of medical knowledge about the disease had made it spread to where it claimed millions of lives in Europe in the 14th century.

"The pick and choose method of treating Ebola patients by Western countries is partly responsible for the increased spread of the disease," an African health official said. Infected Westerners are treated with more care and attention than infected non-westerners. When a Scottish nurse, Cafferkey, tested positive, she was immediately flown by a military plane to London, using a specially equipped ambulance "with a police escort to the high-level isolation unit at London's Royal Free Hospital, in accordance with established procedure" for dealing with infectious diseases such as Ebola. The nurse was treated with utmost care, with proper care and attention. Protective gear and clothing were provided to make sure the healthcare workers attending to her were protected. "A designed tent with controlled ventilation surrounds the bed and allows medical staff to provide care without any physical contact with the patient to contain the infection," the media reported.

The idea of providing needed care and equipment is to make sure the disease is contained. In sub-Saharan Africa, healthcare workers are exposed to the disease without proper and adequate protective clothing. In Sierra Leone alone, 12 doctors were infected with 11 succumbing to death by Ebola. In the West, especially in the United States, no American healthcare worker has died from Ebola even though more than six Americans were infected with Ebola, and were treated in the U.S.

While special care is often applied when handling patients infected with Ebola in the West, the same cannot be said of the healthcare workers in West Africa who often work with inadequate protective clothing and gear, in Sierra Leone, Liberia and Guinea. "The Ebola disease will likely spread to the West at the same rapid rate it is spreading, if the West does not come to the aid of sub-Saharan African countries," a doctor with Doctors without Borders said in a recent interview.

Though reports abound that "the U.S., Britain and other countries around the world have mobilized in an effort to combat the largest outbreak of Ebola in West Africa," little of that mobilization of effort is really seen in West Africa. In Sierra Leone, many districts are still without medical clinics and facilities to treat those infected with Ebola. In some cases, in the remotest part of some districts in Sierra Leone, unsafe burials are still prevalent. Unsafe burials can lead to increased spread of Ebola, according to the World Health Organization, and it doesn't seem enough effort is being made by the West to help West African governments to eradicate the disease.

Just like the Black Death had rendered many Europeans helpless in the 14th century, so it will be for Westerners of the 14th century, if concerted efforts are not made to quickly contain the disease before it becomes a global disease that could claim millions of lives like the Black Death of the 14th century. Many scientists have compared the symptoms that cause Ebola with the symptoms that caused the Black Death in the 14th century.

Apart from Ebola and its associated stigma, other infectious diseases have surfaced that bore slight resemblance to the disease that caused millions of Europeans to die from Black Death in the 14th century. Enterovirus disease continues to make headlines for the havoc it has wreaked in several parts of the U.S. Unlike Ebola, enterovirus is a small virus that is comprised of ribonucleic acid and protein. It can be found in the respiratory secretions such as saliva, sputum, and nasal mucus, including the stool of an infected person. Also unlike Ebola, children are mostly susceptible to enterovirus.

Though enterovirus does not kill people the same way Ebola does, it is equally dangerous and can take lives within days. A recent study shows that enterovirus disease has killed over 16,000 in ten states, compared with deaths caused by Ebola.

The reason enterovirus is worth discussing in this page is because it can be as dangerous as any infectious disease if left unchecked and uncontained.

Chapter 18

Conclusions

Ebola continues to wreak havoc in West Africa, especially in Sierra Leone where new infections continue to surface in most of its 14 districts. Though Ebola has subsided in neighbouring Liberia where it was reportedly the country with the most infections and most deaths a few months ago, there are still ongoing infections albeit at a smaller scale. Western countries have pledged billions of dollars but the money does not appear to be making huge impacts as Ebola continues to claim lives in Sierra Leone, Guinea and Liberia. According to the World Health Organization, over 11,000 people have lost their lives to Ebola since its outbreak in West Africa.

The Geneva based agency stated that an estimated 3,915 deaths have occurred in Sierra Leone; 3,471 deaths in Liberia and 2,767 deaths in Guinea. In addition to the deaths in the three countries, the disease has also claimed the lives of more than 14 people outside the three countries. So far, Ebola has reportedly infected over 30,000 people across the world, with most of it in West Africa. A small proportion compared to the Black Death that claimed millions of lives in Europe and Asia in the 14th century.

Ebola, according to the United Nations, is often transmitted through body fluids such as blood, vomit and feces, among many others. Ebola death, according to Fox12 Oregon, represents a mortality rate of 39 percent. BBC News Africa reported that the fatality rate of Ebola can reach 90%, "with mortality rate of between 54% and 62%." If the trend is not immediately stopped, experts believe new infections will continue to resurface in places where it had subsided. To ensure that Ebola is contained and totally eradicated, West African countries must be assisted by wealthy Western countries with preventive and curative drugs.

So far, effective experimental drugs that have saved the lives of those who were infected in the U.S. and Europe have not been made available to West African countries to help them combat the disease. The West cannot make these effective drugs available to their own citizens only. Africans fighting the disease in West Africa need to also have access to these drugs. The excuse that the drugs are still at the experimental stage is not good enough as lives have been saved with the drugs, especially the Zmapp drug.

The World Health Organization recently reported that an Ebola vaccine developed by Canada's public health agency will be tested on humans in Guinea. According to the Wall Street Journal: "The United Nations' health agency said Thursday that Phase III trials of the rVSV-EBOV vaccine would begin in Basse Guinée, the region of Guinea that currently has the highest number of Ebola cases. Phase III trials are the last stage of human testing before drugs are submitted to regulators for approval."

While the effort to develop the rVSV-EBOV vaccine is commendable, the fact that it is being tested on humans poses another health risk as the disease could mutate and flare up to create new infections. It happened in 1976 when Belgian nuns injected pregnant women with vitamins that led to increased infections. It would have been safer if animals, rather than humans, were used for the testing.

The reported billions of dollars pouring into West Africa from Western donors need to be used in buying protective gears and clothing for healthcare workers in the three most affected countries of Liberia, Sierra Leone, and Guinea. Currently, most of the healthcare workers in Sierra Leone, Guinea and Liberia are often scantily clad with protection gears that are barely enough to protect them against the deadly disease. If the West is going to help stop the disease then they need to put their money and efforts in the right places.

Most districts in Sierra Leone do not have hospital beds and medical clinics for Ebola patients. In some cases the patients are forced to live at home with their relatives, thereby infecting those uninfected, and increasing the rate of infections. More medically equipped ambulance vehicles need to be provided to the Ebola hot zones so that the rate of infection can be reduced and possibly eradicated. Ebola related deaths among healthcare workers in the three countries reached unprecedented proportion with the death of the 11th doctor in Sierra Leone in December 2014. If the healthcare workers had had access to effective curative drugs, the lives of those 11 doctors would have been saved. West African countries need courageous doctors like those fighting the disease in the region. Exposing them to needless deaths and risks will only discourage others from helping to fight the disease.

The best hope West Africa and Western countries have of fighting the disease is to supply drugs and medical equipment to the affected countries in West Africa, not money. African leaders have, in the past, developed the habit of misappropriating funds. The billions of dollars pouring into West Africa to fight the disease should not be allowed to fall into the hands of those unscrupulous African leaders who have developed the knack for embezzling funds meant for good causes. The poor and the unprotected, including the courageous healthcare workers, are the ones exposed to the disease, not the rich and the elite.

The son of the president of Liberia who is a medical doctor is reportedly working in a clinic in Georgia while Ebola rages in his homeland. He reportedly refuses to go and join forces to help fight the disease in his home country, for fear of contracting the disease. If the president will not allow her son who is a qualified medical doctor to use his skill where it is most needed, why should other doctors risk their lives in Liberia and elsewhere in the region to fight the disease? It so happens that those doctors risking their lives in the Ebola hot zone in sub-Saharan Africa are doing so, not for money, but for the love of humanity. They answered the clarion call of the poor and the helpless for help; and they abandoned everything, including the safety and love of their family and loved ones, to treat those infected. Many of those brave and courageous doctors sacrificed their lives.

And there are those courageous healthcare workers from Cuba, Nigeria, U.S., U.K. and several other countries who have risked their lives; and continue to do so, to help treat the infected patients of Ebola in Sierra Leone, Liberia and Guinea. A British nurse, Will Pooley, who was infected with Ebola and who was cured of the disease, had returned to West Africa to continue the selfless sacrifice of saving lives. According to Sky News, Pooley said it is "something I have to do." He could have stayed back in England to enjoy the comfort and luxury of the English society but he chose to save lives in West Africa.

Selfless global citizens with conscience like nurse Pooley are the reason Ebola is still manageable. They could have stayed back in the luxury confines of the safety of their advanced countries and ignore those infected patients in West Africa like the son of the president of Liberia, James Sirleaf, who refused to go to Liberia to help save those infected with the disease. They knew that being a medical doctor means saving lives and doing so courageously.

And there are the nurses who have also risked their lives in West Africa. They left the comforts and safety of their countries to go to West Africa to treat those infected with Ebola in the region.

Will Ebola eventually go away and leave the sub-Saharan African shores? That question has been asked by so many Africans, and non-Africans, who see the Ebola scourge as a curse that has brought misery and untold hardship, including adding backwardness to the African continent. Ebola has proven to be resilient and hard to eradicate. Since its first outbreak in 1976, Ebola has often visited sub-Saharan Africa with its attendant havoc and deaths. In 2014 alone, Ebola wreaked deaths that claimed over 11,000 lives so far. And at the same token, the disease has infected over 30,000 people in West Africa. Countries like Liberia, Sierra Leone, and Guinea experienced the worst Ebola outbreak, with dead bodies littering the streets of Liberia at the height of its outbreak in the summer of 2014.

As if that wasn't enough, Africans at home and in the Diaspora were subjected to the most humiliating stigma ever experienced by any race on earth. In some cases, some Africans were fired from their jobs in their workplaces in the U.S. and in Europe. Some Africans who had mistakenly visited their homelands were made to stay off work for a 21 day incubation period until they were deemed healthy, and certified to be so, by a qualified doctor or CDC, to return to work. Many were asked not to return to work! For those Africans, life was difficult and miserable in their chosen homelands in the U.S. and Europe.

There was the case of an African nurse living in New York who was told not to return to work because her country, Liberia, was infected with Ebola. Her co-workers had refused to have anything to do with her because of her country of origin. Her only fault was being born in Liberia! And there were reported cases of Africans who owned businesses that were shunned by customers because of the Ebola scare.

For those African nurses who were fired from their jobs, and African business owners whose businesses were shunned because of the Ebola scare, the U.S. was not the same open-minded country they had fallen in love with, and had sacrificed everything they owned to come to. To them, it was a different U.S. – one that they were unfamiliar with. It was the U.S. that was a total stranger to them; that treated them like aliens from another planet, who were undeserving of living in their midst. For some, a life that was once very promising became endangered and threatened with insecurity and stark discrimination. These Africans were looked down upon, scorned, and openly humiliated. To make things worse, African doctors who gave up lucrative practices to fight Ebola in West Africa were denied access to experimental drugs and medical equipment. Some of these doctors died while treating Ebola patients. There was the case of Dr. Martin Salia, a Sierra Leonean who was living in the U.S. who went home to help combat Ebola. Dr. Salia had become ill in Sierra Leone while working in a hospital in that country. He had paid for his own medical transportation and flight back to the U.S. for treatment at the Nebraska Medical Centre where he expected a cure. Little did he know that cure will not be readily made available to him at the hospital! He died days after he had arrived at the hospital.

For Dr. Salia, death was not what he had bargained for, when he had used his hard-earned money to transport himself back to a country he trusted and loved, that he had come to call his home. Little did he know that being a doctor was not going to differentiate him from other Africans! Even his arrival was treated with marginalization. Unlike the other American doctors who had been infected with Ebola and were treated like heroes and given heroic welcome, he arrived like a thief in the night, without the same excitement that had met Dr. Brantly and Writebol. There were no fire trucks, police escorts, pomp and pageantry that his American counterparts who had contracted the same disease had received.

The worst part was that Dr. Salia did not even receive the same drugs that had been used to treat American Ebola patients in the same hospital. The lame excuse that was given for his death was that his infection had reached an advanced stage for any medical succour. His death was marked with somber as if there was little significance to him. Patients of lesser significance had received presidential embrace and reception; but not Dr. Salia who would only be remembered in a 2014 New Year's Day Parade, to celebrate his death and heroism!

And there was Thomas Eric Duncan who had travelled to the U.S. to marry his long-time fiancée; and to attend his son's graduation ceremony. Days before leaving Liberia, he had heroically helped transport a convulsive pregnant woman to the hospital where she was refused admission. He had also helped to transport the convulsive pregnant woman back home where she had died quietly in the night, for lack of medical attention and care. Her death had been ruled an Ebola-related death even though she was never tested nor confirmed to have Ebola. She was stigmatized with Ebola in death! And because Duncan had helped the pregnant woman who later died, Duncan who was reportedly diagnosed with Ebola, days after arriving in the U.S. on September 20, 2014; and days after helping the convulsive pregnant woman, would be accused of lying that he had had contact with anyone with Ebola. Duncan had been stigmatized with Ebola and left alone to die in an isolation unit at the Texas Presbyterian Hospital; where he had been placed on a ventilator and sedation until his organs failed!

Duncan was accused of bringing Ebola to the U.S. even though Ebola had already been brought to the U.S. by American healthcare workers returning from West Africa, long before his arrival. He was threatened with prosecution and legal repercussions for knowingly bringing Ebola to the shores of the United States. His country's government had threatened to prosecute him for infecting the U.S. with Ebola. It didn't matter that the immediate relatives of Duncan whom he had lived with never contracted Ebola!

And there was the case of the West African woman who had self-admitted herself to Ben Taub hospital in Houston, Texas, for cold, thinking the worst. The woman had immediately been isolated and the hospital evacuated, even though she hadn't tested positive for Ebola. Another West African travelling from Gabon was taken off an international flight because he had coughed while in the aircraft. He had immediately been quarantined for 21 days before he was allowed to proceed with his journey.

The Ebola scare did not only affect West Africans at an unprecedented rate but also damaged the psyche of Africans, especially sub-Saharan Africans. Ebola put Africa back in a blacklist the continent has been trying to improve over the years. The origin of several diseases and infections has always been attributed to Africa. HIV (human immunodeficiency virus infection and acquired immune deficiency syndrome) was said to have originated from Africa. Many Africans had contracted the disease and had subsequently died, in large numbers, at the beginning of the outbreak, before the rate of infection had subsided to a more manageable rate. Though not entirely eradicated, the rate of the infection had slowed down because of the preventive measures the World Health Organization introduced and also because of the awareness of the danger of promiscuity, and the reduced use of unsterilized intravenous needles.

The Ebola epidemic has been around almost as long as the HIV/aids epidemic has been around. Though HIV/aids had killed more people than Ebola during the apex of the disease, the scourge has also marginalized Africans who were reportedly avoided as publicly as they have been avoided during the apex of the Ebola infection.

While Ebola has created more damaging hypes and stereotypes than any other infectious disease in recent times, HIV/aids had also caused its own panic about associating with Africans during its height of infections. For a while in some states in the U.S., Africans and those involved with them were not allowed to donate blood. "My girlfriend was asked if she dates an African during a blood drive at her job, and when she said yes, she was told she couldn't donate blood," a Nigerian student said. For most Africans living in the U.S. in the 1990s, the stigma of the HIV/aids trailed their every endeavour. It was felt by all and sundry that one out of every 10 Africans had the HIV/aids infection. Towards the middle of the 1990s, and the beginning of the new millennial, the stigma had gradually reduced.

Just as Africans were smeared with the stigma of the HIV/aids so were African Americans in the United States. A CNN report of July 29, 2008 indicated that the Aids epidemic among African Americans in the United States was comparable and as "severe as in parts of Africa." Though the report was not a surprise, it added to the stigma that "AIDS in America today is a black disease." It was just a decade and a half ago that AIDS was an African disease. That stigma has since shifted to become a black disease in the millennia. A CDC data indicated that more than half of those living with HIV/AIDS in the U.S. are blacks; a number that is staggering just as it is shocking. It is shocking because the population of blacks is only 14.2% of the total U.S. population. Of that number, only 13.1% identified themselves as African Americans while the remaining percentage identified themselves as just blacks, according to the CDC.

"I can tell you that some blacks do not see themselves as African Americans because of the stigma that continues to trail and bedevil Africa. If Africa were to be a well organized continent with the countries in it well developed financially, those blacks that refused to identify themselves as African Americans would not have done so," a Nigerian student said. No one likes failure. The African continent, especially black Africa, is seen as a failure by some blacks in America.

To them it is a continent where nothing good comes out of. If it is not a disease sprouting out of Africa it will be famine or terrorism! Not to mention war and anarchy! "When you really look at it, why should any black in America who is barely surviving racial profiling, police brutality and marginalization, be saddled with the added stigma coming out of Africa? It is bad enough being a marginalized black in America. It is even worse to be tagged with the African problems of diseases, terrorism and wars," a Zambian nurse living in the U.S. said. The Zambian nurse was re-echoing the sentiment that had openly been expressed by several African Americans and blacks in the U.S.

While Africa has been marred by several setbacks such as HIV/AIDs, Ebola, terrorism, corruption and fraud, the continent has also been striving very hard, amid the detractions, to prove itself. Economically, many African countries are doing well, despite the odds that stack against them. Many African businesses and commerce continue to make global headlines because of the cutting edge competitiveness they have brought to the world stage of commerce. And in the last two decades many Africans have joined the ranks of the world's wealthiest individuals. Many Africans are so outstandingly successful that Africa is beginning to showcase itself as a continent to reckon with, despite its obvious setbacks.

The modern technology that has made life easy for Westerners is also being developed by Africans in Africa. Many Africans have developed computers and tablets that continue to make a difference and even compete, albeit at a smaller scale, with more advanced technologies.

If Africans will look inward instead of always looking outward for a better life, there will be less brain drain and wealth leaving the continent. African leaders need to use the resources available to them to create a better life for the citizenry, and to establish industries that will provide employment for the teeming youth population in Africa. If African leaders would channel most of the continuously embezzled wealth in African towards creating infrastructures and employment for the youth in the region, there will be less terrorism and armed robberies, as there will be less incentive for the youths to join armed robberies and terrorism. Most of all, the youth will not be gullible and susceptible to terrorist recruitments.

The high rate of unemployment among African youths has made them vulnerable to recruiters from al-Qaeda, ISIS, Boko Haram, al-Shabaab, and many nefarious organizations that target unemployed youths in Africa. For Africa to develop, African leaders must be unselfish and willing to not only enrich their own pockets but meaningfully contribute towards the development of their countries. The wisdom of John F. Kennedy, the 35th President of the United States, that Americans should "ask not what America will do for you, but what, together, we can do for the freedom of man," can also apply to Africans and African leaders. African leaders should be more concerned with what they can do for Africa rather than what they can do for themselves, in order to get Africa up and running like other continents of the progressive world in the 21st century.

Looking inward will enable Africans and African leaders to see where things have gone awry with the continent. They will also be able to see what they can "do for the freedom of man," especially the African children and youth that are being recruited and used for suicide bombings by Boko Haram in the northeast of Nigeria, and also in Somalia where Al-Shabaab continues to use children as militants and suicide bombers. African leaders can stop the trend by being relentlessly unselfish and willing to serve their nations rather than line their pockets with their countries' resources and revenues.

Apart from the Ebola epidemic, West Africa is also faced with reduced revenues as the oil glut threatens to once again set the continent back economically. As the U.S. becomes the highest oil producer in the world, surpassing Saudi Arabia, there is reportedly an ongoing oversupply of oil in the market. The reason for the oil glut is not entirely because the U.S. has surpassed Saudi Arabia as the leading oil producer in the world but because there is a low demand for oil in the oil market. Part of the reasons, according to experts, is due to the alternative energy and electric cars that are making their way into the automobile market, and also because more countries now produce oil than ever before. As supply chases few demands, the resultant effect will be a glut, because of the low demand for oil.

Though experts believe the oil stockpile and oversupply is only temporary as the volatile oil industry is known to be, West African countries will, in the meantime, have to grapple with the sudden fall in their budgeted revenues. West African countries like Nigeria, Angola, Libya and Algeria, largely depend on the oil revenue for over 90% of their expenditures, and other fiscal responsibilities. The absence of the once reliable enormous oil revenue will make those African countries more dependent on Western countries for aids and borrowing, to meet their fiscal responsibilities. The 21st century was supposed to be Africa's century to shine and grow, economically but the threat of Ebola and ongoing oil glut threatens to set the region back several years.

In the years Africa has come to be known as the Dark Continent, the continent has improved significantly. The economic output has grown exponentially while unemployment has been reduced proportionately. Before the advent of Ebola, African countries had a semblance of peace, save for the growing terrorism in the continent. The attendant prosperity, even though it was at a smaller scale, was much better than most economists predicted for African. The outbreak of Ebola created a new devastation that set Africa back by several years, so much so that the future of Africa has never been bleaker than it is today, in the first quarter of 2015.

Countries like Nigeria, Angola, Libya and Algeria depend on oil mostly for their foreign exchange earnings. In Nigeria for example, over 90% of its revenue comes from oil. In Angola, it is 95% while Libya and Algeria derive over 92% of their revenues from oil, according to the World Bank. With oil price plummeting like a house of cards, the once promising African economy faces greater economic disaster than in recent times.

As the United States gradually overtakes Saudi Arabia as the world's foremost oil producer in the world, African countries are finding themselves saddled with oil glut and oversupply. Oil producing countries like Nigeria and Angola that had calculated their present and future revenues on prices hovering around $100 per barrel have suddenly found their revenues reduced by more than 50% as supply outpaces demands. Nigeria is not only finding out that its economic growth has been hampered by the oil glut but also finding out that it cannot meet most of its financial obligations without resorting to borrowing. To meet its fiscal responsibilities, Nigeria will need to borrow more than 30% of its lost revenue (from oil), from International banks and the IMF.

Most observers have opined that the oil glut is an economic conspiracy to further weaken Africa and to make the continent more dependent on foreign aids. "The way I see it is that the West hates to see a prosperous Africa. The United Nations had predicted that Africa was on the rise, especially as most African countries' economies were growing at 7%, competing with countries like China whose growth rate hovers around 7.5% and the U.S.'s 5%," a U.K. based Nigerian economist said. Though the conspiracy theory is a little extended, the facts cannot be ignored that fracking in the U.S. is one of the reasons for the current oil glut.

Fracking or the process of injecting fluids into shale beds at high pressure in order to release oil resources such as petroleum and natural gas, has gained momentum in the U.S. as modern technology has made oil drilling from rocks and solid materials even more profitable. Though fracking is expensive, the process allows oil companies to drill oil from abundant and limitless shale beds. According to Bloomberg News, U.S. oil production has exceeded 7 million barrels of oil per day; the highest since March 1993. At 7 million barrels per day, the U.S. not only becomes the highest oil producer in the world but also becomes energy independent, as well as having a robust economic growth.

The U.S. Energy Department reports indicated that oil production in the U.S. has continued to grow year after year, with a weekly average rising to 7.002 million barrels a day. This unprecedented drilling technique now makes oil discoverable in every part of the country, one energy observer said. In 2013, the U.S. oil production was 1.16 million barrels per day less than it is now and continues to increase every month. In one year, between 2013 and 2014, oil production in the U.S. increased by 1.16 million barrels a day, and if the trend continues, expert predict that the U.S. will no longer have any reason to treat Saudi Arabia with the same reverence that it has done in the past. Saudi Arabia is still a significant ally of the U.S. as it remains one of the highest importers of U.S. goods.

As to whether energy independence in the U.S. will result in increased Africa dependence on foreign aids due to the global falling prices of oil will remain to be seen. The shift in U.S. energy needs will no doubt hurt oil producing countries in the developing countries. The U.S. will no longer be prone to OPEC's perennial oil embargos as was the case in the 1980s. With the U.S. meeting most, if not all, of its energy needs of about 83% in 2013 and over 85% in 2014, experts predict that oil production could grow as much as 9 million barrels per day in 2016. The increased use of horizontal drilling, hydraulic fracking will continue to unlock the limitless oil trapped in the bowels of the earth in places like North Dakota's Bakken shale. According to the Energy Department North Dakota's oil production increased by over 40% in 2013 while oil production also increased in Texas by over 30% in 2013. The oil production in Utah rose by over 20% during the same period as Texas and North Dakota. As more areas are being explored for hydraulic fracking and horizontal drilling, oil production will continue to grow at an unprecedented pace in the U.S.

African countries like Nigeria, Angola, Libya and Algeria will be faced with new challenges of how to find alternative foreign exchange earning sources as revenues from oil continue to plummet. The theory of a conspiracy that increased oil production in the U.S. is an attempt to make Africa more dependent and marginalized was debunked by economists and energy experts who opined that increased oil production in the U.S. has nothing to do with Africa. "The U.S. is trying to increase its production to boost its revenue and economic growth; and it has nothing to do with Africa or any country. It does not benefit the U.S. to see Africa or any country therein, to suffer. A suffering African continent can be a breeding ground for terrorism which can become another problem for the U.S.," an energy official with the U.S. Department of Energy said.

"I don't think anyone expected the magnitude of the change in global oil production in just one year," said Andy Lipow, president of Lipow Oil Associates LLC, a Houston-based consulting firm. "It's extraordinary." As the stockpiles of oil continue to increase, oil glut may be the norm in 2015 and onward, unless environmental concerns become a political issue. As Congress reopens its new 114th session on January 6, 2015, with a republican majority, there will be more debates over the controversial keystone pipeline. High oil prices may permanently become a thing of the past in the West. Though there has never been oil scarcity in the U.S. or Western countries, cheap oil prices at filling stations may become the norm.

African countries like Nigeria that always experience oil scarcity will continue to do so because of the absence of, or inadequate, refineries. Though Nigeria is the 6th oil producer in the world, oil scarcity is almost the norm in that country. The problem with Nigeria and other oil producing countries in Africa is that they export their oil only to import the same oil (refined), at exorbitant prices for local consumption! Rather than build refineries to refine their own oil, governments in Africa often prefer to import their own oil for local consumption! The problem, according to experts, will be how to fund imported oil for local consumption while grappling with falling oil prices in countries like Nigeria.

Can Nigeria and other African countries survive oil glut? Analysts believe oversupply of oil is only temporary as oil prices will eventually go up. "You have to understand that oil prices will not remain low for a long time; just as it did not remain high for a long time. Eventually the prices will go up. Right now, the oversupply has saturated the market, with low demands. And because the demand is lower than it was predicted to be, prices are forced to go down because there are very few buyers. Oil price is pretty much based on the law of demand and supply. When supply chases demand, prices often goes down. When demand chases supply, prices will go up and keep climbing," an oil analyst said.

The notion that oversupply of oil is a conspiracy to weaken the economies of African countries is as far-fetched as the accusation by Venezuelan government that McDonald is deliberately refusing to serve French fries as a conspiracy to deny Venezuelans French fries when the truth is that there is a shortage of potatoes in Venezuela. The current oil production in the U.S. is based on economic necessity and needs than on conspiracy. "There is no such thing as conspiring to overproduce in order to weaken another country's economy. I have heard that some Russian officials, including President Vladimir Putin, saying there is a conspiracy to weaken Russian's economy by the West – which is not true. I have never heard it said by any African government. If it is said, then it will be borne out of ignorance as there is no such policy among policymakers or oil companies in the U.S. to destabilize or weaken any economy with oversupply of oil," a U.S. Department of Energy official said.

Oil prices have always been susceptible to the law of demand and supply. The nature of the oil market is that it is essentially driven by economic factors. Though some critics have attributed the current oil production to greed on the part of the oil companies, the truth is that the forces of capitalism are motivated by greed. The same forces of capitalism that drive growths and free markets are the same forces that have contributed to increased oil production in the U.S.

Another reason the conspiracy theory is far-fetched is because it does not benefit oil companies to oversupply the market and then have a huge stockpile with subsequently reduced prices and revenues. Oil companies often lose money when there is an oversupply of oil or when supply is chasing demands in the oil market. Oil companies want oil prices to be high so that they can maximize profits but it is sometimes hard to maintain a high production and expect a high price per barrel. With a huge stockpile and low demand, oil companies are sometimes forced to cut supply by reducing production, to increase demand, and subsequently to increase price. "But that is if it is within the power of the oil companies to do so, i.e. to control supply. If other countries are producing oil to keep up revenue or in some cases, are producing more to make up for the reduced prices, then it is hard for any region's oil companies to control supply," an oil analyst said.

Sometimes, politics and government policies can also factor in, in oil production. For example, experts had predicted that Saudi Arabia will cut back in its oil production to reduce the amount of supply of oil in the market or to counter the U.S. oil production. But the Saudis have not done that. They have instead kept up with their normal production capacity. Experts believe that may change with the death of King Abdullah, on January 23, 2015, and the installation of King Salman, the half brother of King Abdullah. King Abdullah had been against cutting back on oil production to reduce the oil glut in the market. Though the new king, King Salman, said he will maintain the same policy as the late king, time will tell.

For struggling African countries whose revenues are mostly derivable from oil, it will be hard to cut back on oil production as that will worsen their already low revenue. To make up for the losses from reduced oil prices per barrel, countries like Nigeria, Angola, Algeria and Libya may double their supply and production. Though Nigeria and Angola are part of the OPEC and have to abide by the quota set by the organization, other forces may destabilize that quota. In Nigeria for example, illegal oil production is rampant in the Niger Delta where insurgency is very palpable.

There are other forces that have also contributed to the oversupply of oil in the market. In war-torn and weary nations of Iraq and Syria where ISIS (Islamic State of Iraq and Syria) controls large swatches of oil fields in Iraq, Syria and Libya, the terrorists now control oil production in those oil fields. According to media reports, ISIS controls the amount of oil it produces and sends to the market from the oil fields it controls through the black market. The jihadist group is reportedly supplying oil to the market below market prices in the black market, to attract buyers.

The consequences of excessive fracking can sometimes create a drawback and devastating results, such as the recent earthquake that happened in north Texas in which a cluster of small earthquakes rattled a Dallas suburb in an unprecedented manner. Though earthquakes are not common in Texas, hydraulic fracking has contributed to its frequency, experts said. According to ABC News, its occurrence made experts wonder what may have caused the cluster of small earthquakes to occur, on January 7, 2014. Though the temblor was not fatal, it raised many questions about the safety of fracking and shale oil in Texas.

The U.S. geological survey indicated that over 11 cluster of small earthquakes hit north Texas on January 7, 2015. The earthquakes were so numerous and overwhelming that residents in the areas affected were told to stop calling 911 unless someone was badly hurt or injured. With such devastation and environmental concerns, it is just a matter of time before safety takes precedence over profits in fracking and drilling areas in Texas and other parts of the U.S.

When earthquake and contamination of the earth is considered, the economic rewards far outweigh the environmental issues, one oil company official said. For the residents in north Texas, earthquake was not a normal occurrence in the area. The shakings and rumblings that occurred in Irving Texas was not something that happens often.

The Associated Press reported that the magnitudes of the earthquake ranged from 1.6 to 3.6. The 3.6 magnitude was enough to raise concerns as small earthquakes usually average between 2.5 to 3.0 ranges of magnitude. Geologists opined that 2.5 to 3.0 magnitudes are the smallest earthquakes ever felt by humans.

Since fracking became a part of oil drilling in some parts of Texas and Oklahoma, earthquakes have become a common occurrence. ABC News reported that in October, Texas officials took the initiative of amending the rules for fracking in the area where hydraulic fracking is often operated. Texas residents have long protested against the process of hydraulic fracking which includes injecting fluids into shale beds at high pressure in order to free up petroleum resources. The process, according to experts, can trigger earthquakes such as the cluster of small earthquakes that happened in north Texas.

Though some experts believe earthquakes that range from 2.5 to 3.0 magnitudes can happen anywhere and in any place, scientists will be investigating the Texas earthquakes to examine the parameters, magnitudes, depth and location of each occurrence to see if there is a correlation between the earthquakes that occurred and hydraulic fracking. For now, according to ABC News, experts are calling the small earthquakes in north Texas "a swarm swarm, because we've had multitude events happen."

As some electorates in Texas have indicated, fracking is counterproductive because of the environmental issues and pollutions that are associated with hydraulic fracking. The Guardian recently reported that Denton, Texas "where America's oil and natural gas boom began has voted to ban fracking, in a stunning rebuke to the industry." Though the overwhelming vote will not mean a ban of hydraulic fracking it however rekindles the notion that hydraulic fracking is not popular amongst many Texans. Though hydraulic fracking has been one of the factors responsible for the lower oil prices in the U.S., most people feel there is too much at stake with hydraulic fracking.

A recent survey indicated that more than "15 million Americans now live within a mile of an oil gas or well," the Guardian reported. But an overwhelming majority of Americans are happy about the lower prices of oil at gas stations across the country. Critics believe that the 59% vote to ban fracking in Denton, Texas will be the start of a new anti-fracking campaign that will eventually limit fracking across the U.S.

Epilogue

On March 5, 2015, the President of Liberia, Ellen Johnson Sirleaf, declared that Liberia has treated its last patient with Ebola. The purported last patient, Beatrice Yardolo, a 58-year old school teacher, was released from a Chinese-run Ebola treatment center, on Thursday March 5, 2015. Though there are currently no new infections in Liberia, President Ellen Johnson Sirleaf said "no country can be declared Ebola free until all the other countries have no cases."

According to the Associated Press, reported by the Daily News, "Liberia has also successfully traced all known contacts of Ebola cases, compared with just 49 percent for Guinea and 78 percent for Sierra Leone. Not being able to trace potential cases means health officials in Guinea and Sierra Leone don't know where many new cases are coming from." Having treated its last patient, Liberia, according to the World Health Organization, can now begin the countdown to 42 days of zero infection to declare itself free of Ebola.

Though Liberia has started its countdown to a 42-day zero infection, Vickie Hawkins, director of Medecins Sans Frontieres UK, warned about complacency with the disease, saying "there is no room for complacency as the number of new Ebola cases in the region has risen this week." She said the porosity of the borders between the three affected countries could still make it possible for the disease to return to Liberia, if people continue to move easily over the porous borders, without the governments in the region monitoring it.

As Liberia celebrates the release of its last patient, on Wednesday, the World Health Organization reported "132 new Ebola cases last week, an increase from the 99 cases reported the previous week." The agency further reported that the spread of Ebola remains rampant; in Sierra Leone and noted that "cases have jumped both there and in Guinea," the Daily News reported.

Sebastian Funk, an Ebola expert at London's School of Hygiene and Tropical Medicine, warned that "There is always the risk of re-infection. We're still seeing a lot of suspected and probable cases in Liberia." She noted that "Ebola was first introduced to Liberia from Guinea and I see no reason why that wouldn't happen again if it is still circulating in Guinea."

With the end of Ebola in sight, in Liberia, the U.N. said it will start testing an experimental drug in Guinea on Saturday March 14, 2015, to prevent future outbreaks, in West Africa. According to the Daily News, "The health agency's vaccination strategy in Guinea aims to create a buffer zone around an Ebola case to prevent its further spread. Officials will vaccinate people who have already been exposed to Ebola cases and are at risk of developing the disease."

The vaccine, VSV-EBOV, that will be tested in Guinea, was developed by Canada and is reportedly licensed to Merck. Another vaccine was developed by the U.S. National Institute of Health and GlaxoSmithKline, and is scheduled to be tested on a separate study at a future date, when "supplies become available."

In Ferguson, Missouri, the police chief and several city officials were forced to resign from their positions for racism within the police department, following an investigation conducted by the Department of Justice. During a protest to remove the mayor of the city of Ferguson, two police officers were shot, and injured. They were released from the hospital two days later. Eyewitness accounts pointed out that the shooting was carried out by officers within the Ferguson police department to shift, and put the blame on the protesters.

References

American is beating Ebola: every patient taken to an elite U.S. facility has survived. (October, 29, 2014). Forbes. Retrieved from: Forbes.com

Americans agree with Donald Trump, 58 percent want flights banned from Ebola outbreak countries. (October 9, 2014.). Inquisitr. Retrieved from http://www.inquisitr.com/1529569/americans-agree-with-donald-trump-58-percent-want-flights-banned-from-ebola-outbreak-countries/

A tenth Sierra Leonean doctor dies from Ebola. (December 08, 2914). Voice of America. Retrieved from: http://www.voanews.com/content/a-10th-sierra-leone-doctor-dies-from-ebola

Ask not what your country can do for you: great Speeches of the 20th century. (April 22, 2007). The Guardian. Retrieved from: http://www.theguardian.com/theguardian/2007/apr/22/greatspeeches

Are cruise ships floating petri dishes? (February 3, 2014). CNN. Retrieved from: http://www.cnn.com/2014/01/29/travel/cruises-sanitation/index.html

3rd American with Ebola to return to U.S. (September 4, 2014). CNN. Retrieved from: http://www.myhighplains.com/story/d/story/3rd-american-with-ebola-to-return-to-us

British Ebola nurse to return to West Africa. (October 15, 2014). Sky News. Retrieved from: http://news.sky.com/story/1353916/british-ebola-nurse-to-return-to-west-africa

British national in Sierra Leone tests positive for Ebola virus. (November 30, 2014). Q13 Fox News. Retrieved from: http://q13fox.com/2014/08/23/british-national-in-sierra-leone-tests-positive-for-ebola-virus/

Black or African American populations: (October 11, 2014). CDC. Retrieved from: www.blackafricanamerican.com

Cuban doctor infected with Ebola to be treated in Switzerland: (November 19, 2014). Bloomberg News. Retrieved from: http://www.bloomberg.com/news/2014-11-19/cuban-doctor-infected-with-ebola-to-be-treated-in-switzerland.html

Dallas nurse battling Ebola says she's 'doing well.' (Oct 14, 2014). ABC News. Retrieved from ABCNews.com.

Dallas DA Considering charges against Ebola patient. (October 4, 2014). NBC 5. Retrieved from: http://www.nbcdfw.com/news/health/Dallas-DA-Considers-Charges-Against-Ebola-Patient

Dallas nurse Nina Pham reunites with 'best friend' – Bentley after Ebola scare. (November 1, 2014). Daily News. Retrieved from: http://www.nydailynews.com/news/national/nurse-nina-pham-reunites-dog-bentley-ebola-scare-article-

Ebola: 11th Sierra Leone doctor dies; fire destroys supplies. (December 18, 2014). ABC News. Retrieved from: http://abcnews.go.com/Health/wireStory/11th-sierra-leonean-doctor-dies-ebola

Ebola patient dies in German hospital. (October 14, 2014). New York Times. Retrieved from: http://www.nytimes.com/2014/10/15/world/europe/ebola-patient-dies-in-german-hospital

Ebola patient Dr. Craig Spencer enters 'next phase' of illness. (October, 25, 2014). Daily News. Retrieved from: http://www.nydailynews.com/life-style/health/dr-craig-spencer-experimental-anti-viral-drug-brincidofovir-fight-ebola-officials-article-

Ebola in Guinea: travelers' health r(November 16, 2014). CDC. Retrieved from: http://wwwnc.cdc.gov/travel/notices/warning/ebola-guinea

Ebola in Sierra Leone. (November 16, 2014). CDC. Retrieved from: http://wwwnc.cdc.gov/travel/notices/warning/ebola-sierra-leone

Ebola in Nigeria: A survivor's story. (November 17, 2014). The Wall Street Journal. Retrieved from: http://online.wsj.com/articles/ebola-in-nigeria-a-survivors-story.

Ebola outbreak in Senegal over: WHO. (October 17, 2014). Huffington Post. Retrieved from: http://www.huffingtonpost.com/2014/10/17/ebola-senegal-over Retrieved October 29,

Ebola crisis: Liberia holds postponed senate election. (December 20, 2014). BBC News Africa. Retrieved from BBCNews.com/mobile

Ebola cruise ship 'in utter panic' as Mexico and Belize refuse to let it dock. (October 19, 2014). The Independent. Retrieved from: http://www.independent.co.uk/news/world/americas/ebola-cruise-ship-in-utter-panic-as-mexico-and-belize-refuse-to-let-it-dock

Ebola-infected Italian doctor 'recovering. (December 22, 2014). Yahoo News. Retrieved from: http://news.yahoo.com/ebola-infected-italian-doctor-recovering-

Europe's first Ebola victim: (October 8, 2014). The Economist. Retrieved from: http://www.economist.com/blogs/charlemagne/2014/10/ebola-spain

Fifth local doctor in Sierra Leone has died of Ebola. (November 3, 2014). Daily News. Retrieved from: http://www.nydailynews.com/life-style/health/local-doctor-sierra-leone-died-ebola-article

Fracking pushes U.S. oil production to highest in 20 years: (January 9, 2013). Bloomberg News. Retrieved from: http://www.bloomberg.com/news/2013-01-09/fracking-pushes-u-s-oil-production-to-highest-level-in-20-years.html

Florida man shoots and kills 17-year-old teen after argument over loud music at gas station. (November 28, 2012). Daily News. Retrieved from: Florida man shoots and kills 17-year-old teen after argument over loud music at gas station

Fighting Ebola. (October 13, 2014). Time Magazine. Retrieved from Time Magazine.

French police storm hostage sites, killing gunmen Charlie Hebdo suspects dead in raid: hostage taker in Paris is also killed. (January 9, 2015). New York Times. Retrieved from: http://www.nytimes.com/2015/01/10/world/europe/charlie-hebdo-paris-shooting.html?

French forces kill gunmen, end terror rampage; woman suspect still at large: (January 10, 2015). The Times of India. Retrieved from: http://timesofindia.indiatimes.com/world/europe/French-forces-kill-gunmen-end-terror-rampage-woman-suspect-still-at-large/articleshow

De Blij, H. J. Muller, P. O. (December, 2003). Geography: Realms, regions and concepts. New York: John Wiley.

Global alert and response (GAR): (October 30, 2014). World Health Organization. Retrieved from: http://www.who.int/csr/don/archive/year/2014/en/

Guinea: Ebola epidemic declared; MSF launches emergency response. (March 22, 2014). Medecins Sans Frontieres. Retrieved from: http://www.msf.org/article/guinea-ebola-epidemic-declared-msf-launches-emergency-response

Global economic prospects: Sub-Saharan Africa. (December 29, 2014). The World Bank. Retrieved from: http://www.worldbank.org/en/publication/global-economic-prospects/regional-outlooks/ssa

Guinea Ebola outbreak: Bat-eating banned to curb virus. (March 25, 2014). BBC News Africa. Retrieved from: http://www.bbc.com/news/world-africa.

How did nurse Amber Vinson get Ebola? 'It is a mystery to me,' she tells CNN (November 6, 2014). CNN. Retrieved from: http://www.cnn.com/2014/11/06/health/amber-vinson-ebola-nurse-interview

Harvard Professor arrested, trying to get into his home. (July 21, 2009). Islandmix.com. Retrieved from: http://www.islandmix.com/backchat/f6/harvard-professor-arrested-trying-get-into-his-home-

King Leopold's legacy of DR Congo violence. (July 14, 2007). BBC News, 2004. Retrieved from: http://news.bbc.co.uk/2/hi/africa

'It's like Michael Brown all over again.' (December 25, 2014). The Atlantic. Retrieved from: http://www.theatlantic.com/national/archive/2014/10/officer-shoots-and-kills-teen-in-st-louis

Liberia GDP per capital. (November, 2014): Trading Economics. Retrieved from: http://www.tradingeconomics.com/liberia/gdp-per-capita

Liberia's last Ebola patient released from treatment center.(March 5, 2015). Daily News. Retrieved from: http://www.nydailynews.com/life-style/health/liberia-ebola-patient-leaves-treatment-center-article-

Liberia releases last Ebola patient. (March 5, 2015). BBCNEWS Africa. Retrieved from: BBCNewsAfrca.com.

Missouri: Black teen killed by police reportedly drew gun; violent protests break out. (December 24, 2014). San Jose Mercury News. Retrieved from: http://www.mercurynews.com/crime-courts/ci_27200513/missouri-black-teen-killed-police-violent-protests

Mali confirms eighth Ebola case. (November 25, 2014). Fox News. Retrieved from: http://www.foxnews.com/health/2014/11/25/mali-confirms-

eighth-ebola-case/
Mali: Household energy and universal access: (December 11, 2014).
News and Broadcast: The World Bank. Retrieved from:
http://web.worldbank.org/WBSITE/EXTERNAL/NEWS/
Mali travel warning: U.S. passport & international travel. (March 21,
2014). U.S. Department of State: Bureau of Consular Affairs.
Retrieved from:
http://travel.state.gov/content/passports/english/alertswarnin
gs/mali-travel-warning.html
Nigerians, other Africans rescued by Italian navy. (January 2014).
Thisday Newspaper. Retrieved from:
http://www.thisdaylive.com/articles/nigerians-other-africans-
rescued-by-italian-navy
New Ebola cases may soon reach 10,000 a week, officials predict.
(October 14, 2014). New York Times. Retrieved from:
http://www.nytimes.com/2014/10/15/world/africa/ebola-
epidemic-who-west-africa.
New Ebola vaccine to be tested in Guinea: Phase III trials of the
rVSV-EBOV vaccine will begin Saturday in Basse Guinea.
(March 5, 2015). The Wall Street Journal. Retrieved from:
http://www.wsj.com/articles/new-ebola-vaccine-to-be-tested-
in-guinea-
2 NYPD police officers 'assassinated'; shooter dead. (December 20,
2014). CNN. Retrieved from:
http://www.cnn.com/2014/12/20/us/new-york-police-
officers-shot/index.html
Norwegian infected with Ebola in Sierra Leone. (October 6, 2014). YAHOO
News. Retrieved from: http://news.yahoo.com/norwegian-infected-ebola-
sierra-leone-144344869.html
Nigerian doctor dies of Ebola. (August 20, 2014). PM News.
Retrieved from:
http://www.pmnewsnigeria.com/2014/08/20/nigerian-doctor-
dies-of-ebola-virus/
N.C. family says son was lynched: N.C. teen's death a lynching,
mother says. (December 15, 2014). CNN. Retrieved from
CNN.com/mobile
New Ebola outbreak in Sierra Leone raises fears of new infection
chain. (November 2014). The Guardian. Retrieved from:
http://www.theguardian.com/world/2014/nov/04/ebola-
outbreak-sierra-leone

No federal civil rights charges in Trayvon Martin case. (February 24, 2015). CBSNEWS. Retrieved from: http://www.cbsnews.com/news/department-of-justice-no-civil-rights-charges-trayvon-martin-case/

No indictment for Houston officer who shot Jordan Baker. (December 23, 2014). CBS News. Retrieved from: http://www.cbsnews.com/news/jordan-baker-no-indictment-for-police-houston-officer-who-shot-unarmed-black-man/

Oil thieves of the Niger Delta. (February 20, 2014). Bloomberg Business-week-Global Economics. Retrieved from: http://www.businessweek.com/articles/2014-02-20/nigerias-delta-oil-thieves-scrape-out-a-precarious-living

Ohio Wal-Mart where cops shot black man pulls pellet guns from shelves. (September 30, 2014). NBC News. Retrieved from: http://www.nbcnews.com/news/investigations/ohio-wal-mart-where-cops-shot-black-man-pulls-pellet

Obama says Ebola travel ban could make things worse: (October 18, 2014). Reuters. Retrieved from: http://www.reuters.com/article/2014/10/18/us-health-ebola-obama-idUSK

Pope on Paris: 'You cannot insult the faith of others.' (January 15, 2015). USA today. Retrieved from: http://www.usatoday.com/story/news/world/2015/01/15/pope-islam-paris-charlo-hebdo

Pope Francis: freedom of expression has limits. (January 16, 2015). The Guardian. Retrieved from: http://www.theguardian.com/world/2015/jan/15/pope-francis-limits-to-freedom-of-expression

Police killings highest in two decades. (November 11, 2014). USA Today. Retrieved from: http://www.usatoday.com/story/news/nation/2014/11/11/police-killings-hundreds

Past legal problems of George Zimmerman: The big story. (November 18, 2013). Associated Press. Retrieved from: http://www.bigstory.ap.org/article/past-legal-problems-george-zimmerman

Police outside cop funeral turn backs on Mayor de Blasio. (December 27, 2014). NBC4 News. Retrieved from: http://www.nbcnewyork.com/news/local/NYPD-Police-Officers-Turn-Backs-Mayor-Bill-de-Blasio-Funeral-Rafael-Ramos-286927811.html

Protests after N.Y. cop not indicted in chokehold death: Feds reviewing case. (December 4, 2014). CNN. Retrieved from: http://www.cnn.com/2014/12/03/justice/new-york-grand-jury-chokehold/index.html

Rate of new Ebola infections in Liberia is slowing, WHO says. (December 28, 2014). Washington Post. Retrieved from: http://www.washingtonpost.com/national/health-science/rate-of-new-ebola-infections-in-west-africa-is-slowing-who-says

Report: Black U.S. AIDS rates rival some African nations. (July 29, 2008). CNN. Retrieved from: http://www.cnn.com/2008/HEALTH/conditions/07/29/blac k.aids.report/

Spain ramps up Ebola response; Norwegian tests positive in Sierra Leone. (October 8, 2014). CNN. Retrieved from: http://www.cnn.com/2014/10/07/world/europe/ebola-spain/index

Sierra Leone Ebola outbreak 'catastrophic': aid group MSF. (October 31, 2014). (YAHOO News. Retrieved from: http://news.yahoo.com/leone-ebola-outbreak-catastrophic-aid-group-msf

She's lost everything: Duncan's fiancée declared Ebola free and released from isolation. (November, 2014). Mail Online. Retrieved from: http://www.dailymail.co.uk/news/article

Sierra Leone overview. (November 01, 2013). The World Bank. Retrieved from: http://www.worldbank.org/en/country/sierraleone/overview

Sierra Leone's leading doctor dies of Ebola. (December 18, 2014). Reuters. Retrieved from http://www.reuters.com/article/2014/12/18/us-health-ebola-leone-

Scottish Ebola patient transferred to unit in London. (December 30, 2014). Morning Star News. Retrieved from: http://news.morningstar.com/all/printNews.aspx?article

Scientists warn potential Ebola treatments could be hindered by mutations in virus. (January 20, 2015). Public Health Watch. Retrieved from: https://publichealthwatch.wordpress.com/2015/01/20/scientists-warn-potential-ebola-treatments-could-be-hindered-by-mutations-in-virus/

Chamberlain, M.E. (1974). The scramble for Africa. Hong Kong: Longman Group Ltd.

The horizon: History of Africa, American. (1971). Heritage
    Publishing Co., New York.

Two Americans infected with deadly Ebola virus in West Africa.
    (July 27, 2014). CBS News. Retrieved from:
    http://www.cbsnews.com/news/american-doctor-in-west-
    africa-contracts-deadly-ebola-virus/

The most corrupt countries in the world. (July 14, 2013). USA
    Today. Retrieved from:
    http://www.usatoday.com/story/money/business/2013/07/1
    4/most-corrupt-countries

Trayvon Martin shooting: What do we know? (July 10, 2013).
    CBSNews. Retrieved from cbsnews.com

Timeline for a body: 4 Hours in the Middle of a Ferguson street.
    (August 21, 2014). New York Times. Retrieved from:
    http://www.nytimes.com/2014/08/24/us/michael-brown-a-
    bodys-timeline-4-hours-on-a-ferguson-street.html?

Teens describe burglaries that targeted Montana man charged in
    slaying of German student. (December 4, 2014). US News.
    Retrieved from:
    http://www.usnews.com/news/us/articles/2014/12/04/man-
    faces-trial-in-exchange-students-death

The Black Death of 1348 to 1350. (2014). Retrieved from:
    http://www.historylearningsite.co.uk/black_death_of_1348_to
    _1350.htm

There are 53 drugs that could treat Ebola. (December 17, 2014).
    Time.com. Retrieved from: http://time.com/3638494/ebola-
    drugs/#3638494/ebola-drugs/

Texas oil town makes history as residents say no to fracking.
    (November 5, 2014). The Guardian. Retrieved from:
    http://www.theguardian.com/environment/2014/nov/05/birt
    hplace-fracking-boom-votes-ban-denton-texas

Ugandan doctor with Ebola arrives in Germany for treatment. (October 3, 2014).
    The World Post/Huffington Post. Retrieved from:
    http://www.huffingtonpost.com/2014/10/03/ugandan-doctor-ebola-
    germany

U.S. CDC boosts national stockpile of Ebola protective gear.
    (November 7, 2014). Sierra Leone News.net. Retrieved from:
    http://www.sierraleonenews.net

UN: Ebola kills 8,153 people in West Africa, infects 20,650. (January
    9, 2015). Fox 12. Retrieved from:

http://www.kptv.com/story/27762742/un-ebola-kills-8153-people-in-west-africa-infects-

US geological survey records cluster of earthquakes in Texas. (January 7, 2015). ABC News. Retrieved from: http://abcnews.go.com/US/wireStory/us-geological-survey-records-small-quakes-north-texas-

What we know about Thomas Eric Duncan. (October 6, 2014). Huffington Post. Retrieved from: http://www.huffingtonpost.com/2014/10/06/thomas-eric-duncan-dallas-ebola-patient

WHO medic with Ebola taken to Germany for treatment. (August 27, 2014). (YAHOO News. Retrieved from: http://news.yahoo.com/staffer-ebola-taken-germany-treatment

Why Niger Delta oil theft can't stop – Boyloaf. (September 7, 2014). (Vanguard. Retrieved from: http://www.vanguardngr.com/2013/09/why-niger-delta-oil-theft-cant-stop-boyloaf/

Worst Ebola outbreak in history: What you need to know. (December 10, 2014). CNN. Retrieved from: http://edition.cnn.com/interactive/2014/12/world/ebola/

12-year-old boy dies after police in Cleveland shoot him. (November 23, 2014). New York Times. Retrieved from: http://www.nytimes.com/2014/11/24/us/boy-12-dies-after-being-shot-by-cleveland-police-officer.html?